DESERT

STUDIES IN MORAL, POLITICAL,
AND LEGAL PHILOSOPHY

General Editor: Marshall Cohen

DESERT

George Sher

PRINCETON UNIVERSITY PRESS

PRINCETON, NEW JERSEY

Copyright © 1987 by Princeton University Press
Published by Princeton University Press,
41 William Street,
Princeton, New Jersey 08540
In the United Kingdom:
Princeton University Press, Guildford, Surrey

Library of Congress Cataloging in Publication Data
will be found on the last printed page of this book

ISBN 0-691-07745-2
ISBN 0-691-02316-6, pbk.

First Princeton Paperback printing, 1989

This book has been composed in Linotron Aldus

Clothbound editions of Princeton University Press books
are printed on acid-free paper, and binding materials
are chosen for strength and durability. Paperbacks,
although satisfactory for personal collections,
are not usually suitable for library rebinding

Printed in the United States of America
by Princeton University Press
Princeton, New Jersey

For my mother and my father

CONTENTS

PREFACE

Desert is central to our pre-reflective thought. Most people find it simply obvious that persons who work hard deserve to succeed, that persons of outstanding merit deserve recognition and reward, and that persons harmed by wrongdoers deserve to be compensated. Such outcomes seem morally fitting and please us when they occur. Moreover, though some resist the feeling, I suspect that most people also react with gratification when some especially vicious criminal is apprehended and punished. Conversely, I suspect that most feel disturbed when such a criminal—some wanton destroyer of lives—eludes punishment and escapes to live well while far better people suffer. Such outcomes suggest that the world is out of joint, that things are somehow not working out as they should.

What are we to make of these reactions? Do they reflect genuine moral concern, or are they mere vestiges of a primitive tendency to wish our benefactors well and our malefactors ill? If the reactions are genuinely moral, are they rationally defensible? If rationally defensible, to what degree, and how, should they shape our behavior? And how are they related to other sorts of moral judgments? Though the answers to these questions are far from obvious, what should be obvious, given the importance we attach to desert, is the need to ask them. Yet when we do ask them—when we seek a theoretical understanding of desert—we find a striking omission. For, in stark contrast to the recent outpouring of work on rights and justice, desert has received very little philosophical attention. There has, of course, been some important work—Joel Feinberg's seminal papers and John Rawls's influential discussion come immediately to mind—but none of it adds up to a full-scale and constructive treatment. And, as a glance at a few representative works reveals, desert often is not merely glossed over, but altogether ignored.

Why this neglect? I suspect that the reasons for it lie partly in the heterogeneity of the claims and principles that fall under desert—a heterogeneity that will become all too apparent in what follows—and partly in the temper of the age. This temper I take to include both a concern with equality that conflicts with the differentiations imposed by desert and tendencies to downgrade individual responsibility and to doubt the efficacy of individual acts in a complex world. There may also be something to Alisdair MacIntyre's suggestion that "the notion of desert is at home only in the context of a community whose primary bond is a shared understanding both of the good for man and of the good of that community and where individuals identify their primary interests with reference to those goods."[1] But whatever truth these speculations may contain, I shall not pursue them further. Instead, my aim is simply (or, rather, not so simply) to provide the sort of comprehensive treatment of desert that has so far been lacking. To orient the reader, I begin with some remarks about the problem as I conceive it and about my operating assumptions.

What, then, is the problem of desert? There are, I think, several. The most familiar, and the one on which the most progress has been made, is to clarify the logic of claims that persons deserve things (hereafter called "desert-claims"), and to classify these in illuminating ways. On these matters, the work of Feinberg is invaluable. But analysis, however necessary, is not the only task that must be performed. Also required, but much less often attempted, is an account of the moral underpinnings of desert. We need to understand not only how desert-claims should be classified, but also what they imply about what persons should have and how they should be treated. Moreover, and crucially, we need to know how (if at all) these implications are to be justified. Answering this question requires substantive normative inquiry, and a good half of this book will be devoted to it. But even exposing the normative roots of desert will not complete our task; for here, as elsewhere, the ground of ethics is metaphysics. As we will see, desert presupposes both a particular vision of the self and a specific view of the relation between

---

[1] Alisdair MacIntyre, *After Virtue* (Notre Dame, Ind.: University of Notre Dame Press, 1981), p. 233.

reasons and time. At the deepest level, a full-scale account must expose and defend these metaphysical presuppositions.

As these remarks suggest, one of my central aims is to display the underlying justification of desert-claims. It is only by actually doing this that we can show desert to be morally significant. But what, exactly, should qualify as justification here? As a first attempt, we might equate justifying desert-claims with the unearthing of moral principles that obligate us to provide deserving parties with what they deserve.[2] But thinking of justification in this way begs important questions. It prejudges both the question of whether desert always is associated with specific moral obligations and the question of whether all obligations are backed by quasi-legal moral principles.[3] In addition, it promises to invite further questions about how the cited principles are themselves to be justified. For both reasons, we shall need a wider conception of justification.

To arrive at a more suitable conception, I shall do two things. First, to avoid tying desert too closely to moral obligations, I shall introduce, as a term of art, the broader notion of *normative force*. Under this heading, I shall include any significant implication that something ought, or ought not, to be the case. Given this stipulation, a desert-claim will indeed have normative force if a specific person (or arm of society) is obligated to provide the deserving party with what he deserves. But a claim will also have normative force if the deserving party's having what he deserves would, for reasons connected with the basis of his desert, be an especially good thing. A desert-claim's normative force may thus be either a matter of right or a matter of (moral or nonmoral) value. But in neither case will justification consist simply of citing the value or obligation that supplies the normative force. Instead, I shall try to show, with some rigor, how that value or obligation (or a related principle) illuminates a whole range of associated intuitions. Where the value,

---

[2] Here and in most other places, I shall use "obligation" and "duty" interchangeably. Any deviations from this usage will be either expressly noted or made clear by the context. In general, then "X is obligated to do A" and "X has a duty to do A" will both be used to mean "X morally ought to do A."

[3] For a statement (perhaps an overstatement) of the dangers of this assumption, see Joel Feinberg, "Supererogation and Rules," in Feinberg, *Doing and Deserving* (Princeton: Princeton University Press, 1970), pp. 3–24.

obligation, or principle is itself controversial, I shall argue for it in turn. In so doing, I shall sometimes appeal to a more general principle or value whose validity is, at least for the moment, beyond dispute. At other times, I shall appeal instead to requirements of practical reason; at still others, to persuasive analogies and metaphors. Although I shall not defend it here, I accept, and find liberating, a metaethic that holds that there are no a priori limits to what counts as an acceptable philosophical account. What will turn out to be intellectually satisfying often cannot be known in advance.

As should be apparent, the approach to be taken is in several ways pluralistic. I acknowledge a plurality both of legitimate modes of argument and of values and obligations. I also acknowledge that different values and obligations may be independent of one another in a sense strong enough to threaten commensurability.[4] Most important, I acknowledge that desert need not have any single normative basis. Instead, the different classes of desert-claims may owe their justification to irreducibly different principles and values. By starting from the various desert-claims we actually make, and by letting these guide the quest for a unifying account, I hope to avoid the opposing dangers of over-systematization and conceptual anarchy. It would, of course, be most satisfying if all major desert-claims turned out to have a single compelling normative base; but here, as elsewhere, what would be most satisfying may simply not be the case.

Whatever the truth about the normative basis of desert-claims, an adequate understanding of desert should illuminate not only a much-neglected area of moral thought, but also various ancillary matters. It was, indeed, concern with quite separate issues that originally led me to this project. I began with an interest in action theory which, I now realize, was directed primarily at the all-important notion of responsibility. More recently, I have pursued normative projects both on topics such as preferential treatment, punishment, and subsidized medical care and on broader issues concerning compensatory justice and the dispute between consequen-

---

[4] Here, my thinking is influenced by Thomas Nagel, "The Fragmentation of Value," in Nagel, *Mortal Questions* (Cambridge, England: Cambridge University Press, 1979), pp. 128–41.

tialist and non-consequentialist moralities. While thinking about these normative topics, I was repeatedly impressed with both the centrality of desert and the inadequacy of existing treatments of it. Finally, I decided to face the issue head-on, and this book is the result.

Because I am reluctant to show my work in its early stages, writing the book was, for a long time, a solitary exercise. Still, I have incurred a variety of debts, and I am very pleased to acknowledge them. The longest-standing is to my teacher Arthur Danto, whose stimulating lectures and writings greatly influenced my thinking. More recently, I have benefited from discussions of pertinent topics with my colleagues William Mann and Chad Hansen, and with my former colleagues Steven Cahn, Patricia Kitcher, and Philip Kitcher. More recently yet, three acute philosophers, Arthur Kuflik, Hilary Kornblith, and Alan Wertheimer, read the entire manuscript in draft, and I am grateful to them for their comments. Each in his own way has greatly improved the final product. I have also received helpful advice from Derk Pereboom and invaluable practical assistance from Leslie Weiger.

Parts of two of the book's chapters have appeared elsewhere. A version of most of Chapter 2 was published in *Philosophy & Public Affairs* under the title "Effort, Ability, and Personal Desert"; and much of Chapter 10 appeared in *Philosophical Studies* under its present title, "Why the Past Matters." That paper was written in the stimulating environment of the National Humanities Center, where I spent my sabbatical year of 1980–1981, and I am pleased to acknowledge the Center's support. I am also grateful to the University of Vermont, which provided a research grant in the summer of 1982. But my greatest debt is to my wife, Emily Gordon Sher. Though she is not a professional philosopher, I have long relied on her keen sense of what is philosophically important, and of what does and does not ring true. In the later stages of writing, I also depended heavily on her unsurpassed stylistic sense. For these things, and for much else, I thank her.

January 1987

DESERT

O N E

INTRODUCTION: THE DIMENSIONS
OF THE PROBLEM

Desert is uncharted philosophical territory, and my aim in this book
is to explore it. But before I begin, I want to take some time to scout
the terrain. In any philosophical inquiry, the answers one gets are
largely dictated by the questions one asks. Thus, to get the right answers, we must be sure to ask the right questions. In the current
context, this means getting clear about both the special puzzles that
desert raises and the full range of desert-claims that people actually
make. In addition, it requires that we be clear about the difference
between an explanatory and a justificatory account; the relations
between desert, utility, and social institutions; and the proper evi-
dential role of our intuitions. In this introductory chapter, I shall
have something to say about each of these things. In addressing
them, I shall be setting the agenda for the fuller discussion to follow. To end, I shall briefly anticipate the course of that discussion.

I

Let us begin with some puzzles. Although desert-claims raise many
problems, four seem especially perplexing.

   1. The first puzzle is one that most often is associated with retributive desert. When we say that wrongdoers deserve punishment,
we clearly imply that they ought to be punished, that it would
somehow be a good thing if they were. Furthermore, we imply that
it is at least permissible for suitably situated persons *to* punish
them. However, punishing people typically involves harming
them, either by causing them pain or by depriving them of their

freedom, property, or life. Harming people in these ways is ordinarily not morally permissible. Thus, to say that wrongdoers deserve punishment is to imply that their own past wrong actions have made it legitimate to treat them in ways that would ordinarily be illegitimate. But how can this be? How can one impermissible act annul or cancel the normal impermissibility of another? What is this "mysterious piece of moral alchemy in which the combination of the two evils of moral wickedness and suffering are transmuted into good"?[1] Until we can explain this, the claim that wrongdoers deserve to be punished will remain opaque.

As just stated, our first puzzle is a staple item in the philosophy of punishment. Its standard use is to discredit those versions of retributivism that justify punishment on grounds of desert. Yet this puzzle is not restricted to desert of punishment. We encounter it again, in a slightly different guise, when we say, for example, that a wrongdoer's victim deserves compensation, or that a best-qualified job applicant deserves to be hired. In these cases, too, the basis of a given person's desert is often felt to affect what others ought to do. In most people's view, the fact that someone has wrongfully harmed another obligates the wrongdoer to provide compensation. And, though the case is more controversial, the fact that a job applicant is best qualified is widely thought to imply that the hiring officer ought to appoint him. Because these and other sources of desert are also believed to alter structures of obligation, it would be inconsistent to resolve the puzzle by abandoning only retributive desert.[2] Barring some further argument, the negative and positive desert-claims must stand or fall together.

---

[1] H.L.A. Hart, "Postscript: Responsibility and Retribution," in Hart, *Punishment and Responsibility: Essays in the Philosophy of Law* (Oxford: Oxford University Press, 1968), pp. 234–35.

[2] There are also, of course, important disanalogies between the bases of desert of punishment and desert of compensation and opportunity. For one thing, neither one's job qualifications nor one's previous suffering implies anything about one's moral character, while the wrongness of one's actions clearly does. For another, neither qualifications nor suffering lift what would otherwise be moral prohibitions, while previous wrongdoing apparently does. Yet these differences, though important, do not affect the basic fact that all three factors—wrongdoing, being wrongly harmed, and being best qualified—seem to alter what would otherwise be a prevailing structure of obligations.

4

2. Our first puzzle turned on the connection between desert and obligation. Our second turns precisely on their lack of connection. For, in many cases, what is most striking about desert-claims is precisely that they do *not* imply anything about what particular persons ought to do. When we say that an especially hard-working self-employed farmer deserves to succeed, or that a person of fine moral character deserves to fare well, we typically do not mean that anyone is obligated to take steps to provide what is deserved. Similarly, when we say that a superior athlete deserved to win a contest he lost on a fluke, we do not imply that anyone has failed to act as he should have. In these and many other cases, desert seems *not* to bear on anyone's obligations. And this is puzzling for two reasons; first, because these desert-claims behave so differently from others, and second, because their failure to alter obligations seems at odds with the moral significance we attach to them.

3. A third puzzle about many desert-claims concerns their orientation to the past. When we say that wrongdoers deserve punishment, or that their victims deserve compensation, we clearly imply that what someone has done or undergone at an earlier time provides a reason for some later action or occurrence. The same applies when we say that a hard worker deserves success, that a victim of misfortune deserves some good luck, or that a hero deserves a reward. In all such cases, we imply that past actions or events bear directly on what ought to occur now or in the future. But this backward-looking orientation, though often noticed, is itself extremely puzzling. For why *should* past acts or events function in this way? Why should what has already happened, and what is now beyond alteration, nevertheless affect the moral status of other possible occurrences? Why is it not more rational to ignore the past, and to concentrate solely on doing as well as possible from now on? Why does the past matter at all?

4. One additional puzzle warrants mention. As we have seen, many desert-claims are grounded in actions. Persons are said to deserve things as a result of their transgressions, superior performances, sustained efforts, and displays of moral excellence. Yet persons could not perform such actions if they were not born with suitable initial sets of abilities, or if they were not conditioned to

5

acquire the relevant character traits or trained to develop the relevant skills. Since persons can claim credit for neither their native abilities nor their conditioning and training, all the actions that determine desert are made possible by various factors that are themselves undeserved. But how can this be? How, if people do not deserve what makes their actions possible, can they deserve what they obtain *through* those actions? And how, a fortiori, can they deserve anything for such traits as the ability to do a job, which may have nothing to do with what they have (yet) done?

Of these four puzzles, only the last is raised by all desert-claims and only by desert-claims. As we saw, the first and second puzzles are disjoint, and so do not apply across the board. The third puzzle is not raised by the desert of the best-qualified, since job qualifications cannot be equated with any past performances. On the other hand, both the first and the third puzzles do arise in some *non*-desert contexts; for promises and agreements create no desert, yet they do alter the promisor's later obligations to the promisee. But these facts, though significant, do not diminish the overall force of the puzzles. Indeed, if anything, they make things more difficult, for they raise the additional, disturbing possibility that there may *be* no single notion of desert to which the puzzles apply. This possibility looms larger, moreover, when we turn from the puzzles to a more systematic examination of desert-claims themselves.

II

For consider the range of contexts in which we naturally assert that people deserve things. Among the sorts of assertions that fall within this range, we find (at least) the following:

1. Jones deserves his success; he's worked hard for it.
2. Smith deserved more success than he had; he gave it his all.
3. Walters deserves the job; he's the best-qualified applicant.
4. Wilson deserved to be disqualified; he knew the deadline for applications was March 1.
5. Jackson deserves more than minimum wage; his job is important and he does it well.

6. Baker deserves to win; he's played superbly.
7. Miss Vermont deserves to win; she's the prettiest entrant.
8. Anderson deserves his twenty-year sentence; he planned the murder.
9. Brown may have known he wouldn't be caught, but he still deserves to be punished.
10. Winters deserves some compensation; he's suffered constant pain since the shooting.
11. Lee deserves a reward; he risked his life.
12. Benson deserves some good luck; he's a fine person.
13. Gordon deserves some good luck; he's had only bad.
14. McArthur deserves a hearing; he's an expert on the subject.
15. Cleveland deserves better publicity; it's an interesting city.

As John Kleinig has noted, all such claims have a common structure, in that they all assert that some person or thing deserves some occurrence or mode of treatment in virtue of some fact about him or it.[3] Schematically, they all display the form "M deserves X for A." In addition, the claims all imply that A has altered what would otherwise be the normative status of M's having X (although in no case is it implied that M thereby acquires a *right* to X). In all these ways, the fifteen claims are alike. However, when we attend to details, important variations emerge. Thus, consider first the factor that is said to create the desert—what Feinberg has called the "desert basis."[4] In some cases (1, 2, 4, 5, 6, 8, 9, 11), this is clearly one or more act or omission of the deserving party—his hard work, his lateness in applying, his crime, and so on. However, in other cases (7, 10, 12, 13, 15), it is clearly *not* an action, but rather a characteristic—being attractive, having had bad luck, being interesting, and the like. Moreover, in still other cases (3, 14), it falls somewhere in between. As I have already noted, being best-qualified (and, I might add, being knowledgeable) cannot simply be equated with anything

[3] John Kleinig, *Punishment and Desert* (The Hague: Martinus Nijhoff, 1973), chap. 3. According to Kleinig, some desert-claims have a fourth element, in that they specify a set of rules in virtue of which the relevant mode of treatment is deserved.
[4] Joel Feinberg, "Justice and Personal Desert," in Feinberg, *Doing and Deserving*, pp. 55–94.

one has done. Still, in many cases, these desert-bases are closely *related* to one's past acts; for skill and knowledge are both acquired and demonstrated through purposive activity. The fact that desert-bases encompass both actions and characteristics not involving actions is often given less emphasis than the fact that the relevant actions and characteristics are those of the deserving party. However, if we want to explain how a desert-basis can affect an outcome's normative status, then the action/characteristic distinction may well be crucial. At least some explanations will not work unless a person's desert can be traced back to his own actions.

Just as claims 1 through 15 vary with respect to desert-bases, so too do they vary with respect to the bearers of desert, and with respect to what those bearers deserve. Concerning the bearers of desert, the main dimension of variation is personhood. The inclusion of Cleveland shows that the deserving party need not always be a person. With regard to what is deserved, the dimensions of variation are more complex. First, the deserved item may or may not already be in the possession of the deserving party. The hard-working Jones (1) is already successful, and the murderer Anderson (8) is already in prison. However, the diligent Smith (2) has decisively failed to achieve his deserved success, and in other examples the situation is unclear. Second, the acquisition of what is deserved is sometimes antecedently predictable and sometimes not. Wilson's disqualification (4) clearly *was* predictable from his lateness in applying, and the same appears true in some other cases; but it is Brown's *avoidance* of his deserved punishment (9) that appears to have been predictable. Third, what is deserved may vary in specificity. "Some good luck," deserved by Benson in (12) and Gordon (13), is much less specific than the twenty years in prison deserved by Anderson (8). And fourth, as we have already seen, the deserved items may vary in their impact on others' obligations. The facts that Walters (3) deserves the job for which he is best qualified and that Miss Vermont (7) deserves to win the beauty contest do appear to affect the obligations of the hiring officer and the contest judge; but the fact that Benson and Gordon deserve good luck does not appear to affect anyone's obligations toward them.

III

Taken together, this disorderly array of beliefs, implications, and puzzles makes up our subject matter. Our problem is to make as much sense of it as possible. But what sort of sense? When we examine our familiar beliefs about desert, should we attempt to understand why people *do* hold these beliefs, or rather why they *ought* to? Should we seek the socio-psychological genesis of the prevailing attitudes, or their rationale? Should our efforts be merely explanatory, or should they be primarily justificatory?

As posed, these questions are seriously misleading. They mislead by wrongly implying that explaining the acquisition of beliefs and justifying those beliefs are always disparate activities. In fact, under certain common conditions, to justify a belief also is to explain why it is held. In particular, this is often the case when the holder of the belief is rational, has some interest in learning the truth, and is capable of following the justificatory argument on some (not necessarily conscious) level. If these conditions obtain, and if we lack a compelling alternative explanation of how a belief has come to be held, then any demonstration of how it *could* have been rationally acquired is in effect an explanation of how it *has* been acquired. Of course, we often do have an alternative explanation of the genesis of a moral belief, in that we know that nonrational techniques were employed in the moral education through which the belief was acquired. However, if these techniques were used to enhance the subject's ultimate receptivity to reasons, then our rational explanation of that person's belief may still be dominant.[5] In addition, a compelling justification may indirectly account for a person's moral beliefs by explaining why those responsible for his moral education (or those responsible for his teachers' moral education, and so on) proceeded as they did.

Because every justification of a belief provides a prima facie explanation of why it is held, while the converse is not true, there is a sense in which the justification of moral beliefs is clearly prior to

[5] For discussion of ways in which nonrational techniques may enhance receptivity to reasons, see George Sher and William J. Bennett, "Moral Education and Indoctrination," *The Journal of Philosophy* 79, no. 11 (November 1982), pp. 665–77.

their explanation. Justification is also prior in the sense that no matter what explains why we came to hold our moral views, we may become culpable in continuing to hold them if we acquire good reason to believe that they cannot be justified. Moreover, one good reason to believe that a moral belief cannot be justified is precisely the decisive failure of our attempts *to* justify it. Thus, the first task of anyone who seeks an adequate theoretical account of desert is to try to justify our considered beliefs about it. He must thoroughly canvass the possible reasons for believing that various desert-bases really do affect what people ought to have or how they ought to be treated. In so doing, he may well find himself forced to abandon the ideal of a single unifying rationale in favor of a number of different justifications which together cover (most of) the field. Given our less-than-perfect consensus about the particulars of what people deserve, he will almost certainly have to dismiss some familiar desert-claims as metaphorical or simply unsustainable. However, rather than attempting to predict this, it seems most sensible to proceed by trying to justify as much as possible of what we believe about desert. There will be time enough to fall back on non-justificatory explanations if our attempts at justification fail.

IV

Given that our aim is to establish whether (and how) desert-claims can be justified, what attitude should we take toward utilitarian accounts of desert? This question is not as straightforward as it seems. On the one hand, utility and desert do seem to face in opposite temporal directions. Because an action's utility is determined by the future benefits it will bring, while what a person deserves ordinarily depends on his past or present actions or characteristics, it is not obvious that a consistent utilitarian can allow for desert. On the other hand, utilitarians have displayed considerable ingenuity in showing how apparently nonutilitarian attitudes might have a utilitarian base. Thus, we cannot simply assume that any adequate justification of our backward-looking moral beliefs must itself appeal solely to backward-looking considerations. Utilitarian accounts of desert cannot be dismissed out of hand, but must be examined on their merits.

Generally speaking, all such accounts begin by emphasizing the incentive effects of reward and punishment. Given these effects, we generally can maximize utility by rewarding people for their efforts and contributions, and by punishing them for their misdeeds. Moreover, although rewarding and punishing in these ways some-times fails to maximize utility, our attempts to isolate the cases in which it will fail, and to refrain from rewarding and punishing in such cases, often do more harm than good. Thus, many utilitarians have held that we can best promote utility by inculcating in our-selves and others a general propensity to reward effort and contri-bution and to punish wrongdoing. This would mean, among other things, producing a disposition to feel guilty when we fail either to reward the hard-working and productive or to punish the guilty, and to feel indignant when others fail to do so. In view of this, many utilitarians would hold that our belief that punishment and reward are called for by past actions—our belief that they are *deserved*—is only to be expected. This belief, like all others that are defensible, is ultimately grounded in utility.[6]

Though many accept it, this account raises some serious ques-tions. We may wonder, for example, whether it really does maxi-mize utility to inculcate a disposition always to reward the hard-working and productive and always to punish wrongdoers. Might we not gain even greater utility by inculcating a disposition always to act in these ways *except* when not doing so will very clearly max-imize happiness? And, again, even if it does maximize utility to in-culcate unconditional beliefs and attitudes, this will not account for our actual beliefs unless our actual teachers were utilitarians (or un-less their teachings were shaped by utilitarianism in some less con-scious way);[7] neither will it justify inculcating those beliefs unless

[6] For an account along these general lines, see R. M. Hare, *Moral Thinking* (Ox-ford: Oxford University Press, 1981).

[7] For discussion, see Allan Gibbard, "Inchoately Utilitarian Common Sense: The Bearing of a Thesis of Sidgwick's on Moral Theory," in *The Limits of Utilitarianism*, ed. Harlan B. Miller and William H. Williams (Minneapolis: University of Minne-sota Press, 1982), pp. 71–85, and A. John Simmons, "Utilitarianism and Uncon-scious Utilitarianism," same volume, pp. 86–98.

utilitarianism itself can be justified. Whether utilitarianism is justifiable and the degree to which it shapes our moral thinking are themselves major outstanding questions of moral theory. Thus, at best, the utilitarian approach to desert leads directly to deeper unresolved issues.

By itself, this does not disqualify the utilitarian approach. The ability to generate new and deeper puzzles is characteristic of all philosophical doctrines, including those that will be advanced here. However, a related problem does suggest that the proposed utilitarian approach is not where we should start. We have seen that this approach invokes utility to justify inculcating the belief that reward and punishment should be administered on the basis of past activities, and not to promote future utility. However, it is one thing to justify *inculcating* this belief and quite another to justify the belief itself. As long as the utilitarian's basic tenet is that the rightness of acts depends ultimately on their consequences, he must still maintain that punishing and rewarding in accordance with desert is wrong whenever its costs outweigh its benefits. However, it is central to our beliefs about desert that a person may deserve reward or punishment (and, hence, that he *ceteris paribus* ought to receive it) even if his receiving it will not maximize overall utility. Thus, whatever it does justify, the proposed utilitarian account does *not* succeed in justifying our most fundamental belief about desert. Where that belief is concerned, the account remains merely explanatory, and hence irrelevant to our purpose.

V

The account of desert we have just rejected is that of the sophisticated act-utilitarian. But act-utilitarianism is not the only version of utilitarianism. Its rival, rule-utilitarianism, is often preferred precisely because of its greater justificatory resources. Can a rule-utilitarian justification of desert-claims succeed where act-utilitarianism fails?

Although rule-utilitarianism itself takes various forms, one of these warrants special mention. According to this approach, justifications of desert-claims can be offered at two different levels. At the level of individual action, treating someone as he deserves is justified not in terms of utility, but rather in terms of the demands of some practice or institution within which the treatment is administered. However, one level up, the existence of that practice or institution is itself justified in utilitarian (or related) terms. Because this approach ties individual desert to the demands of social institutions, I shall refer to it as the "institutional" approach.

Like much else that is said about desert, the institutional approach has its recent origins in the theory of punishment. In an article written in 1939, J. D. Mabbott made the important suggestion that the debate between utilitarians and retributivists is misconceived—that the parties are addressing entirely different questions about punishment.[8] The utilitarian, who insists that the justification of punishment must lie in its social benefits, is arguing that we should institute or retain legal *systems* involving punitive sanctions, while the retributivist, who insists that the obligation to punish follows directly from the wrongdoer's guilt, is answering the different question of how individuals should be treated *within* such systems. Once this distinction is made clear, Mabbott contends, we can say both that "[t]he only justification for punishing any man is that he has broken a law,"[9] and that "[c]onsiderations of utility come in on two quite different issues. Should there be law, and what laws should there be."[10] As actually expressed, Mabbott's discussion contrasts utilitarianism with retributivism rather than with appeals to desert; but, in Hugo Bedau's words, "[r]etributivism without *desert* . . . is like *Hamlet* without the Prince of Denmark."[11] Thus, Mabbott's approach to retributive obligation leads directly to an institutional account of desert.

Mabbott's suggestion that the demands of retribution are requirements of institutions which in turn are justified non-retributively is echoed by others. It is clearly present in the work of

---

[8] J. D. Mabbott, "Punishment," *Mind* 48, no. 190 (April 1939), pp. 150–67.

[9] Ibid., p. 158.

[10] Ibid., p. 161.

[11] Hugo Bedau, "Retribution and the Theory of Punishment," *The Journal of Philosophy* 75, no. 11 (November 1978), p. 608.

H.L.A. Hart and in the early work of John Rawls.[12] Moreover, the institutional approach has recently been extended beyond desert of punishment. In his major work, *A Theory of Justice*,[13] Rawls argues that desert of reward and recompense are also artifacts of social institutions which in turn are justified in quite different ways. Instead of imposing constraints upon our choice of social institutions, personal desert is only established within and by such institutions. As Rawls himself puts it:

> [T]he concept of moral worth is secondary to those of right and justice, and it plays no role in the substantive definition of distributive shares. The case is analogous to the relation between the substantive rules of property and the law of robbery and theft. These offenses and the demerits they entail presuppose the institution of property which is established for prior and independent social ends. For a society to organize itself with the aim of rewarding moral desert as a first principle would be like having the institution of property in order to punish thieves.[14]

In this and other passages, Rawls's statement of the institutional approach is weakened by his unwarranted assumption that the only possible desert-basis for distributive shares is moral worth or virtue. Moreover, unlike Mabbott, the mature Rawls is not a utilitarian of any sort. However, setting this aside, it seems clear that Rawls's later position represents a natural broadening of Mabbott's original suggestion about punishment, and that this broadened position has several very attractive features.

For suppose we accept it. In that case, we can explain how a person's actions can alter others' obligations to punish or reward him (and, more generally, how his actions can affect what he ought to have) in either of two ways. We can say, with Mabbott, that the ob-

---

[12] H.L.A. Hart, "Prolegomenon to the Principles of Punishment," in Hart, *Punishment and Responsibility*, pp. 1–13, John Rawls, "Two Concepts of Rules," *The Philosophical Review* 64, no. 1 (January 1955), pp. 3–32.

[13] John Rawls, *A Theory of Justice* (Cambridge, Mass.: Harvard University Press, 1971).

[14] Ibid., p. 313.

ligations or demands thus created are not moral obligations or demands at all, but rather are constituted solely by the relevant (legal or other) institutions; or we can say, with the later Rawls himself, that they *are* genuinely moral obligations or demands which devolve *from* the justification of the relevant institutions. In either case, our account will accommodate both consequentialist and nonconsequentialist beliefs and intuitions. It will also explain variations in the content of desert-claims by attributing them to variations in the demands of different social institutions.

But despite its undeniable attractiveness, the institutional approach raises new problems. If desert-claims do reflect only the demands of institutions, then we will *not* be able to justify any desert-claim that lacks an institutional base. This means that persons will not deserve punishment for acts that are not proscribed by actual institutions, and that they will not deserve wages that are not dictated by our economic system. It also rules out all forms of desert-claims that cannot plausibly be tied to institutions at all—claims that heroes deserve rewards, that superior characters deserve happiness, that hard workers deserve to succeed, and so on. But while some pruning of desert-claims seems inevitable on any account, the potential loss here is surely excessive. Furthermore, if desert *is* determined by the demands of institutions, then it will be unintelligible to criticize institutions on the grounds that they themselves are insensitive to desert. We will be unable to say, for example, that certain acts should be criminalized precisely *because* those who perform them deserve to be punished. However, even where such assertions are false, they are surely intelligible.

These objections may seem to miss the point. In response, the utilitarian or Rawlsian might reply that it is not the demands of actual institutions, but rather those of ideal institutions, that really determine what people deserve. According to this rejoinder, the reason a criminal deserves punishment, or a worker deserves a certain wage, is not because any actual institution demands these outcomes, but rather because the outcomes *would* be demanded by a utility-maximizing or entirely just social order. Because desert does not depend on the demands of actual institutions, the fact that actual institutions do not support a given desert-claim does not force

15

us to dismiss that claim as unjustified. For similar reasons, we need not deny the possibility of criticizing actual institutions for not treating people as they deserve.

Although this rejoinder improves the institutional approach, it leaves the basic problem unresolved. For consider such merely ideal institutions as the economic system that would maximize utility or the criminal justice system that would be chosen from the original position. Although the details are unclear, it is not far-fetched to suppose that these institutions might themselves dictate wages and punishments that systematically diverge from what persons intuitively deserve. If they did, then we would again have to dismiss as unjustifiable whole classes of deviant desert-claims. And, setting this aside, even the most ideal of criminal justice systems must incorporate procedural safeguards whose effect is to acquit some guilty persons. If the ideal institutional account were correct, then we could not say that such guilty individuals would fail to receive the punishment they deserve. More generally, we would have to dismiss as unintelligible the charge that an (otherwise) ideal set of institutions fails to treat people as they deserve. But, once again, even if such criticism is false, it is surely intelligible.

The ideal institutional account also raises a further worry. Precisely because it does detach justification from the demands of actual institutions, this account lacks the justificatory impact of its simpler relative. Since actual institutions clearly impose actual demands, any desert-claims which they undergird will receive a recognizable sort of justification. Since merely possible institutions do not clearly impose actual demands, the justifications they provide are correspondingly less clear. In favor of such justifications, it may be said that if a possible institution really is ideal, then there is a strong moral case for bringing it into existence. However, as presented, this argument establishes only that the ideal institution, and so too its demands, *should* exist. We need a further argument to show that, despite the institution's nonexistence, its demands are nonetheless now operative in the actual world. Hence, pending further discussion, the account leaves it unclear why anyone should have what he deserves, given the world as it is.[15]

[15] Rawls would not necessarily disagree, for he holds that non-ideal theory (that

These objections do not decisively disqualify the institutional approach. Despite its problems, some version of it may ultimately be defensible, and may provide the best obtainable justification of desert-claims. Yet if is does, our project will have failed; for we will have to concede that desert is merely a derivative category of moral thought, and that it plays no basic role in determining what justice requires. At this early point, such concessions are surely premature. Because they are, I shall not pursue further the idea that desert is a purely institutional notion. Instead, I shall adopt the working hypothesis that it involves both natural *and* conventional elements, and that any adequate account must illuminate the connections between them. According to this hypothesis, the institutional and conventional aspect of desert does not eliminate our justificatory task. It is, if anything, itself a major part of our problem.

VI

One further approach to desert is popular enough to warrant preliminary mention. According to many philosophers who accept a non-institutional conception of desert, the fact that people deserve things—the fact that their past acts and characteristics determine the ways in which they now ought to be treated—is not a thesis to be established by argument, but rather something known directly by intuition. It is a ground-level fact of ethics, not susceptible to further justification. In an earlier day, explicit appeals to intuitions about desert and related notions were very common. They were, for example, the basis both of G. E. Moore's doctrine of organic unities and of W. D. Ross's corresponding view about the duty of reward and punishment.[16] More recently, such explicit appeals have become less frequent, although their echo can be heard in assertions such as the following:

---

is, the branch of the theory of justice that deals with, among other things, "adjustments to natural limitations and historical contingencies") is "worked out after an ideal conception of justice has been chosen" (Rawls, *A Theory of Justice*, pp. 245–46).

[16] G. E. Moore, *Principia Ethica* (Cambridge: Cambridge University Press, 1962), esp. chaps. 1 and 6; W. D. Ross, *The Right and the Good* (Oxford: Oxford University Press, 1965), pp. 56–64.

That a retributivist theory, which is a particular application of a general principle of justice, can account more satisfactorily [than a utilitarian theory] for our notion of justice in punishment is a positive reason in its support.[17]

Explicit or not, however, we can ascribe something like the intuitionist approach to everyone who takes for granted the nonderivative truth of desert-claims, yet does not attempt to explain *how* people's acts or characteristics can alter the ways in which they ought to be treated.

How seriously should we take the intuitionist approach to desert? Construed uncharitably, it may appear to be simply a rejection of the philosophical stance, a substitution of blind prejudice for reason. But with a little help, it can be made to look more respectable. Sympathetically understood, it says that (some of) our considered beliefs that people deserve things are the best available evidence, and are sufficient evidence, that people actually do deserve these things and thus should be treated in the requisite ways. Thus understood, the intuitionist's position rests on a variant of our earlier observation that, under plausible assumptions, any demonstration of how a belief could have been rationally acquired is in effect a prima facie explanation of how it *has* been rationally acquired. Read backwards, this implies that the fact that a belief is held by a rational person is itself a prima facie basis for believing that there is reason to hold it.

Given this reconstruction of intuitionism, it will not do to assert, with R. M. Hare, that moral intuitions "have no probative force."[18] To establish this about specific intuitions, one must show why they in particular are unlikely to be grounded in reason or appreciation of truth. One possible way to show this about desert-intuitions is to stress the variability of their content: for every retributivist who finds it natural to say that wrongdoers deserve punishments that fit their crimes, there is a utilitarian who finds such intuitions barbaric; and the diversity of our intuitions about 'good desert' has

[17] H. J. McCloskey, "A Non-Utilitarian Approach to Punishment," *Inquiry* 8 (1965), p. 239.
[18] Hare, *Moral Thinking*, p. 12.

been impressively chronicled by Henry Sidgwick.[19] Alternatively, one may try to discredit our intuitions about desert by offering competing explanations of them. In particular, one may either re-invoke the act-utilitarian account considered above or else attribute the relevant beliefs to individual or class interest. But while all these gambits must be taken seriously, none is obviously conclusive. Someone sympathetic to the intuitionist approach will argue that the alternative explanations are on the whole less plausible than the claim that our intuitions stem from an awareness of truth, and that any conflicts among these intuitions can be sorted out by giving preference to those intuitions that best satisfy the conditions under which beliefs *are* evidence for their own truth.

However, when intuitionism is reconstructed as a respectable approach to desert, it ceases to compete with the view that our beliefs about desert can be independently justified. The view that a moral intuition is evidence for the truth of the intuited proposition is neutral between the claim that the intuition shows that we are directly acquainted with a moral fact and the claim that it points the way to a deeper and independently intelligible justificatory argument. Moreover, given the problems raised by the direct acquaintance view, the latter claim is surely the more plausible. However, if so, then appeals to intuition are best understood as a prologue to reconstructing the justificatory arguments that have given rise to the intuitions. Thus understood, such appeals lead naturally back to attempts to produce independent justifications of our beliefs about desert.

All this suggests that it is reasonable to assign only a secondary role to our intuitions about desert. Although I believe that many such intuitions do have "probative force," I will not appeal to them alone, but will instead try to unearth the justificatory arguments that underlie them. This will involve establishing why specific actions and characteristics have specific effects on the ways people ought to be treated. Where there are conflicting intuitions about what is deserved, it is obviously impossible to justify every belief

[19] Henry Sidgwick, *The Methods of Ethics*, 7th ed. (London: Macmillan, 1922), bk. 3, chap. 5, secs. 5 and 6.

that every person holds; but even here, we may hope to display the rationale for every important belief by showing how inconsistent beliefs can be derived from a justifiable core belief plus plausible but conflicting secondary assumptions. Throughout, people's intuitions will be invoked only to suggest which beliefs are candidates for justification, and to serve as a check on the justifications produced.

VII

What, finally, is the book's actual argument? Since our topic is the justification of desert-claims, the natural starting point is John Rawls's influential argument that nobody (pre-institutionally) deserves anything because nobody deserves the talents and abilities that make his actions possible. By exposing the defects of this argument, I attempt in Chapter 2 to defuse the most urgent of our puzzles. Having done that, I turn in Chapter 3 to the first of a series of justificatory arguments. Taking my cue from the widely noted but elusive connection between desert and autonomous action, I first consider an argument that attributes the normative force of desert-claims to the value that is conferred on deserved outcomes by agents' own free choices. As it turns out, this argument does justify some significant desert-claims, but it fails to justify many others. To account for these, I try in Chapters 4 through 8 to match different justifications to different sorts of desert-bases. In Chapter 4, I argue that hard workers ought to succeed because their attainment of what they strive for acquires value, in a recognizable way, from their striving itself. In Chapter 5, I defend a purified version of Herbert Morris's suggestion that deserved punishment annuls the unfair advantage which wrongdoers have acquired over others. In Chapter 6, I generalize the principle of diachronic fairness that underlies this contention and apply it to desert of such other things as compensation and wages. In Chapter 7, I argue that what look like homogeneous claims about desert for nonmoral merit are really grounded in a variety of different values and principles. And in Chapter 8, I defend a similar thesis about desert for moral virtue. Although these chapters may leave some marginal desert-claims unjustified, I believe the most significant types of cases are all covered.

Problems remain. For one thing, our puzzle about the past, and why it matters, remains unresolved. Worse, the diversity of desert's normative sources threatens the notion with disintegration. If desert-claims are justified in many different ways, what, if anything, do they have in common? In what sense, if any, is desert a single notion at all? And why, if it is morally significant, does desert systematically give way to rights when their claims conflict? Taken together, these questions define the problematic of the book's final part. In Chapters 9 and 10, the discussion takes a metaphysical turn. In Chapter 9, I argue that one important thing that desert-claims share is a unifying vision of the self. They all presuppose that persons are both closely enough related to (some of) their attributes to deserve things for them and the actions they generate and stable enough over time to deserve things at later moments for actions performed earlier. This vision is not a historical accident, but is forced upon us by our status as deliberating agents. Moreover, in Chapter 10, I argue that coherency in deliberation also forces us to regard features of occurrences as continuing to provide reasons for acting even when the occurrences are past. This resolves our puzzle about time. Since the arguments of both chapters appeal to the requirements of agency, they provide a satisfyingly deep explanation of the connection between desert and free action.

In the final chapter, I take up a further, more normative commonality among desert-claims. Besides sharing a single vision of the self, most desert-claims, I argue, are grounded in values rather than in obligations. Where desert affects what persons ought to do, it generally does so only indirectly. This means that, despite appearances, desert-claims and rights-claims seldom conflict. And just as desert and rights are complementary, so too, in a different way, are desert and justice. In the end, the three notions do not offer competing accounts of what persons should have, but are complexly related elements of a single scheme.

T W O

RAWLS'S ATTACK ON DESERT

Attempting to provide a constructive account of the philosophical basis of desert is only reasonable if there is no a priori reason to deny that desert-claims are what they seem, and that they reflect a moral phenomenon of the first importance. Yet, as we have seen, there is a general argument which, if correct, would preclude this possibility. That argument, advanced by John Rawls, asserts that nobody deserves the advantages that his character or natural abilities make possible, because nobody deserves his character or abilities themselves. As Rawls himself puts it:

> It seems to be one of the fixed points of our considered judgments that no one deserves his place in the distribution of native endowments, any more than one deserves one's initial starting place in society. The assertion that a man deserves the superior character that enables him to make the effort to cultivate his abilities is equally problematic; for his character depends in large part upon fortunate family and social circumstances for which he can claim no credit. The notion of desert seems not to apply to these cases.[1]

If these contentions are correct, and if Rawls is correct in concluding that nobody deserves "the greater advantages he could achieve with [his natural endowments],"[2] then there will be no room for pre-institutional desert. At best, a social system which is justified on quite different grounds may determine a (logically secondary) sense in

[1] Rawls, *A Theory of Justice*, p. 104. See also pp. 15, 75–76, 310–15, and passim.
[2] Ibid., p. 104.

22

which people deserve things. Since this conclusion would vitiate our enterprise from the outset, we must carefully consider the argument that leads to it.[3]

I

We know that Rawls wants to move from the premise that people do not deserve their character or abilities to the conclusion that people also do not deserve the advantages that those "natural assets" make possible. But why, exactly, does he deny that people deserve their character and abilities? Because Rawls mentions the social causes of our effort-making ability, and because our possession of other talents and abilities seems also to be caused, he may appear to be claiming that our "natural assets" are undeserved simply because our possession of them is caused. This interpretation draws some support from its affinity with the incompatibilist claim that persons do not act freely, and are not responsible for what they do, when their actions are caused. Yet exactly because it turns Rawls into a kind of incompatibilist, the interpretation makes one of his premises extremely controversial. If we construe his argument this way, it will not convince anyone who believes that freedom and determinism can be reconciled.

If all our abilities and traits were the result of our own past acts, then the best way of showing we do not deserve to have those abilities and traits might be to argue that we did not induce them in ourselves freely. But the whole thrust of Rawls's position is that we *cannot* be the authors of all our abilities and traits. Since we must

---

[3] Although Rawls has presented the most developed version of the anti-desert argument, an abbreviated version of it also appears in Richard Wasserstrom, "The University and the Case for Preferential Treatment," *American Philosophical Quarterly* 13, no. 2 (April 1976), p. 167. For related discussion, see also Thomas Nagel, "Equal Treatment and Compensatory Discrimination," *Philosophy and Public Affairs* 2, no. 4 (Summer 1973), pp. 348–63; John Schaar, "Equal Opportunity and Beyond," in *Equality: Nomos IX*, ed. J. Roland Pennock and John W. Chapman (New York: Atherton Press, 1967), pp. 228–49; and John Hospers, "What Means This Freedom?" in *Determinism and Freedom in the Age of Modern Science*, ed. Sidney Hook (New York: Collier, 1961), pp. 126–42.

have ability and motivation in order *to* act, we cannot acquire all our abilities and motives *through* action. We may do things to develop our talents, to alter our motives, or to increase our effort-making ability; but all such steps must depend on some earlier complement of talents, abilities, and traits. Once this is made clear, the issue of freedom, and so too of causation, drops out as irrelevant. Properly interpreted, Rawls's claim that our "natural assets" are undeserved rests not on the fact that they are uncaused, but simply on the fact that our possessing them is not the result of anything *we* have done. If their causal genesis is significant, it is only because this highlights our lack of complicity in their production. It is because our talents and abilities antedate our actions that we cannot "claim credit" for them.

When an agent's possession of a given ability is not the result of anything he has done, I shall refer to that ability as a *basic* ability. Formulated in terms of basic abilities, the complete anti-desert argument looks something like this:

(1) Each person has some basic set of abilities, including an ability to exert effort, which does not belong to him as a result of anything he has done.

(2) If a person's having X is not a result of anything he has done, then he does not deserve to have X.

Therefore,

(3) No person deserves to have his basic abilities.

Moreover,

(4) Each action a person performs is made possible, directly or indirectly, by some subset of his basic abilities.

(5) If a person does not deserve to have X, and X makes Y possible, then that person does not deserve Y.

Therefore,

(6) No person deserves to perform his actions, and neither does anyone deserve to enjoy any of the benefits that his actions in turn make possible.

I do not know if Rawls would endorse this version of the argument as his own. However, whether or not he would, it is the version that initially seems most likely to yield his conclusion, and in any event it is worthy of consideration in its own right. For these reasons, I shall confine my discussion to it. Is this argument, or some further refinement of it, sound?

II

Although each step has some intuitive appeal, the argument surely cannot be accepted as it stands; for premise (5), at least, is implausibly strong. If deserving the benefits of our actions did require that we deserve everything that makes our actions possible, then all such desert would immediately be canceled by the fact that no one has done anything to deserve to be born or to live in a life-sustaining environment.[4] If this were the case, then Rawls's insistence that people do not deserve their natural assets would be quite superfluous. Moreover, as Alan Zaitchik has pointed out, anyone who accepts both (5) and "the truism that all deserving is deserving in virtue of some ground or other" will immediately be led to a vicious regress: in order to deserve Z, a person must deserve Z's ground Y, in order to deserve Y, he must deserve Y's ground X, and so on.[5] This regress shows again that (5) rules out the possibility of personal desert for reasons quite independent of the (alleged) fact that we do not deserve our natural talents or abilities.

According to Zaitchik, the fact that (5) rules out the possibility of personal desert, and so contradicts many people's "pre-theoretical certainty that at least some people deserve something,"[6] is itself a *reductio* of (5). It seems to me, however, that this particular way of dismissing (5) proceeds too quickly. If Zaitchik has correctly represented Rawls as intending to produce "a completely general argument which alleges that *no* desert theory could be true for the simple reason that no one ever deserves things,"[7] then we cannot appeal to our intuitive conviction that people *do* deserve things without begging the question against Rawls. What we can ask,

---

[4] I owe this point to Wendy Lotz.

[5] Alan Zaitchik, "On Deserving to Deserve," *Philosophy and Public Affairs* 6, no. 4 (Summer 1977), p. 373.

[6] Ibid., p. 373.

[7] Ibid., p. 371.

however, is that Rawls's premises about personal desert should themselves not be question-begging in turn. Although they must of course be strong enough to yield the desired conclusion, Rawls's premises should also be uncontroversial enough to be acceptable even to persons initially sympathetic to personal desert. As we have stated it, premise (5) fails to satisfy this requirement. Can any alternative premise do better?

Perhaps one can. The basic problem with (5) is that it promiscuously allows a person's desert of Y to be canceled by *all* undeserved necessary conditions for his having Y. Intuitively, this seems excessive, because many such conditions are satisfied not only by the person in question, but also by everyone else. *All* claimants to goods must satisfy such conditions as having been born and existing in life-sustaining environments; and so these conditions, though undeserved by the possessor of Y, have not given him an unfair advantage over anyone. In light of this, the obvious way to amend (5) is to construe it as requiring not that a person deserve *all* the conditions necessary for his having Y, but rather only that he deserve any of those conditions that are not shared by all rival claimants. This modification will in effect transform (5) from a statement of the conditions necessary for a person's deserving Y *simpliciter* into a statement of the conditions necessary for his deserving to have Y while someone else does not. When desert is consistently interpreted as involving a relation of this sort, (5) becomes:

(5a) If one person does not deserve to have X while another does not, and if having X enables the first person to have or do Y while the second does not, then the first person does not deserve to have or do Y while the second does not.

By shifting from (5) to (5a), we can avoid both the charge that this premise is violated by universally satisfied necessary conditions for having Y and the charge that it leads to a vicious regress. Yet despite these gains, the shift to (5a) brings costs of its own. For one thing, since (5a)'s antecedent is now cast in comparative terms, the anti-desert argument's earlier premises will also have to be recast if they are to mesh with (5a). More seriously, the shift to a comparative conception of desert will also require us to make new distinc-

26

tions among the elements of a person's basic abilities. As long as personal desert was construed non-comparatively, it was quite permissible to speak of one's whole basic package of abilities as either deserved or undeserved. However, once we shift to a comparative conception of desert, we must go beyond this. If a person M has a set of basic abilities $a_1 \ldots a_5$, while another person N has the smaller set $a_1 \ldots a_4$, then only special ability a_5 will give M an advantage over N. Because of this, the argument's earlier premises must be reformulated to factor out such shared basic abilities as $a_1 \ldots a_4$.

When both of the required alterations are made, the anti-desert argument emerges looking like this:

(1a) Each person has some basic set of abilities, including an ability to exert effort, which does not belong to him as a result of anything he does. Suppose M's basic abilities include $a_1 \ldots a_5$ while N's include only $a_1 \ldots a_4$.

(2a) If a person's having X is not a result of anything he has done, then he does not deserve to have X while another does not.

Therefore,

(3a) M does not deserve to have a_5 while N does not.

(4a) Let A be an action that a_5 enables M, but not N, to perform.

(5a) If one person does not deserve to have X while another does not, and if having X enables the first person to have or do Y while the second does not, then the first person does not deserve to have or do Y while the second does not.

Therefore,

(6a) M does not deserve to perform A while N does not, and neither does M deserve to enjoy the benefits of A while N does not.

There may be problems with the assumption that abilities are goods that people can deserve relative to other people; for abilities, unlike other goods, are not transferable among persons. But instead of pursuing these problems further, I want to raise a different sort of question. Assuming that its treatment of abilities can be made intelligible, what, if anything, will this version of the argument tell us about desert in particular cases?

By demonstrating that the Rawlsian argument must be reformulated in comparative terms, we have already compelled a measure of retreat from its initial unqualified conclusion that nobody ever deserves anything. In its current form, the argument does leave room for desert in cases in which all the relevant parties have equivalent sets of basic abilities. However, if basic abilities are in fact generally *unequally* distributed, then this concession will leave essentially intact Rawls's central conclusion that personal desert counts for little or nothing. If we are to challenge this conclusion, we must examine more closely the claim that people's basic abilities vary systematically in significant ways. Since this claim is most controversial as it applies to the ability to exert effort, we may begin by considering this aspect of it. On what basis, exactly, can people be said to differ in effort-making ability?

Although Rawls is plainly committed to an environmental explanation of *how* people come to differ in effort-making ability, he offers no explicit defense of the prior claim that they *do* differ in this ability. Thus, any discussion of the rationale for this claim must be quite speculative. As a first attempt at reconstructing that rationale, let us consider the argument that people are shown to differ in effort-making ability by the great differences in the efforts they actually make. If M applies himself assiduously to whatever task is at hand while N's efforts are interspersed with evasion and procrastination, the argument might run, then M must have some effort-making ability that N lacks. N must indeed have *some* effort-making ability, since he does try sporadically; but whatever such ability N has, M must have that much ability plus some additional ability. For how else are we going to account for M's additional industry?

Although this argument may have some initial plausibility, a closer look reveals its weakness. If we are going to infer directly from M's additional industry to his superior effort-making ability, then we will have to do so on the basis of the more general principle that people are not capable of making any more effort than they actually do make. But this principle seems simply to be false. Even persons who would be acknowledged to have superior effort-making abilities are often inclined not to make the efforts necessary to accomplish their goals. Many goals, though desirable, are not worth the effort it would take to attain them; and others, though worth the effort, are blocked by conflicting goals. In light of this, there is obviously room for a distinction between the *possession* of an ability to exert effort and the *exercise* of that ability; and given this distinction, it is easy to understand the difference in M's and N's efforts without supposing that they differ in effort-making ability: we need only view the difference in their efforts as stemming from the different degrees to which they have exercised their common effort-making ability.

Given these considerations, we clearly cannot infer directly from the fact that people differ in their efforts to the conclusion that they also differ in effort-making abilities. However, it remains possible to defend the different-ability thesis in another way. While persons who exert different amounts of effort always *can* be viewed as drawing differently upon similar effort-making abilities, this suggestion may seem implausible when the difference in their efforts is pronounced, systematic, and obviously disadvantageous to the less industrious. In such a case, there is simply no good reason for N to refrain from exercising his effort-making ability; and so it may seem most reasonable to suppose that he does not have a full measure of that ability to begin with. If we defend the unequal-ability thesis in this way, we will in effect be deriving it not as a logical consequence of the difference between M's and N's efforts, but rather via an inference to the best explanation of that difference.

This second way of defending the different-ability thesis is considerably more sophisticated than the first. It is not, however, notably more successful; for even when N's failure to try as hard as M is clearly disadvantageous to him, there remain plausible ways of accounting for it that do not commit us to anything as momentous as a difference in effort-making ability. For one thing, N's comparative lack of effort may simply reflect the fact that he is not as consistently attentive to his interests as M. For another, it may reflect the fact that he is (sometimes or always) less concerned than M to further those interests—that, at least at some moments, he has other priorities. Given these (and no doubt other) alternatives, the different-ability thesis will only provide the best explanation of N's comparative lack of effort in cases in which M and N are equally attentive to their own interests, and in which they are equally concerned to further those interests. But why, in any given case, should we say that M and N *are* equally attentive to, and consistently concerned to further, their respective interests? We surely cannot infer this from the different amounts of effort they make; neither does it seem to be supported by any other easily imaginable fact about them. Moreover, simply to assume it would be to beg the question against the equal-ability thesis. Thus, the proposed explanatory inference seems problematical at best.[8]

There is a further difficulty here. Even if we grant the contention that people commonly differ in effort-making abilities, its conjunction with the other Rawlsian premises still will not entail that M does not deserve the benefits of his superior efforts. According to (5a), a difference in M's and N's effort-making ability will rule out M's desert relative to N only if the difference in their abilities makes it *impossible* for M and N to exert equal amounts of effort. But not every difference in effort-making ability need have this effect. It is easy to see how M and N might differ in effort-making ability, but N might still take steps to match M's superior efforts. For one thing, N can maintain a special vigilance against those distractions that he but not M finds attractive; for another, if N foresees difficulty in avoiding these temptations, he can always take action to avoid them, or to increase his ability to resist them. Of course, Rawls could always maintain that these steps, as well as N's efforts themselves, are blocked by N's lesser effort-making ability; but this contention becomes progressively more difficult to maintain as the range of N's inability is said to increase. Whatever it is that N cannot do, there are surely many things that he *can* do; and since there is no theoretical limit to the steps one can take to increase one's effort-making ability, the number of cases in which

---

[8] Although I have argued against Rawls's uncritical assumption that people differ in effort-making abilities, I do not wish to suggest that Rawls has been the only philosopher to fall into this error. For another example of it, see my own earlier paper, "Justifying Reverse Discrimination in Employment," *Philosophy and Public Affairs* 4, no. 2 (Winter 1975), pp. 165–67.

differences in such ability render differences in effort inevitable seems minimal at best. In light of this, even genuine differences in effort-making ability, should they exist, would seem unlikely to have the moral significance attributed to them by Rawls.[9]

IV

So far, we have seen that Rawls's anti-desert argument is plausible only if desert is understood comparatively; that the argument under this interpretation implies that desert is threatened only by unequal basic abilities; and that it is doubtful whether people's abilities to exert effort are unequal in the relevant way. The Rawlsian argument has thus evidently failed to discredit the thesis that personal desert may be established by conscientious effort. However, people manifestly *do* differ in abilities like physical strength and intelligence, and so a parallel defense does not seem available for the further thesis that personal desert is established by superior achievement. Thus, it is tempting to view Rawls's argument as showing, in effect, that personal desert is properly associated with effort rather than with achievement. Although Zaitchik's approach to the Rawlsian argument differs substantially from mine, he has drawn from it a qualified version of this conclusion. It seems to me, however, that the truth lies elsewhere.

Let us again consider the argument advanced at the end of the preceding section. There, I contended that even if people *did* differ in effort-making abilities, those differences would not inevitably lead to differences in efforts actually expended. By suitably compensating for his lesser effort-making abilities, N might have put himself in a position to exert the same amount of effort that M made; and if N could have done this, then his lesser effort-making ability was not a violation of (5a) at all. But surely something similar can be said for other differences in initial ability as well. Even if M is initially stronger or more intelligent than N, this difference will only entail that M does not deserve what he has achieved rela-

---

[9] For the argument of this paragraph, I owe an obvious debt to Stuart Hampshire, *Thought and Action* (New York: Viking, 1959), chap. 3.

tive to N if the difference between them has made it impossible for N to achieve as much as M. However, differences in strength, intelligence, and other native gifts are rarely so pronounced as to have this effect. The far more common effect of such differences is merely to make it more *difficult* for the less talented person to reach a given level of attainment. He must work harder, husband his resources more carefully, plan more shrewdly, and so on. Because the latter differences do *not* combine with (5a) to yield any conclusions about desert, the Rawlsian premises are evidently compatible with desert for achievement in at least a large number of cases.

The conclusion is reinforced, moreover, by a careful reconsideration of (5a) itself. We were initially led to accept (5a) because intuitively it seems unfair for one person to enjoy benefits from which another has been barred through no act or omission of his own. However, on second glance, this unfairness may be largely mitigated if there is another, comparable benefit that the second person can enjoy instead. It is merely perverse for someone to remain deeply upset over his inability to become a professional athlete when he is perfectly capable of making a successful career in education or business. Because this is so, (5a) is actually *im*plausible when it is applied to particular benefits without regard to alternatives available. To make (5a) generally plausible, we must insist that it range not over particular benefits, but rather over general levels of well-being. Properly understood, (5a) should assert only that if M does not deserve to have X while N does not, and X makes it possible for M to achieve a particular level of well-being which N does not share, then M does not deserve to exist at *that level of well-being* while N does not. Since this alteration will permit even persons with superior talents to deserve the benefits of their achievements as long as others are capable of attaining equivalent levels of well-being in other areas, its result will be to relax still further the constraints that the Rawlsian premises place upon desert for achievement.

But despite this loosening, some constraints clearly do remain. Even after we have allowed both for the greater efforts of the less talented and for the possibility of equivalent achievement in alternative areas, there will remain many cases in which one person has achieved a level of well-being that another could not possibly have achieved. This may be either because the first person's talents were great, because the second person's talents were minimal, or because the first person was just lucky enough to be in the right place at the right time. Moreover, there will remain many other cases in which a person of meager attainments could indeed have achieved more, but only through efforts that it would have been unreasonable to expect of him. In the former cases, and perhaps even in the latter, premises like Rawls's will indeed suggest that the person who has achieved more does not deserve the full benefit of his achievement relative to the other, but rather deserves only the proportion of it that the other could reasonably have been expected to match. Since every high achiever can be paired with some low achiever in this way, it seems to follow that few people can lay absolutely full claim to all the benefits they have achieved.

These considerations suggest that if the Rawlsian premises are correct, we cannot allow people to enjoy the full benefits of their achievements without permitting many persons to be better off than they deserve to be with respect to at least some others. Assuming that undeserved inequalities that do not bring appropriate compensating benefits are unjust, this concession may seem to tell heavily against allowing people to enjoy whatever they have achieved. In fact, however, the situation is more complicated than this; for even if allowing people to enjoy the benefits of their achievements does permit some undeserved inequalities, it may still come closer to giving everyone what he deserves relative to everyone else than any alternative. To see why, consider a simplified situation in which M has much talent and has achieved much, while N has much talent but has achieved little, and O has little talent and has achieved little. In this situation, N and O may well deserve the same amount relative to each other, but M will deserve more relative to N than he does relative to O. Because of this, M's getting precisely what he deserves relative to N will require that he *not* get precisely what he deserves relative to O, and vice versa. Such cases show that it is almost certainly impossible to allow everyone to get exactly what he deserves relative to everyone else. At best, we can try to design a system in which as few people as possible get more or less than they deserve relative to others. Nothing in Rawls's argument suggests either that such a system will not allow most or all people to enjoy most or all of the benefits they have achieved or that its remaining undeserved inequalities will be so weighty as to render it unjust. Hence, there remains at least one version of the claim that people deserve what they have achieved which the Rawlsian argument leaves quite untouched.

V

Up to now, my criticism of the Rawlsian argument has been mainly internal. I have contended that even if we grant that people only deserve things relative to others when having those things is of their own doing [(2a)] and when it is not the result of further undeserved differences [(5a)], we are still not forced to deny that people commonly do deserve things. To conclude, I will abandon this internal perspective and examine premises (2a) and (5a) themselves. Despite their surface plausibility, I will argue that both are questionable.

Of the two premises, (2a) has the more immediate appeal. There is clearly something attractive about the idea that the ways people fare should not be determined by factors beyond their control—by factors that are "arbitrary from a moral perspective."[10] Yet upon further inspection, this suggestion is neither consistent with Rawls's own reasoning nor clearly defensible on its merits. It is not consistent with Rawls's own reasoning because after dismissing all particular facts about persons, he goes on to derive his own principles of justice from abstract and hypothetical facts that are even further removed from anything persons have done or can control. In particular, his own principles are grounded in choices that *would* be dictated by the abstract features of free and rational agency if persons were placed in a certain constrained choice situation. Because these choices are merely hypothetical, and not choices anyone has actually made, they are plainly not within the control of actual agents. Thus, if Rawls's criterion of moral arbitrariness is correct,

---

[10] Rawls, *A Theory of Justice*, p. 74.

these choices must be no less morally arbitrary than a person's actual abilities or character traits. Conversely, if his criterion is incorrect, then there is no reason to say that a person's lack of control over his abilities and traits renders *them* morally arbitrary.

Because this rejoinder is merely ad hominem, it does not settle the question of whether characteristics not involving actions really are morally arbitrary. At most, it shows that saying they are arbitrary cuts deeper than many have thought. But there are also other reasons to view Rawls's criterion of arbitrariness with suspicion. If we accepted it, we would in effect be saying that how a person fares may legitimately depend on what he *does*, but never on what he *is*. Yet even if it is an overstatement to say, with R. E. Hobart, that one's actions are morally significant only insofar as they reveal one's character,[11] it certainly is plausible to say that one's character and other traits may have a moral significance that does not *reduce to* the significance of one's acts. In defense of this statement, we may note both that an agent's character and other traits are more stable and enduring than his acts and that they are, in a familiar sense, more central to his identity. In addition, we may cite our common practice of evaluating character as well as acts. Given all of this, our intuitions and practices do not unqualifiedly support Rawls's claim that all traits beyond one's control are "arbitrary from a moral point of view." To be defensible, that claim would require far more discussion than Rawls provides.

As tenuous as the case for (2a) is, the case for (5a) seems weaker yet. As we have seen, the intuitive reason for accepting (5a)—for saying that M does not deserve to have something N lacks if M has acquired it through the use of an ability N lacks—is that M's greater ability seems to have given him an unfair advantage. But an advantage is only unfair when it prevents one person from competing on equal terms with another. Once this is made clear, the defense of (5a) is seen to presuppose a single (and overly simple) view of the way desert is acquired. Properly understood, it presupposes a wholly competitive model of desert-acquisition. Yet while com-

[11] R. E. Hobart, "Free Will as Involving Determinism and Inconceivable Without It," *Mind* 43, no. 169 (January 1934), pp. 1–27.

petition is certainly *one* important context which gives rise to desert, it is clearly not the *only* such context. Instead, anyone initially sympathetic to desert will hold that people may also come to deserve things in many other ways. They may acquire desert by working hard, acting wrongly, behaving virtuously, performing heroic acts, and so on. There is, of course, much room for disagreement over this list, but the basic point is beyond dispute. Extending effort, acting wrongly, and exhibiting virtue are not variant forms of winning. Hence, where they are concerned, the notion of unfair advantage is hopelessly out of place.

And thus the only plausible general defense of (5a) collapses. If that premise is ever to be acceptable, it will be only in those comparatively few contexts in which desert does arise through victory in competition. Some such contexts—for example, those in which the best-qualified are said to deserve jobs and other opportunities, and entrepreneurs to deserve profits made in competitive markets—are extremely important. However, even in these contexts, the truth of (5a) is hardly obvious; for although some undeserved competitive advantages are plainly unfair, it is far from clear that all of them are. Indeed, if we follow Rawls in construing anything that leads to victory, including superior effort-making ability, as a competitive advantage, then all competitive advantages cannot be unfair. To say that they are would be to preclude the possibility of anyone's winning, and so would rule out the idea of competition itself.

There is obviously much more to be said about fair competition and its role in determining desert. There is also more to be said about the relation between persons and their traits and abilities. Indeed, I believe Rawls is clearly right to stress the importance of this relation for a full understanding of desert. But, having said enough to defuse his general anti-desert argument, I would like to defer further discussion of the issue. For us now, the more pressing question concerns justification. Given that pre-institutional desert is not ruled out, can we find justificatory arguments that are sufficiently compelling to imbue desert-claims with real normative force? And, if so, what will these arguments be like?

THREE

FREEDOM, ACTION, AND DESERT

There are two ways in which we might approach the justification of desert-claims. To demonstrate their grounding, we might attempt either to derive each type of claim from some defensible principle or value associated with its desert-basis—different derivations for different desert-claims—or else to derive many or all of them from a single principle or value associated with some suitably generic feature of desert. Of these approaches, the second is the more elegant. If successful, it would decisively show that there is an important unity beneath the apparent diversity of desert-claims. Moreover, there is one near-generic feature of desert that does seem morally significant enough to have a chance of bearing the argument's weight. This is the connection between desert and autonomous action. Let us begin by exploring it.

I

It is widely recognized that free action has some important link to desert. Ironically, even Rawls acknowledges this. As we saw, his anti-desert argument assumes that a person cannot deserve to have X while another does not unless his having X is the result of something he has done. Here, Rawls implies that desert, if it exists, is somehow rooted in free choice or agency. And similar connections have been noticed by philosophers more sympathetic to desert. James Rachels, for example, writes that

[t]reating people as they deserve is one way of treating them as autonomous beings, responsible for their own conduct. A

person who is punished for his misdeeds is *held responsible* for them in a concrete way. . . . [T]he recognition of deserts is bound up with this way of regarding people. (Emphasis his)[1]

In what sense is recognizing deserts "bound up with" treating persons as autonomous agents? One possibility, suggested by Brian Barry, is that "a person's having been able to have done otherwise is a *necessary condition* of ascribing desert" (emphasis his).[2] But this suggestion, though sensible, is far too weak to justify any specific desert-claims. To do that, the desert-autonomy link must provide some positive reason for persons to have what they are said to deserve. Since it is widely agreed that persons ought to have and exercise autonomy itself, the most natural way of giving such a reason is to argue that the value of a person's acting autonomously is somehow transmitted to, or inherited by, what he is said to deserve. In other words, it may be possible to infer from the premise that it is good that persons act autonomously the conclusion that it is good that they have certain things that flow from their autonomous acts. Although Robert Simon does not (here) mention desert, he seems to have something like this argument in mind when he says:

> Since our performances and appraisals express our choices, evaluations and decisions, since they are our actions, we would not be treated as persons—as autonomous agents—if they were to be dismissed as illegitimate or were totally ignored. . . . [I]f an individual is to be treated as a person . . . the individual's own purposes, goals, intentions and judgments should determine his or her fate, consistent with similar regard for others.[3]

Can we make this argument work? To do so, we must show, first, that autonomous acts have real value, and second, that the link between such acts and the outcomes we take to be deserved is a suit-

[1] James Rachels, "What People Deserve," in *Justice and Economic Distribution*, ed. John Arthur and William H. Shaw (Englewood Cliffs, N.J.: Prentice-Hall, 1978), p. 159.

[2] Brian Barry, *Political Argument* (New York: Humanities Press, 1965), p. 108.

[3] Robert Simon, "An Indirect Defense of the Merit Principle," *The Philosophical Forum* 10, nos. 2–4 (Winter-Summer 1978–1979), p. 237.

able conduit for this value. The first task need not detain us long. Few would deny that persons ought to be able to choose and act freely, and indeed that their doing so is of paramount importance. These claims, whatever their exact interpretation, are central to our shared moral scheme. But if the opportunity to act freely has value, then so too must its exercise. We can hardly say that it is a good thing when someone *can* determine his own fate, but not a good thing when he does. The more difficult question is how the value of autonomous acts is transmitted to particular outcomes. Why should the value of anyone's exercise of freedom mean that he should have one thing rather than another? Indeed, however valuable autonomy is, why should its exercise imply that a person should have anything at all?

To answer these questions, we must look more closely at free action itself. There has, of course, been much discussion of the conditions under which persons act freely, and of the bearing of causality and reasons upon an agent's freedom. For our purposes, though, what matters is not a free act's antecedents, but its projected consequences. Before acting, we typically weigh alternative acts whose consequences extend from the present into the intermediate and more distant future. Our deliberations thus encompass both possible initial acts and the various later events we expect them to cause. But if our deliberation itself displays this complexity, then the contents of the resulting choices must be similarly complex. Because we deliberate with an eye to consequences, our free choices must encompass not just our immediate doings, but also the later lines of development to which we expect them to lead. Thus, at least one connection between free acts and their consequences is internal to the notion of free agency itself.

And, given this connection, we can indeed see why any value that attaches to an autonomous act might carry over to that act's consequences. Because (at least some of) those consequences are part of what an agent chooses, it would be quite arbitrary to say that it is good that the agent perform the act he has chosen, but not good that he enjoy or suffer that act's predictable consequences. Since choices encompass both acts and consequences, any value that attaches to the implementation of choice must belong equally to both.

If someone did *not* have to live with the predictable consequences of his choices—if he were able to go through the motions of deciding what to do, but was invariably shielded from his actions' easily foreseeable results—then he would have only a semblance of freedom. His "autonomy" would be worth little; and if ours is worth more, it is only because we do inhabit a world in which choices have consequences. In light of this, one natural reason for saying that free agents ought to enjoy or suffer specific consequences is that those consequences, where predictable, have acquired value from the fact that they are part of what the agent has chosen. And where the consequences are what the agent intuitively deserves, our belief that he ought to have what he deserves will also fall into place. In that case, what justifies our desert-claim will be the value of the retrospective aspect of freedom itself.[4]

I I

I have just proposed that the value of a person's getting what he deserves may sometimes be attributed to the fact that it is a predictable consequence of his earlier free choice. For ease of reference, let us call this the "expected-consequence account."

At least formally, the expected-consequence account seems well suited to capture the peculiarities of desert. As we have seen, many desert-claims do not correlate with moral obligations. The claim that X deserves A often does not imply that anyone is obligated to

---

[4] Because my argument here distinguishes between an initial act and its later consequences, it may appear to presuppose what Alvin Goldman has called a "fine-grained" approach to act-individuation. However, because the argument aims only to show that *free choice* is directed at foreseeable consequences, the act-consequence distinction is not essential to it. The main point could be made as well by stating that an agent's choices often include *his movements'* foreseeable consequences—a formulation that seems, if anything, to favor a "coarse-grained" approach to act-individuation. For elaboration and defense of the coarse- grained approach, see Donald Davidson, "Actions, Reasons, and Causes," *The Journal of Philosophy* 60, no. 23 (November 7, 1963), pp. 685–700; Donald Davidson, "The Logical Form of Action Sentences," in *The Logic of Decision and Action*, ed. Nicholas Rescher (Pittsburgh: University of Pittsburgh Press, 1967), pp. 81–95; and G.E.M. Anscombe, *Intention* 2d ed. (Oxford: Basil Blackwell, 1963). For a development of the fine-grained approach, see Alvin Goldman, *A Theory of Human Action* (Englewood Cliffs, N.J.: Prentice-Hall, 1970).

provide X with A, to refrain from interfering with X's efforts to acquire or retain A, or to do anything else of this sort. These considerations are sometimes cited as difficulties, as when Mabbott objects that "[i]t takes two to make a punishment, and for a social wrong I can find no punisher. . . . I cannot see how there can be duties which are nobody's duties."[5] But on the expected-consequence account, these facts are not surprising, for the normative implications of freedom are themselves diffuse. Like desert, freedom impinges on our moral scheme not primarily by creating tightly structured sets of obligations, but rather as a value whose promotion always tells for an act or institution. Thus, if desert is grounded in the value of freedom, then its failure to correlate with obligations will also be comprehensible.

The expected-consequence account is the *sort* of account we want. But does it mesh with our intuitions about specific cases? In many instances it does. It coincides, for example, with the intuition that Wilson, who knowingly submitted his application late, now deserves to be disqualified. If this desert-claim is to have normative force, it is surely because one *ought* to suffer the predictable consequences of one's earlier carelessness. And the most straightforward way of explaining this is precisely to say that such predictable consequences inherit the value of the free choices that led to them. For similar reasons, the account correctly accommodates claims of this type: Harris, who didn't bring his raincoat, now deserves to get wet; Simmons, who didn't study for his exam, now deserves to fail. It also accommodates the claim expressed by a reader of the Burlington [Vermont] *Free Press* (in a letter headed "Fate Deserved"):

> With all of the warm weather we have been getting lately, who in their right mind would go out on the ice much less drive a car or truck? . . . Anyone who is crazy enough to drive their vehicle out on the ice deserves to have the vehicle go through the ice.[6]

And the account does not accommodate only desert-claims involving bad outcomes. Just as the man who leaves his umbrella home

[5] Mabbott, "Punishment," p. 154.
[6] Letter to the Editor, March 5, 1984.

when it rains deserves to get wet, so too does the man who brings his umbrella deserve to reach his destination dry. More important, we believe that persons who resourcefully seize opportunities deserve the resulting benefits, that persons who carefully make and execute plans deserve success, and that persons who forego immediate benefits in expectation of longer-range gains deserve those gains. In all such cases, the expected-consequence account explains not only why the deserving party should have something, but also why he should have what we intuitively feel he deserves.

Of course, in the actual world, people seldom have exact foreknowledge of their acts' consequences. Far more often, they know only that each available act has various possible outcomes, and that each such outcome has a given (subjective) probability. Thus, the man who leaves his umbrella at home is apt to know only that there is a certain rough probability that it will rain and a certain probability that it will not. If the probability of rain is high, his getting wet may still be fully a part of what he has chosen. In that case, it may inherit value from his choice even before it occurs. But if the prior probability of rain is roughly .5, then his choice not to bring the umbrella will not distinguish his getting wet from his staying dry. How, then, can we say which outcome inherits the value of his choice?

To answer this question, we must refine our notion of what is chosen. When there is both a significant probability that it will rain and a significant probability that it will not, a person's decision not to bring his umbrella clearly encompasses both possibilities. Properly understood, what he chooses is neither to get wet nor to stay dry, but rather the combination of a certain risk of getting wet and a certain chance of staying dry. Since the magnitude of a risk equals its probability times its (dis)utility, what inherits the value of his choice is not *all* the discomfort of being rained on, but only an amount of it proportional to the probability of rain. As Robert Goodin remarks about two similar examples:

> If [someone] bought 1 out of 1000 tickets for a lottery, the only prize in which is $1000, his or her statistical expectation is a

payoff of $1. That is what he or she deserves—and that is all he or she deserves . . .

Consider, again, someone who takes risks with his or her health—driving without fastening the seat belt, for example. He or she has done something silly, and in some sense deserves to suffer the consequences of such silliness. But being thrown through the windshield is surely far more punishment than he or she could be said to deserve. He or she was, after all, running only a 1 in 10,000 chance of crashing. His or her deserts, calculated as in the lottery example above, would be only 1/10,000th of the pain he or she suffers going through the windshield.[7]

In these and many other cases, the suggestion that the amount of an outcome that is deserved is proportional to the outcome's antecedent probability is in line with our intuitions.

Sometimes, however, our intuitions are different. For example, even if a person does deserve 1/10,000th of the pain that he suffers after not fastening his seat belt and thus running a 1 in 10,000 risk of having an accident, he may not seem to deserve *any* proportion of the pain that he suffers from an accident in which his seat belt was fastened. This is puzzling, since the risks of driving with one's seat belt fastened in some situations are surely just as high as the risks of driving without a seat belt in others. Thus, before we can agree that some risked consequences do inherit value, we must understand why others do not.

To explain this, we must distinguish between risks that are necessary elements of all reasonable lives and risks that are more nearly optional. Quite obviously, the risks of driving under normally hazardous conditions fall squarely within the former category. Although we can adopt policies to minimize these risks—and fastening seat belts is surely among these—any attempt to elimi-

---

[7] Robert E. Goodin, "Negating Positive Desert Claims," *Political Theory* 13, no. 4 (November 1985), pp. 584–85. Goodin's general thesis—that what one deserves is what one would receive if the normal course of events were not disrupted—bears obvious affinities to the expected-consequence account. However, according to Goodin, desert-claims serve only to "point the finger at illicit interventions that are undeserved" (p. 580), and they lack independent normative force.

nate the risks would impose severe limitations on what we can do. Under current conditions, a willingness to accept the risks of driving is a prerequisite to implementing most decisions. But if that willingness is a prerequisite for most specific exercises of freedom, then it is itself more nearly forced upon us than a meaningful expression of our will. Thus, it should not be surprising that the mere choice to drive confers no value on its expected consequences.

Thus far, I have tried to explain only why persons do not deserve all the *bad* consequences that they risk. But it should be clear that analogous reasoning applies to improbable *good* consequences. Where good consequences are antecedently unlikely, they are generally ancillary to an agent's main purpose. Hence, they too are seldom meaningful expressions of his will.

Thus, we can say without fear of *reductio* that some antecedently improbable outcomes do inherit value, after the fact, from the agent's choice. This increases the plausibility of the expected-consequence account. Yet other questions remain. The major difficulty is not that we can envision cases in which outcomes are intuitively deserved without being predictable—cases in which criminals deserve to be punished despite the predictability of their not being apprehended, and in which workers deserve wages they have no hope of receiving. Such cases yield only the disappointing but unremarkable conclusion that the expected-consequences account cannot fulfill its promise of justifying all desert-claims. The more pressing problems involve outcomes that seem undeserved even though they *are* expected—the careful criminal's enjoyment of his spoils, the success of a mediocre scion of a well-connected family, and the like. If *these* examples cannot be disarmed, then we will have to withdraw our claim that value flows from free acts to their expected consequences. And if we do that, our account will justify no desert-claims at all.

III

In what contexts do the predictable consequences of free acts seem undeserved? In general, there are five types of troublesome cases. Expected consequences seem undeserved when they are

1. very easily acquired.
2. the disastrous results of merely careless acts.
3. the spoils of wrongful acts.
4. the harmful effects of self-sacrificing acts.
5. the results of choices made under threat, or in some other illegitimately structured choice situation.

In each case, we may conjecture that something prevents the expected consequence from inheriting value. But what are the interfering factors, and how do they affect our account?

Consider first persons who merely take advantage of readily available opportunities. Such persons include pedestrians who find valuable objects at their feet, heirs who claim inheritances by signing legal documents, and entertainers who earn millions of dollars for single concerts. In each case, the agent does something which he rightly expects to benefit him; but in no case does he thereby come to deserve the benefit. Indeed, heirs—even those who must sign documents to collect their money—are stock examples of persons who do *not* deserve their wealth.

Yet these cases, though technically counterexamples, are easily accommodated. On the proposed account, what initially has value, and thus what confers that value upon expected consequences, is an agent's genuine exercise of autonomy. But exercises of autonomy, whatever they amount to, are surely more than unimpeded acts that will obviously yield large benefits at little cost. Where no more is involved—where the agent neither has to choose among real alternatives nor has to exercise thought or ingenuity nor has to do anything difficult—his choice is too easy, too automatic, to be significant. Though not unfree, it is also not a meaningful expression of his will. Hence, we should not be surprised that it confers no value upon its consequences.

The second sort of case, in which an act's predictable consequences involve great harm or loss, requires different treatment. We may agree that the ice fisherman who has not first tested the ice deserves to lose his truck, but few would say that he deserves to lose his life. Even if both outcomes are equally predictable, the latter desert-claim seems unduly harsh. Similarly, we would balk at the claim that a daredevil who tries to leap a twenty-foot chasm deserves to be paralyzed, or that a heavy smoker deserves to get lung cancer. In part, our hesitation may reflect doubt that these outcomes are predictable with sufficient certainty, but it also has another explanation: that any value which these outcomes inherit is overmatched by their disvalue. To say that personal autonomy is a great good is not to deny that suffering and death are great evils. Thus, when a free act's consequences include such misfortunes, there comes a point at which the value they inherit from the agent's exercise of freedom is outweighed by their intrinsic disvalue. Hence, the feeling that such consequences are not deserved is only to be expected. Far from damaging the expected-consequence account, this intuition is a harmless manifestation of the plurality of value.

The next two sorts of counterexamples are again different. Of these, the third involves undeserved benefits acquired through wrong acts, while the fourth involves undeserved harms suffered as the results of virtuous acts. As examples, we may suppose that Adams has made a fortune as a predictable consequence of his exploitation of the poor and uneducated, while Johnson has predictably suffered a broken leg while rescuing a child from the path of a truck. Taken at face value, the expected-consequence account implies that Adams deserves his wealth and Johnson his injury. This implication is not canceled by the fact that these acts are too trivial to be meaningful expressions of the agents' wills; and neither is either outcome sufficiently tragic to outweigh the value of the agent's exercise of freedom. (Under other circumstances, a predictably broken leg might well be deserved.) Nevertheless, we are intuitively inclined to reject both desert-claims.

But this inclination, too, can be explained; for even if neither agent has suffered a misfortune whose disvalue is great enough to outweigh the value of his free choice, both actions have other aspects whose disvalue seems to do just this. In the Adams case, the positive value of the agent's exercise of freedom is plausibly said to be offset by the negative value of the way he has *exercised* that freedom. Although it is good that Adams has acted freely, it is bad that he has freely chosen to do what is wrong. And because this is bad—

because it would have been far better if Adams had not made this choice—it would also have been better if the consequences of the choice had not played themselves out. In the Johnson case, it is not *what* he has chosen, but rather the necessity of his *making* that choice, that is disvaluable. Although it is good that Johnson has chosen freely, and good also that his choice was a virtuous one, it is bad that the price of virtue is harm or injury to a good man. It would have been far better if Johnson had not *had* to choose between injury and saving the child; and so it would have been better also if the consequences of his choice had not played themselves out.

So far, our counter-examples have neither damaged nor forced us to amend the expected-consequence account. But what, finally, of choices made in illegitimately structured situations? If someone surrenders his money at gunpoint, he may accurately foresee that he will lose it forever. Nevertheless, he clearly does not deserve to lose his money. Why, on our account, is this so?

On one level, the answer is straightforward. If very easy decisions are not significant expressions of an agent's will, then neither, a fortiori, are decisions made at gunpoint. However we analyze coercion, the victim's response to the gunman is surely a paradigm of it. Hence, his response is also a clear case of (one type of) lack of freedom. But the expected-consequence account asserts only that *free* acts confer value on their consequences. Thus, it plainly does not imply that the consequences of the victim's "choice" have any value.

If an agent's options were affected only by the acts of other individuals, then this response would be sufficient. But options are also shaped in other ways. Notoriously, they are influenced by the social institutions under which we live. Opportunities for schooling and training are shaped by society's educational system; career opportunities and potential rewards depend on society's economic institutions; and the types of people with whom one is likely to associate are determined by one's social class. In addition, the activities one can perform without risk of punishment are of course determined by the law. Thus, individually imposed restrictions are arguably not the only sources of unfreedom. If threats can undermine freedom, then so too can the constraints imposed by unjust institutions.

This acknowledgment that the justice of social institutions can affect what people deserve is a necessary concession to Rawls. As such, it may seem to diminish considerably the appeal of the expected-consequence account. We introduced that account to show that desert-claims may have pre-institutional justifications, and so may themselves affect the justice of institutions. But if persons can deserve only the expected consequences of choices that are structured by just institutions, then would it not be circular to say that respect for desert, as determined by the expected-consequence account, is part of what makes institutions just? If we do say this, then would we not be unable to establish whether an expected outcome is deserved without first establishing whether a society is just, but also unable to establish whether a society is just without first establishing whether its agents can enjoy or suffer the expected outcomes they deserve?[8]

One possible rejoinder is that this objection overemphasizes the importance of social institutions. No matter what their society is like, people will always face choices between bringing and leaving their umbrellas, driving and not driving on thin ice, and meeting and missing deadlines. Thus, there may appear to be many choices whose freedom does not depend on the justice of the agent's society. Yet the distinction between options that are and are not socially structured is far from clear. Even if all societies allow certain

---

[8] In posing the problem in this way, I assume that whether someone is coerced depends on whether others have acted wrongly in structuring his situation. If this "moralized" approach to coercion is rejected, it will not be necessary to evaluate the *justice* of one's society to determine whether one has acted freely. Needless to say, this will not invalidate either the claim that a paucity of options restricts freedom or the claim that social institutions are central determinants of options. For a statement of the moralized approach, see Robert Nozick, *Anarchy, State, and Utopia* (New York: Basic Books, 1974), p. 263 and passim. For more detailed discussion and defense, see Alan Wertheimer, *Coercion* (Princeton, N.J.: Princeton University Press, forthcoming). For criticism of the moralized approach, see G. A. Cohen, "Robert Nozick and Wilt Chamberlain: How Patterns Preserve Liberty," in *Justice and Economic Distribution*, ed. Arthur and Shaw, pp. 246–62; and David Zimmerman, "Coercive Wage Offers," *Philosophy and Public Affairs* 10, no. 2 (Spring 1981), pp. 121–45.

choices, the consequences of those choices will differ with the societies' background institutions. This becomes clear when we compare the consequences of risking one's health in a society that provides health insurance with those in a society that does not. And even if an act's consequences include only such natural occurrences as getting wet, those consequences would be very different if the act were against the law. Finally, restricting the expected-consequence account to purely natural outcomes would prevent it from justifying any desert-claims with educational, economic, or legal dimensions. Since these include many of the most significant desert-claims, our difficulty would remain substantially intact.

There is a better way out of the circle. To break out, we need to distinguish between the claim that desert—as justified by the expected-consequence account—plays a *role* in determining what justice requires and the much stronger claim that such desert is the *sole* determinant of justice. Quite clearly, our thesis about the relation between desert and justice requires only the former, more modest interpretation. But once we thus restrict ourselves, our difficulty immediately disappears. We can now consistently say (1) that the other determinants of justice (which may include both reasonable levels of opportunity for all and respect for other forms of desert) must be present before an agent can act freely enough to deserve his acts' expected consequences and (2) that his and others' receiving the deserved consequences of their acts is an additional determinant of their society's justice. Thus construed, the fact that desert presupposes other aspects of justice does not prevent it from being an independent and significant source of normative force. Rather, desert and the other elements may work in tandem to determine the proper structuring of the social order.

IV

Thus, the value of freedom is one genuine source of desert. Yet although many desert-bases are autonomous acts, the value of such acts justifies only a small subset of the corresponding desert-claims. I will end by surveying some types of action-based claims that are not justified by that value.

A first class of cases involves effort. Persons often are thought to deserve things because of the duration, difficulty, or single-mindedness of their efforts. Yet even the most diligent of efforts may not presage success. Scholars who spend years at their studies may deserve secure jobs in their fields, but if their fields are overcrowded, it may be quite predictable that they will not find them. Athletes who train with great dedication may deserve to do well in competition, but no amount of training can overcome a basic lack of coordination. Shopkeepers or farmers who work long hours may deserve to prosper, but some enterprises are just not viable. Moreover, even where success is predictable, hard workers may be no *more* likely to succeed than more talented but less industrious rivals. Even so, we feel that hard workers deserve success more.

A second class of cases concerns not past efforts, but rather reward schedules. In the eyes of many, it is wrong for unskilled laborers to earn minimum wages while advertising executives earn hundreds of thousands of dollars a year. Such differences are felt to be out of line with what is deserved. Similarly, many feel that housewives deserve greater rewards, both material and psychological, than they actually receive for their domestic activities. However, in all such cases, the sizes of the rewards are well known, and hence predictable in advance. Neither laborers nor executives are surprised at their paychecks—indeed, this is just the problem. Hence, what many feel is deserved again fails to coincide with what is antecedently predictable.

We find a similar lack of congruence in a third class of cases. When persons display certain forms of merit—when they act heroically or unselfishly, and when they perform excellently in competitions or on exams—they are commonly thought to deserve various opportunities or goods as rewards. Here again, it seems that they ought to receive what they deserve. But, in many cases, such agents have little prior reason to *believe* that their activities will be rewarded. The person who scores highest on an exam may have good antecedent reason to believe that others will score higher, or that the contested position will be given to the examiner's favorite; the good Samaritan may know nothing about the subsequent behavior of his beneficiary. Since these agents still deserve their rewards, their desert seems unlikely to be grounded in the value that their being rewarded inherits from their autonomous acts.

So far, we have noted three contexts in which the expected-consequence account does not explain why persons deserve benefits. But there are also counterexamples involving deserved burdens and harms. In particular, as we saw, the account sometimes fails to explain why persons deserve punishment. When someone commits a crime, it is indeed predictable that the criminal justice system will attempt to apprehend, convict, and punish him. Because of this, his initial choice does have some connection with his punishment. As Herbert Morris correctly notes:

> [T]here is some plausibility in the exaggerated claim that in choosing to do an act violative of the rules an individual has chosen to be punished. This way of putting matters brings to our attention the extent to which, when the system is as I have described it, the criminal "has brought the punishment upon himself."[9]

Yet construed as a general justification of retributive desert, the expected-consequence account is clearly inadequate; for to apply it, we would have to conflate the prediction that the state will *try* to punish the criminal with the quite different (and often less well-supported) prediction that it will succeed. When a criminal act is carefully planned or the local police are known to be inept, over-burdened, or corrupt, it is unlikely that the state's efforts to punish will be successful. If the criminal knows this, then he chooses to run only a small risk of punishment. On the account developed above, this choice confers value only on an amount of the threatened punishment that is proportional to the probability that it will be administered. But if two persons commit similar crimes, the fact that one is likely to be punished while the other is not does not imply that the former *deserves* more punishment. Thus, once again, there is evidently a source of desert which the expected-consequence account cannot capture.

[9] Herbert Morris, "Persons and Punishment," in Morris, *On Guilt and Innocence* (Berkeley and Los Angeles: University of California Press, 1976), pp. 35–36.

51

This concludes my attempt to derive a justification of desert from the value of autonomous action. In theory, an appeal to some other near-generic feature of desert, or to some other principle or value associated with this one, might yield a more inclusive justification. But I cannot see how such an argument would run. Thus, I shall not pursue this approach further. Henceforth, I will confine myself to the more local principles and values that are associated with specific desert-bases.

F O U R

DESERT AND DILIGENCE

Of all the bases of desert, perhaps the most familiar and compelling is diligent, sustained effort. Whatever else we think, most of us agree that persons deserve things for sheer hard work. We believe that conscientious students deserve to get good grades, that athletes who practice regularly deserve to do well, and that businessmen who work long hours deserve to make money.[1] Moreover, we warm to the success of immigrants and the underprivileged who have overcome obstacles of displacement and poverty. Such persons, we feel, richly deserve any success they may obtain. But what, exactly, does this mean? Do our reactions reflect only admiration and sympathy, or are there more objective reasons why hard workers ought to succeed? What form might such reasons take? Why should the diligent have what they deserve?

I

Let us approach this question indirectly. Before asking how (if at all) our beliefs about the desert of the diligent can be justified, let us look more closely at those beliefs themselves. In particular, let us ask (1) what determines what specific hard workers do deserve and (2) what could be meant by saying they ought to have those things. By starting here, we may both clarify our problem and anticipate its solution.

---

[1] There is of course a difference between deserving to get a good grade and deserving the grade itself. Similarly, we can distinguish deserving to win a prize from deserving the prize. People deserve to get good grades or win prizes if they have worked hard in the past; they deserve the grades and prizes themselves for their actual performances. In this chapter, my topic is the former form of desert; the latter is discussed in Chapter 7.

There is no single answer to the question of what hard workers deserve. A hard-working executive may deserve to be made a vice-president but not to do well on a physics exam. Conversely, a diligent student may deserve to get a high grade but not to be made a vice-president. In each case, what the agent deserves is obviously a function of his particular efforts. But of which aspect of those efforts? We have seen that what he justifiedly expects to achieve is no sure guide; but another feature of his effort holds more promise. Because sustained efforts are always directed at some end—because endeavor is activity with an intentional object—another natural criterion of what hard workers deserve is what they have *tried* to achieve. By this criterion, what any hard worker deserves is just the outcome he has striven to produce. Thus, the reason the student deserves to get a good grade, and the executive to be made vice-president, is that these are the outcomes at which their respective efforts have been aimed. Although this criterion will eventually require refinement, it clearly reflects our basic intuitions.

Assuming that something like this is correct, in what sense might it be true that a hard worker *should have* what he deserves? Like the desert-claims discussed earlier, such claims generally do not imply either that the hard worker has any special right against anyone else or that anyone else has any special obligation toward him. To say that a hard worker deserves something is not to say that anyone is obligated to provide him with it, to refrain from interfering with his efforts to obtain it, or to prevent anyone else from interfering with those efforts.[2] In itself, diligent effort creates no entitlements. It does, however, seem to confer upon one's goal a value it would otherwise lack. When an agent has worked hard to attain a goal, we believe that it would be a good thing if he *did* attain it; and this gives sense to the assertion that he ought to have it. When that assertion has another sense—when others are obligated to promote the goal—the obligations seem merely local and derivative.

As clarified, the thesis whose rationale we want to understand is that diligent efforts confer value upon their intentional objects. But

[2] Cf. Brian Barry: "To say that a venture deserves success does not necessarily commit one to saying that steps ought to be taken to see that it gets it" (Barry, *Political Argument*, p. 106).

when thus framed, it strikingly resembles a more familiar thesis about desires. Like diligent efforts, desires too are directed at intentional objects. What a person wants may not exist when he wants it, and indeed it may never exist at all. Nevertheless, like diligent efforts, desires are widely thought to confer value on their objects. It is widely believed that if M desires X, then, other things being equal, the world would be a better place if M did obtain X than if he did not. This thesis has received its classic statement from Ralph Barton Perry, who argues in *General Theory of Value* that "[a]ny object, whatever it be, acquires value when any interest, whatever it be, is taken in it."[3] And the thesis is held, in only superficially different forms, by many other philosophers.[4]

Given these parallels, a possible normative basis for the desert of the diligent has begun to emerge. Because even idle desires are thought to confer some value on their objects, and because diligent striving is in some sense an extension of desire, we may conjecture that the far greater value of the objects of diligent striving is somehow a function of the way diligent striving surpasses mere desire. Like our earlier proposal that predictable consequences inherit value from autonomous choices, this one links desert-claims to a central element of our moral scheme. However, also like the earlier one, this proposal raises many new questions. Familiarity aside, how can we defend the claim that desires confer objective value on their objects? In what sense is effort an extension of desire? And why, exactly, should this relationship intensify desire's value-conferring effect?

---

[3] Ralph Barton Perry, *General Theory of Value* (New York: Longmans, Green and Company, 1926), pp. 115–16.

[4] Thus, for example: "[I]n no case do we strive for, wish for, long for, or desire anything because we deem it to be good, but on the other hand we deem a thing to be good, because we strive for it, wish for it, long for it, or desire it" (Spinoza, *Ethics* [New York: Dover, 1951], pt. III, Prop. IX, p. 137n); "The sole evidence it is possible to produce that anything is desirable is that people actually do desire it" (John Stuart Mill, *Utilitarianism* [Indianapolis: Hackett, 1979], p. 34); "The immediately good is what you like and want in the way of experience; the immediately bad is what you dislike and do not want" (C. I. Lewis, *An Analysis of Knowledge and Valuation* [LaSalle, Ill.: Open Court, 1946], p. 404). In her recent article "Two Distinctions in Goodness" (*The Philosophical Review* 92, no. 2 [April 1983], pp. 169–95), Christine M. Korsgaard attributes a version of the thesis to Kant.

II

Not all aspects of the connection between desire and value are equally important for us. In the past, philosophers often asked whether value can be *defined* in terms of objects of desire.[5] But this dispute, besides presupposing an analytic-synthetic distinction that many now reject, is irrelevant to our concerns. Even if value cannot be defined at all, we will be as well served if desires *contingently* confer value on their objects. Similarly, we need not decide whether *only* desire-like attitudes confer value; for our argument requires only that desires (and so too diligent efforts) be among the factors that do this. What does matter, though, is that desire be at least *sufficient* for value—that we be able to infer from "*M* desires *X*" to "*M*'s having *X* is valuable in itself."

Can we defend this inference? To do so, we might try arguing, first, that if a person wants something, his getting it is at least a part of *his* good, and, second, that if something is part of any person's good, it must thereby acquire value in itself. Of this argument's steps, the first invites the familiar objection that many desires prove harmful when satisfied; but to this objection, there is an equally familiar reply. In such cases, what is harmful may be not strictly the satisfaction of the desire, but only the *effects* of the occurrence that satisfies it (which of course may include the frustration of other desires). Yet even if this response is satisfactory, the argument's second step raises further problems. In the recent metaethical literature, a number of philosophers have tried to show that reason forces us to make the move from "*X* is good for *M*" to "*M*'s having *X* is good in itself" (or at least the closely related move from "*M* has reason to seek *X*" to "Everyone has reason to promote *M*'s having *X*").[6] But while much of this discussion is extremely interesting, no

---

[5] The thesis that value can be so defined is defended by Perry in *General Theory of Value*. The viability of Perry's definition is criticized by Ross in *The Right and the Good*, chap. 4. For more general arguments against the possibility of defining value, see Moore, *Principia Ethica*.

[6] See, for example, Alan Gewirth, *Reason and Morality* (Chicago: University of Chicago Press, 1978), and Thomas Nagel, *The Possibility of Altruism* (Oxford: Oxford University Press, 1970).

argument along these lines has commanded widespread assent.[7] Moreover, although I cannot here discuss the difficulties the arguments raise, a number of these clearly are serious. Thus, pending further progress, this route to the desires-confer-value thesis seems at best problematical.

Is there any other way of defending the thesis? Given the record, no quick categorical defense seems likely to succeed. But what may be possible—and what would suffice for present purposes—is a hypothetical defense. In other words, we might conditionally justify the thesis by showing that it follows from some *other* belief that is plausible or, in the current context, beyond dispute. Moreover, when we reflect on the preconditions for morality itself, we do encounter a further belief that seems to lead naturally to the desires-confer-value thesis. Put most simply, this belief is that persons themselves matter—that they are, in some sense, "ends in themselves." As Kant famously discerned, we cannot even raise the question of how we ought to act toward others unless we first assume that each person, in and of himself, has some absolute value. Moreover, this assumption clearly draws important support from

---

[7] Indeed, Nagel himself no longer accepts the inference from "*M* has reason to seek *X*" to "Everyone has reason to promote *M*'s having *X*"; neither does he now accept the desires-confer-value thesis. In his recent book *The View from Nowhere* (Oxford: Oxford University Press, 1986), he writes that "[t]hough some human interests (and not only pleasure and pain) give rise to impersonal values, I now want to argue that not all of them do. If I have a bad headache, anyone has a reason to want it to stop. But if I badly want to climb to the top of Mount Kilimanjaro, not everyone has a reason to want me to succeed" (p. 167). In defense of the latter claim, he argues that "[i]t seems too much to allow an individual's desires to confer impersonal value on something outside himself, even if he is to some extent involved in it. The impersonal authority of the individual's values diminishes with distance from his inner condition" (p. 169). This argument against a generalized version of the desires-confer-value thesis trades on (1) Nagel's assimilation of the value-conferring effect of desires to other sorts of effects that diminish with distance, and perhaps also (2) the tacit suggestion that if the value-conferring effect of desire did not diminish with distance, we would be swamped with value ("it seems too much . . ."). But exactly why should we accept any such "radio-signal" model of desires? Is it even clear what Nagel's metaphor of "distance" from the self (as opposed to simple spatial or temporal distance) amounts to? And wouldn't proliferating values remain a problem even if desires did confer value only when their objects were states internal to the desiring party? In light of these questions, the force of Nagel's argument is obscure.

the fact that persons care, intensely and complexly, both about what happens to themselves and other entities and about the outcomes of their own actions. Not only are the beings to which morality ascribes fundamental value capable of taking other things to have value, but their taking those other things to have value is central to what makes them valuable. Thus, it does seem natural to hold that a portion of their value devolves upon what they value— that some of the absolute value of persons is transferred to, or inherited by, the things they care about. If persons themselves matter, then what matters *to* persons should matter as well.[8]

This line of reasoning makes it plausible to say that desires confer some value on their objects. At any rate, I shall henceforth accept that claim. But how does this pertain to the objects of diligent striving? How does it show that *they* have value? At first glance, the relation may seem straightforward, for diligent striving is itself a reliable sign of desire. Persistent attempts to achieve a result, and sacrifices made to obtain it, are the strongest possible evidence of a stable and enduring desire for it. More deeply, desire and effort may be conceptually related; for on various accounts, it is logically impossible to desire something without being disposed to try to get it.[9] If even the former connection holds, then all diligently pursued outcomes are desired. Hence, if all desired outcomes have value, then so too do all outcomes that are diligently pursued.

Does this reasoning provide an adequate basis for our belief that hard workers deserve to succeed? If that belief implied only that the success of hard workers has some value, then the reasoning might indeed suffice. But, in fact, the belief implies much more. When we say that the diligent deserve to succeed, we mean precisely to distinguish them from equally desirous but less industrious persons. We believe, at a minimum, that it is far better for a hard worker to

[8] If this line of reasoning is correct, the contrast between Kantianism and utilitarianism is less stark than is often assumed; for the idea that persons are "ends in themselves" will underlie not only Kantian normative principles, but also the theory of value upon which (one popular version of) utilitarianism rests.

[9] This view is held in common by philosophical behaviorists and by proponents of some versions of functionalism and the identity theory. See, for example, Gilbert Ryle, *The Concept of Mind* (New York: Barnes and Noble, 1949), and D. M. Armstrong, *A Materialist Theory of Mind* (New York: Humanities Press, 1968).

succeed than for any ordinary desire to be satisfied. The value of a hard worker's success, if not different in kind, seems at least vastly different in degree. But why, on our account, should this be?

One possibility, suggested by our earlier discussion, is that the industrious and the idle have relevantly different desires. As we saw in Chapter 2, the mere fact that someone does not steadily pursue a goal suggests that it is not consistently important to him. Even if he sometimes wants it, his distractibility and unwillingness to sacrifice suggest that, at least at intervals, other aims take precedence for him. To this extent, his desire is less strong than that of the diligent striver. But if desires do confer value on their objects, then the amounts of value conferred should vary with the desires' strength and duration. Hence, it may seem only natural that the desires of the diligent confer much greater value than those of procrastinators and idlers.

Yet this suggestion can hardly capture the normative significance of sustained effort. As intense and continuous as a hard worker's motives are, they remain mere desires and nothing more. For this reason, their normative impact seems far too slight to support our judgments about what the hard worker deserves. And this conclusion is reinforced when we compare the desert of persons who actually have worked hard with that of persons who were similarly motivated but could not implement their desires. If a hard worker's strong desire to achieve his goal were the main basis of his desert, there would be no relevant difference between, for example, a violinist who practiced regularly for twenty years, another who would have practiced regularly but for arthritis, and a third who would have practiced regularly but for the need to earn a living. In that case, not only hard workers, but also those who *would* have worked as hard if given the opportunity, would deserve the objects of their (actual or hypothetical) labors. But, in fact, we do not believe anything like this. We regard persons who have not worked hard because they were incapacitated, or because they lacked opportunities, as unfortunate rather than deserving. Intuitively, only actual sustained effort creates actual desert.[10]

[10] For some implications of the view that only actual activity creates actual claims,

III

Thus, we cannot attribute the desert of the diligent to the special quality of their desires. If anything confers sufficient value on their goals, it must be precisely their efforts themselves. But *do* sustained efforts have this effect? And, if so, why?

Let us recall (what was presented as) the rationale for the desires-confer-value thesis. As we saw, that thesis seems ultimately to rest on the value of persons themselves. If persons matter, then what matters *to* persons must matter as well. This seems to be why a person's wanting something invests that thing with a value it would otherwise lack. But if so, then sustained efforts will indeed confer more value than desires if the objects of such efforts matter to persons in a deeper way. Moreover, in at least one sense, the objects of diligent striving do matter to persons more deeply, for diligent striving represents a far greater commitment than does mere desire. First, sustained effort stems from will and judgment as desire typically does not. What someone wants is not directly within his control, while what he does over an extended period of time generally is. Second, sustained effort forecloses other options as mere desire does not. Wanting something, even strongly, is compatible with wanting any number of incompatible other things, while doing something, even something easy, is incompatible with doing many other things.[11] A fortiori, steadfastly pursuing an outcome requires foregoing many other activities that one would find pleasant or worthwhile.

Do these aspects of diligent striving imply that it confers more value on its objects than mere desire? Prima facie, this may not seem obvious; for however committed to his goal a hard worker is, achieving that goal need not be the outcome he most prefers. Even if someone devotes his whole life to a project, he may do so only

---

as that view bears on questions of compensatory justice, see George Sher, "Ancient Wrongs and Modern Rights," *Philosophy and Public Affairs* 10, no. 1 (Winter 1981), pp. 3–17.

[11] "We cannot speak a loyal word and be meanly silent, we cannot kill and not kill in the same moment; but a moment is room wide enough for the loyal and mean desire, for the outlash of a murderous thought and the sharp backward stroke of repentance" (George Eliot, *Daniel Deronda* [New York: Signet, 1979], p. 35).

because other options are closed to him. Thus, a man who single-mindedly pursues a musical career might have undertaken a very different life, and might have changed his course at any point, if he had seen a realistic chance of becoming a professional linebacker. If so, then his consistent preference was surely to play professional football rather than to achieve musical excellence.

The existence of such cases is undeniable. But to concede this is not to concede that strong desire confers more value than (or even as much value as) sustained effort. Indeed, there remains compelling reason to say the opposite. We have already observed that actions (including omissions) foreclose options as mere desires do not. Because actions do foreclose options, it follows that any agent who exerts a sustained effort is making an important sequence of allocative decisions. In diligently pursuing his goal, he is investing a major portion of his scarce time and energy in his goal's achievement. Since his time and energy *are* limited, he is, in a sense, investing his non-renewable resources. But the metaphor of resources should not mislead. Unlike other resources, our time and energy are not just means of augmenting the effects of our actions. They are, instead, the raw materials of those actions themselves. Since our lives are constituted by our actions, our time and energy are thus the very stuff of which we fashion our lives. Hence, any agent who devotes a major portion of his time and energy to achieving a goal is quite literally making that goal a part of himself. By single-mindedly pursuing the goal, he is weaving it into the fabric of his life.

By contrast, the other forms of valuation have no comparable status. Even strong preferences and desires, if never implemented, are external to most aspects of day-to-day life. Moreover, acts that lack consistency—the efforts of persons who cannot stick to things—are too diffuse to be deeply implicated in agents' lives. Thus, of all the modes of caring, only sustained effort both provides a person's life with overall direction and shapes a large range of his sub-goals, preoccupations, and habits. Only such effort is implicated across the broad spectrum of his cognitive, conative, and practical activities. And this fact is surely an adequate basis for the inchoate belief that hard work confers far more value on its objects than other modes of caring. If only sustained effort pervades an agent's life, then only such effort can invest its object with a substantial portion of the agent's value.

With this, we arrive at what I take to be the correct explanation of why the diligent ought to succeed. They ought to succeed because their sustained efforts are substantial investments of themselves—the ultimate sources of value—in the outcomes they seek. Reversing Marx's aphorism that value is congealed labor,[12] we might express the point by saying that (sustained and goal-directed) labor is congealed value. Of course, this suggestion is only as convincing as the view that persons are constituted by the specific acts they perform, and by the specific act-related traits they possess. However, since the grounding of this view is complicated, I shall defer discussion of it. We will return to it in Chapter 9.

I V

For now, we face more immediate worries. I have argued that though all valuations confer some objective value on their objects, diligent effort confers far more value than mere desire. But can the idea of an object of effort—of a hard worker's goal—really bear the argument's weight? Unlike desires, which are individuated by their objects, efforts often seem to be identifiable *without* reference to goals. It seems intelligible to say that someone has worked hard without mentioning anything for which he has worked. Thus, we cannot take it for granted that every hard worker's goal can be unambiguously specified.

To focus the problem, let us introduce some examples. Consider a merchant who keeps his small shop open until eleven o'clock each night. This merchant may at once be trying to: attract new customers, retain old ones, build his bank account, provide for the security of his family, and increase the price he will get when he sells

---

[12] Marx's aphorism is cited by G. A. Cohen in "The Labor Theory of Value and the Concept of Exploitation," *Philosophy and Public Affairs* 8, no. 4 (Summer 1979), p. 346. Cohen argues that the thought expressed in the aphorism is false, and that it tends to be confused with another which is superficially similar. His reference is to *Capital*, vol. 1 (Moscow 1961), pp. 39–40.

his business. Of which outcome, exactly, do his efforts render him deserving? Or consider a writer who spends ten years working on a novel. He may simultaneously be trying to: write a good novel, write a best seller, resolve the problems raised by alternating first- and third-person perspectives, please his mother, and be honored at lots of autographing parties. Which of these outcomes does he deserve, and why?

To answer these questions, we need some way of regimenting diverse aims. Because desert will obviously attach to basic rather than to subordinate goals, we need a principled way of determining which goal is basic or dominant. In many cases, the obvious criterion is hierarchical order. For the shopkeeper, the goals of attracting new customers, retaining old ones, building a bank account, and increasing the shop's value are all subsumed under the more general goal of making money. Moreover, this goal in turn seems to be subsumed under the still more general goal of providing security for his family. Similarly, the writer's goal of combining diverse narrative perspectives appears to be subsumed under the general goal of writing a good novel (of a particular sort). Where these goals are concerned, we can safely conclude that the shopkeeper deserves to earn enough money to provide his family with security and the writer deserves to write a good novel. These conclusions match our intuitions.

If all goals were hierarchically nested, this strategy alone would resolve our problem. But this is not always the case. When our hard-working novelist pursues both artistic and financial success, it may well be that neither goal is subsumed under the other. Even if he expects a good book to bring him financial success, he may not be trying to write a good book (solely) in order to make money. Instead, it may be that he would continue writing to achieve artistic success if he believed financial success were unattainable, and that he would continue writing to achieve financial success if he believed artistic success were impossible: each goal is distinct and independent for him. Moreover, if *two* goals can be independent, then so can numerous others. It is counter-intuitive to say that any agent who simultaneously pursues n independent goals thereby comes to deserve n distinct good outcomes. Thus, where goals are not hierarchically ordered we must find some other way of ascertaining which is dominant, and hence which determines what the agent deserves.

To do so, we must alter our counterfactual question. Instead of asking whether the agent would continue to pursue each goal if he believed the other were unattainable, we must ask which goal he would pursue if he believed that each were attainable *only at the expense of the other*. We must, in other words, imagine a further counterfactual situation in which he believes his goals to be individually attainable but jointly incompatible. This means, for example, imagining that our writer believes that his further pursuit of artistic success will preclude financial success, and vice versa. If the writer believes this, several things might happen. He might, on the one hand, decide to forego financial success because it requires that he sacrifice artistic integrity. In that case, artistic and not financial success is his basic goal, and so is what he primarily deserves. Alternatively, he might sacrifice artistic integrity. In that case, his dominant goal is to make money, and so he deserves primarily this. He might, finally, find it difficult to choose, and continue to pursue both goals or vacillate fruitlessly between them. In that case, there is simply no right answer to the question of which of his goals is more basic. At best, our account will imply that he deserves each outcome to a degree, but neither as strongly as he would if he were more purely motivated.[13]

One further complication warrants mention. So far, we have considered only the problem of multiple goals. But rather different problems arise when continuous efforts are directed at *no* clear goal. Suppose, for example, that someone has little ambition, but for years has had to work hard just to survive. What, on our account, does *he* deserve? We are, I think, pulled two ways. On the one hand, we do not feel that he deserves to achieve financial independence or a position of responsibility, even though others who have worked no longer or more strenuously may deserve these things. Here the explanation is that efforts made only in response to immediate needs are not goal-directed in the more stringent

[13] After writing this section, I discovered that Alisdair MacIntyre makes some of the same points about dominant and subordinate goals in *After Virtue*, chap. 15.

sense of being integrated parts of a larger plan. Yet, on the other hand, even the labors of the unambitious clearly do create some desert. For one thing, all workers, including unambitious ones, deserve reasonable wages for their labors. For another, we feel that, having worked when able, a person deserves to live decently in his old age. Of these intuitions, the first is inexplicable on the current account and must be justified differently if at all. But the second—that workers deserve decent lives when they are old—may indeed receive some justification from this account. Even if one does work primarily to survive, one's survival is desirable in part because it makes possible a later life. Hence, even an unambitious worker's efforts can be viewed as directed at, and so as conferring some value upon, the longer-range goal of his later well-being.[14]

V

Efforts with multiple or ambiguous goals pose no real problem for us. But another class of objections may seem more damaging. As presented, our account seems to imply that *all* diligent efforts confer value on their objects. Yet all hard workers surely do not deserve success. Even if someone has worked hard to achieve a goal, we do not believe he deserves to achieve it if his doing so would badly harm him; neither do we attribute desert to hard workers whose projects are either unrealistic or morally impermissible. If our account cannot accommodate these intuitions, it is badly defective.

The possibility that a hard worker's success might harm him—that, all in all, he might be better off not achieving his goal—should not be overstated. It is true that getting what we want is sometimes

[14] These remarks should not be taken to imply that all diligent efforts are exclusively means to independently specifiable ends. As Charles Fried convincingly argues in *An Anatomy of Values* (Cambridge, Mass.: Harvard University Press, 1970), few purposive acts *are* performed as means alone. Instead, according to Fried, most activities are structured by one or more rational principles, obedience to which is an end in itself. These principles include, but are not exhausted by, those of morality, friendship, art, and the quest for knowledge. Fried's penetrating observations do not discredit our contention that diligent strivers deserve to succeed because their sustained efforts confer value on their goals. However, his observations do suggest that what is deserved often includes the opportunity to follow through on earlier actions as one's rational principles demand.

not, all things considered, in our interest. But because sustained effort involves far more commitment than does desire, it defines an agent's interests to a far greater degree. Hence, its success is far less likely than the satisfaction of any given desire to preclude other outcomes of greater worth to the agent. In addition, where successful effort *is* bad for an agent—where, for example, it causes the disintegration of his marriage or the ruin of his health—the most that generally follows is that the effort was not in his interest *when he undertook it*. Once the effort has been made (the only time an ascription of desert is in place), its bad effects often are already produced or in train. Thus, the best remaining outcome for him generally does include the success of that effort.

Given these considerations, the only cases in which the success of an agent's past effort is not in his overall interest are ones in which *that success itself* will gravely harm him, for example, by destroying the harmony of his family, ruining his health, or irretrievably disrupting his peace of mind. When such effects ensue, we do feel that the agent does not deserve them. Yet this hardly implies that he does not deserve his success. Since losing his health or family is no part of what the agent has diligently sought, it is also no part of what counts as success for him. Thus, we can consistently say both that he does deserve to achieve his diligently pursued goal and that he does *not* deserve the harm that achieving that goal will (contingently) bring.

This rejoinder is possible because harms caused by one's success are conceptually separable from that success itself. But other counterexamples do not yield to such treatment. In other cases, what intuitively seems undeserved is exactly the outcome the agent has diligently sought. Thus, we feel that hard workers do not deserve to succeed when their efforts are directed at blatantly unrealistic goals. We do not believe that an untalented poet deserves to write a great poem because he has striven for years to do so, that a mediocre tennis player deserves to compete at Wimbledon because his long hours of practice have been directed solely at that end, or that a political hack deserves to be elected president because he has sought this goal for so long. Nor, again, do we believe that hard workers deserve to succeed if their projects are morally impermissible. A safecracker does not deserve to escape with the contents of a vault because he has spent five years tunneling into it; neither does a political fanatic deserve to succeed at a painstakingly plotted assassination.

If all diligent efforts confer value on their objects, and if this is why hard workers deserve to succeed, then why do we have these intuitions? Why do we not feel that diligent strivers deserve to achieve even unrealistic or immoral goals? To explain the intuitions without withdrawing the effort-confers-value thesis, we must somehow show that, in these cases, any value that is conferred by the agent's hard work is nullified by disvalue from some other source. This response is not unfamiliar; we also made it in reply to objections to the expected-consequence account. But why, exactly, should the achievement of unrealistic or immoral goals have negative value?

Interestingly enough, the disvalue of unrealistic goals is established by the expected-consequence account itself. When an agent's goal is unrealistic, it is the failure of his efforts that is predictable. But, as we saw in Chapter 3, it is generally sufficient for an outcome's having value, and for the agent's consequently deserving it, that that outcome have been predictable from the agent's earlier activities. In most contexts, this source of value simply operates independent of diligent effort. However, in the cases of the untalented poet, the mediocre tennis player, and the political hack, the two sources of value conflict. If we focus on their diligent efforts, we are led to believe that these agents ought to succeed, while if we focus on the easy predictability of their failure, we are led to believe that they ought to fail. Thus, it is hardly surprising that we are unwilling to say unequivocally that the poet, tennis player, or politician deserves to succeed *or* fail. The explanation is that our two sources of value—our two sufficient conditions for desert—cancel one another out.

And a similar response explains why we feel that diligent agents do not deserve to succeed at morally impermissible projects. Here again, the explanation is that the value conferred by their efforts is offset by the disvalue—this time the *moral* disvalue—that stems from the wrongness of their projects. At first glance, it may seem illegitimate to infer that because an agent's efforts have negative moral value their outcomes must have negative value as well. But when a person's efforts are goal-directed, the negative moral value appears to attach to the whole event-sequence that begins with the formation of his intentions and ends with the achievement of his goal. Thus, the sequence's final element—the achievement of the goal—must itself have negative value given its causal antecedents.

Thus, the last objection falls away, and the explanation proceeds as before. Like our intuitions about unrealistic hard workers, the intuition that diligent but immoral effort creates no desert reflects no defect in the effort-confers-value thesis, but only the plurality of the sources of value.

FIVE

DESERVED PUNISHMENT

We have now discussed two ways in which a person's actions may render him deserving of a particular outcome. Yet even together, these accounts do not come close to justifying all significant desert-claims. Perhaps most conspicuously, neither explains why persons who have acted wrongly now deserve to be punished. Wrongdoers do not diligently pursue their own punishment; neither is it always predictable from their acts. Thus, if their desert is to be understood, it must be in terms of some third sort of justification. But what further principle or value is involved, and how would an appeal to it work?

I

More than other forms of desert, desert of punishment has been much discussed by philosophers. The discussion has no doubt been encouraged by the air of paradox that surrounds the assertion that actions that are wrong in ordinary contexts are permissible or mandatory as punishment. It may also have received impetus from the felt inadequacy of the forward-looking justifications so eagerly proffered by utilitarians. But a cursory historical survey makes it clear that although retributivism has been, and still is, a live philosophical option, its theoretical base has not been clearly articulated.

Of the classical retributivists, the two most famous are Kant and Hegel. According to both, retribution is in some sense a demand of justice. As Kant puts it:

> [W]hat is the mode and measure of punishment which public justice takes as its principle and standard? It is just the principle

69

of equality, by which the pointer of the scale of justice is made to incline no more to the one side than the other. It may be rendered by saying that the undeserved evil which any one commits on another, is to be regarded as perpetrated on himself.[1]

And in Hegel's words:

The injury [the penalty] which falls on the criminal is not merely *implicitly* just—as just, it is *eo ipso* his implicit will, an embodiment of his freedom, his right; on the contrary, it is also a right *established* within the criminal himself, i.e., in his objectively embodied will, in his action. The reason for this is that his action is the action of a rational being and this implies that it is something universal and that by doing it the criminal has laid down a law which he has explicitly recognized in his action and under which in consequence he should be brought as under his right.[2]

In response to Kant, we want to know *why* we ought to regard the wrongdoer's act as "perpetrated on himself" when it is in reality perpetrated on another. Moreover, even if we do so regard the wrongdoer's act, it is not clear why we are entitled to bring about what we envision by actually treating him as he has treated his victim. In response to Hegel, we want to know why justice *should* be thought to confer on any wrongdoer a "right" to be punished, and why, even if such a right exists, the wrongdoer should not be entitled to waive it. It is true that the wrongdoer, in demonstrating his indifference to the rule he breaks, must also demonstrate indifference to a principled prohibition on acts that treat him as he has treated his victim. But even so, it is unclear why this demonstration of indifference, unlike a merely verbal one, should legitimize (or, a

---

[1] Immanuel Kant, *The Philosophy of Law*, Part II, trans. W. Hastie, in *Philosophical Perspectives on Punishment*, ed. Gertrude Ezorsky (Albany: State University of New York Press, 1972), p. 104.

[2] G.W.F. Hegel, *The Philosophy of Right*, trans. F. M. Knox (Oxford: Oxford University Press, 1942), sec. 100, p. 70.

fortiori, mandate) any act that is ordinarily illegitimate.[3] In the absence of well-motivated answers to these questions, neither the pervasive metaphor of scales and balances nor appeals to the criminal's "objectively embodied will" are apt to induce conviction.

Nor do things improve much when we turn to more recent discussions. Of the defenses of retributivism proposed in this century, one of the most interesting is that of G. E. Moore. Because Moore was a consequentialist, it may seem inconsistent to rank him as a retributivist at all. However, Moore's contribution was precisely to show that one *can* combine the two positions if one is liberal enough about the goods that one says should be maximized. More specifically, what one must say is that

> [i]f pain is added to an evil state of either of our first two classes [that is, love of evil or ugliness and hatred of what is good or beautiful], the whole thus formed is *always* better, *as a whole*, than if no pain had been there. . . . It is in this way that the theory of vindictive punishment may be vindicated (emphasis his).[4]

Moore's retributivism, unlike that of Kant and Hegel, views punishment as justified not by considerations of rights or justice, but rather by the value it brings. Thus, if the account is construed as an explanation of why the guilty deserve to be punished, it allows us to assimilate desert of punishment to the other forms of desert that are grounded in value rather than in obligation. However, precisely because Moore's account allows this, it raises serious questions in its turn. For one thing, even if there *is* considerable value in the matching of suffering to evil, it hardly follows that all methods of producing that value are legitimate. Acts of punishment, in particular, are problematical precisely because they are the kinds of acts that are ordinarily impermissible. In view of this, few non-utilitarians will be satisfied with a "defense" of punishment that consists

---

[3] One possibility here is that the wrongdoer's act amounts to a gesture of consent to others acting similarly toward him. For critical discussion, see George Sher, "An Unsolved Problem About Punishment," *Social Theory and Practice* 4, no. 2 (Spring 1977), pp. 161–63.

[4] Moore, *Principia Ethica*, sec. 128, p. 214.

solely of a demonstration that it produces a novel kind of value. And even if we grant Moore's "ideal utilitarian" framework, his defense of punishment is inconclusive; for its central claim, that pain acquires value when appended to previous evil, is given no defense. Since that claim is clearly part of what any non-retributivist will deny, Moore's "theory" at best merely restates what the retributivist needs to explain.

To some degree, these objections apply also to the theory of Moore's contemporary, W. D. Ross. Like Moore, Ross believes that we can "derive the prima facie duty of . . . punishment from the superiority of the state of affairs produced,"[5] but he offers no defense of the claim that there is value in the matching of pain to evil. Unlike Moore, however, Ross is impressed by the difficulty of both ascertaining any individual's degree of vice and defending any state activity whose aim is not "to protect the most fundamental rights of individuals." Given these considerations, Ross insists that any workable defense of institutionalized punishment must appeal not to the value that punishment produces, but rather to the rights it safeguards. To ground punishment in rights, Ross goes on to argue that "the main element in any one's right to life or liberty or property is extinguished by his failure to respect the corresponding right in others,"[6] and that

> [the law] is a promise to the injured person and his friends, and to society. It promises to the former, in certain cases, compensation, and always the satisfaction of knowing that the offender has not gone scot-free, and it promises the latter this satisfaction and the degree of protection against further offenses which punishment gives.[7]

Taken together, these contentions imply that state punishment is legitimate because the wrongdoer has forfeited his right *not* to be punished, and that such punishment is (prima facie) obligatory because the law is a promise *to* punish. This position departs from (and is curiously unintegrated with) Ross's earlier claim that pun-

[5] Ross, *The Right and the Good*, p. 58.
[6] Ibid., p. 60.
[7] Ibid., pp. 63–64.

ishment is justified by the value it brings. Nevertheless, in defending punishment by invoking a *combination* of rights-related principles, it represents a potential improvement over other, simpler accounts.

Yet at least as a rationale for *desert* of punishment, Ross's approach remains unsatisfactory. First, and most obvious, if a wrongdoer ought to receive the punishment he deserves merely because society's laws are a promise to inflict it, then there is *no* reason why wrongdoers ought to be punished when they have broken no laws. However, some wrongdoers, such as high-ranking Nazis, have broken no laws, and yet they *do* deserve punishment in a sense that implies that they ought to receive it. Second, because one cannot incur an obligation to do something wrong merely by promising to do it, society's promise to punish wrongdoers will only obligate if punishing is not wrong. Thus, Ross's overall position is no stronger than his reason for saying that a wrongdoer forfeits "the main element" of any right by violating the corresponding right of another. Yet is Ross really entitled to say this? In his previous discussion of rights, he was led to conclude that

> Taking . . . the obvious division between duties arising out of contract and those that arise otherwise, we must say that while the former are cancelled by breach of the contract on the other side, the latter are not cancelled by the bad behaviour of the other person.[8]

Thus, to maintain that persons who assault or kill have forfeited the "main element" of their right not to be treated in like manner, Ross must maintain that the main element of the right not to be assaulted or killed is contractually based. Yet this is neither implied by anything Ross has said nor independently plausible. More generally, that wrongdoers forfeit some of their rights not to be harmed or deprived of liberty or property is a central part of what any opponent of retributivism will deny. Hence, it is part of what any retributivist must defend in detail. Because Ross provides no such defense, his account too begs at least one crucial question.

[8] Ibid., p. 55.

Are defenses of retributivism unavoidably question-begging? That they are is suggested by Stanley Benn and R. S. Peters.

> It is . . . virtually impossible for [the retributivist] to answer the question "What justification could there be for rules requiring that those who break them should be made to suffer?" . . . [W]e can justify rules and institutions only by showing that they yield advantages. Consequently retributivist answers to the problem can be shown, on analysis, to be either mere affirmations of the desirability of punishment, or utilitarian reasons in disguise.[9]

Yet despite our discouraging results so far, this conclusion is surely not forced on us. To assert that we can justify punishment only by showing that it brings advantages is to beg the question *against* retributivism as blatantly as others beg the question in its favor. Moreover, if it is argued that any retributive justification must ultimately appeal to some deeper backward-looking principle or value, the retributivist can respond that any consequentialist justification must similarly appeal to some deeper *forward*-looking principle or value. As Roger Wertheimer has pointed out, this problem arises for all forms of justification.[10] Thus, the acceptability of any given justification cannot depend on the form of its ultimate principles or values. Instead, it must depend on broader considerations of depth, precision, and plausibility. If classical retributivist arguments fail this test, the proper response is not to abandon retributive desert, but rather to take a fresh look at its foundations.

II

Let us turn to an influential contemporary statement of retributivism. We have already encountered Herbert Morris's justly celebrated essay "Persons and Punishment." In that essay, Morris de-

[9] S. I. Benn and R. S. Peters, *The Principles of Political Thought* (New York: Collier, 1964), p. 204. See also Bedau, "Retribution and the Theory of Punishment," p. 616.
[10] Roger Wertheimer, "Understanding Retribution," *Criminal Justice Ethics* 2 (Summer-Fall 1983), pp. 31–32.

fends the institution of punishment by carefully comparing it with its main alternative. As he notes, any society that wishes to forego punishment, but also wishes to control behavior, will be pressed to regard undesirable acts as forms of pathology. If a thief or rapist is not regarded as blameworthy, the natural alternative is to view him as being afflicted with a serious disorder. Considered in this light, attempts to alter his behavior become forms of therapy. As therapy, they need be neither predictable nor proportional to what the "patient" has done. Indeed, they need not be administered in response to his actions at all. Instead, the mere potential for "pathological" behavior is sufficient to justify such attempts. Moreover, if someone's behavior is a mere symptom, then so too are his protests against treatment, including even protests against being turned into someone with values he (now) abhors. Carried to its natural conclusion, the "logic of therapy" ends by degrading us to the status of animals or things.

These implications, subtly articulated by Morris, compel a reexamination of Hegel's claim that criminals have a right to be punished. Instead of ascribing to criminals an unwanted "right" to be deprived of liberty or property, Hegel may be taken as ascribing to them a more abstract right to the respect implied by the punitive but not the therapeutic outlook. Thus construed, his suggestion becomes much more plausible. Still, when taken as a full-fledged account of retributive desert, it remains unsatisfactory. One problem is that the choice between punitive and therapeutic systems of control is not exhaustive. Morris himself acknowledges the possibility of an alternative system based on shame rather than guilt, and current Chinese practices of "reeducation" suggest further possibilities. [11] Second, even if punitive systems do respect the dignity of the individual more than do any possible rivals, it remains unclear how this respect confers legitimacy on ordinarily impermissible acts. Third, because Morris construes punishment's aim as controlling behavior, his argument has a strongly consequentialist element.

---

[11] For elaboration of these possibilities, see Chad Hansen, "Punishment and Dignity in China," in *Individualism and Holism: Studies in Confucian and Taoist Values*, ed. Donald Munro (Ann Arbor: University of Michigan Press, 1985), pp. 359–83.

And, finally, even if successful, the argument justifies particular punitive acts only by placing them in the context of larger systems of laws. Thus, at best, it fails to capture the pre-systemic and individual nature of retributive desert.

Given these difficulties, Morris's main argument is clearly inadequate to our purposes. But other elements of his discussion are more promising. Recognizing the need to establish the permissibility of particular acts of punishment, Morris mounts independent appeals both to the criminal's own choice and to the fairness of the rules under which that choice is made. As we saw in Chapter 3, he contends that

> [t]he punishment associated with these primary rules paid deference to an individual's free choice by connecting punishment to a freely chosen act violative of the rules, thus giving some plausibility to the claim, as we saw, that what a person received by way of punishment he himself had chosen.[12]

In addition, he argues that the rules of (some) punishment systems are fair because they "apply to all, with the benefits and burdens equally distributed."[13] Since the first contention yields a variant of the familiar expected-consequence account, we need not consider it further. But the second—that punishment distributes benefits and burdens fairly—is Morris's most important suggestion and, I believe, the key to an adequate theory of retributive desert.

Let us look more closely at the way in which punishment may be said to be fair. Morris's view emerges clearly in the following passages:

> The rules define a sphere for each person, then, which is immune from interference by others. Making possible this mutual benefit is the assumption by individuals of a burden. The burden consists in the exercise of self-restraint by individuals over inclinations that would, if satisfied, directly interfere or create a substantial risk of interference with others in proscribed ways.

[12] Morris, "Persons and Punishment," p. 41.
[13] Ibid., p. 48.

A person who violates the rules has something others have—the benefits of the system—but by renouncing what others have assumed, the burdens of self-restraint, he has acquired an unfair advantage. Matters are not even until this advantage is in some way erased. Another way of putting it is that he owes something to others, for he has something that does not rightfully belong to him. Justice—that is punishing such individuals—restores the equilibrium of benefits and burdens by taking from the individual what he owes, that is, exacting the debt.[14]

In these passages, Morris argues that punishment is fair because it removes an advantage that the wrongdoer has but others lack. Those who obey the rules abjure the advantage they could obtain by interfering with others in proscribed ways. Those who break the rules gain this advantage. Because they gain it without giving up the additional advantage they get from the self-restraint of others, they end up with more than their fair share of advantage. In punishing them, we remove their excess advantage, and so restore a fair balance of benefits and burdens.

This suggestion immediately moves the discussion to a new level. By de-coupling punishment from pain and suffering, it defuses the charge that all attempts to exact retribution are mere senseless cruelty. In addition, by justifying punishment in terms of fairness, it casts the debate in terms that are acceptable even to those who are skeptical about punishment. If plausible, it will give content to Kant's metaphor of the scales of justice, and will perhaps also provide a rationale for Ross's claim that persons who violate the rights of others thereby forfeit rights of their own. Furthermore, if punishment does reestablish a fair balance of benefits and burdens, then we can understand the intuition that it is not just permissible but (in some sense) required; for surely we ought to promote distributions that are fair.

Retributivists clearly have much to gain by attempting to ground desert of punishment in fairness. But is the attempt likely to succeed? Before concluding that it is, we must resolve some difficult

---

[14] Ibid., pp. 33–34.

questions, both about the relevant benefits and burdens and about the principle(s) of fairness requiring their equalization. First, because criminal acts may benefit persons financially, psychically, and in other ways, we must get clearer about the sorts of gains that fairness requires criminals to relinquish. Second, because acts are only crimes in relation to particular legal codes, we must explain why this suggestion is any better able than its predecessor to accommodate the pre-systemic nature of retributive desert. And, third, because it requires not only that persons share burdens and benefits fairly, but also that unfair advantages at earlier moments be offset at later ones, the view evidently presupposes at least two distinct principles of fairness, one synchronic and the other diachronic. What do these principles come to, and how are they to be defended?

III

As a vehicle for clarifying the connections between fairness and retributive desert, let us consider some objections to the benefits-and-burdens account. In an interesting recent discussion, Richard W. Burgh has examined the account in some detail,[15] acknowledging that it is powerful and persuasive. But he has serious reservations about its ability to capture our intuitions either about *who* deserves punishment or about *how much* punishment various wrongdoers deserve. By examining Burgh's reservations, we can get clearer about what the account does and does not say.

Burgh's first objection concerns the premise that the wrongdoer gains an unfair advantage by benefiting twice. It may seem obvious initially that any wrongdoer does benefit once from the self-restraint of others and a second time from his own lack of self-restraint. However, as Burgh notes, this premise seems to fail whenever the wrongdoer lacks the capacity to be interfered with as he has interfered with his victim. It fails, for example, in cases of rape, since (for all practical purposes) women cannot rape men. It also fails in cases of embezzlement, since

[15] Richard W. Burgh, "Do the Guilty Deserve Punishment?" *The Journal of Philosophy* 79, no. 4 (April 1982), pp. 193–213.

[t]he sphere of noninterference which . . . [laws against embezzlement] define protects only those who are in a position from which they can be embezzled. Yet clearly the fact that an embezzler happens not to be in a position to be embezzled from should be irrelevant to the question of whether he deserves punishment.[16]

Because the rapist and embezzler cannot be interfered with as they have interfered with their victims, they have not benefited from the restraint of others as well as from their own wrongdoing. Hence, we seem unable to construe their punishment as canceling their unfair additional advantage.

This argument, however, proceeds too quickly. Even if the rapist cannot be raped or the embezzler embezzled from, they may have benefited from their victims' and other persons' restraint in not harming them in closely related ways. In particular, the rapist may have benefited by not being physically assaulted, and the embezzler by not being defrauded (of his labor, if of nothing else). And crucially, even if the examples are doctored to exclude these possibilities, the rapist and embezzler will still have benefited from their victims' and other persons' restraining themselves from many *other* sorts of wrongful activities. In Burgh's own words, they have still obtained "a second-order set of benefits, viz., those received from obedience to law in general"[17] (or, by extension, from general obedience to moral law).

If Burgh acknowledges that the rapist and embezzler have benefited from others' generally restraining themselves from wrongdoing, why does he still deny that these individuals deserve punishment according to the benefits-and-burdens account? The answer is that he regards appeals to generalized benefits as illegitimate. To make such an appeal, he argues, is to imply that all wrongdoers have received the *same* benefits, and, hence, "that all offenders are, regardless of the offense they committed, deserving of the same punishment."[18] In view of this, Burgh maintains that any appeal to

[16] Ibid., p. 205.
[17] Ibid., p. 206.
[18] Ibid.

generalized benefits would fail to capture the intuition that different transgressions call for different penalties.

This rejoinder is confused. The benefits-and-burdens account regards punishment as justified not merely by the wrongdoer's receiving the benefits of others' self-restraint, but by his having these benefits *plus* the benefit of his own lack of self-restraint. Moreover, even if wrongdoers do all receive the same amount of benefit from the self-restraint of others, they can be expected to get differing amounts of excess benefit from their own transgressions. Since it is the latter excess that punishment seeks to remove, the amount of punishment needed to remove it can be expected to vary as well.

This response disposes of the worry that not all wrongdoers receive a double benefit. However, in doing so, it raises a further question. We just saw that the benefits-and-burdens account equates amounts of punishment deserved with amounts of excess benefit received: how are these excess benefits to be measured? Given Morris's stress on self-restraint, it is tempting to say that the wrongdoer's excess benefit is just the amount of extra freedom he has secured by transgressing. But this merely defers the difficulty, for we now need to know what determines the excess freedom gained. According to Burgh, the most natural measure of a wrongdoer's extra freedom is the strength of the inclination he has refrained from inhibiting.

> The stronger the inclination, the greater the burden one undertakes in obeying the law. Hence, if the strength of the inclination to commit one crime is stronger than another, a greater advantage will be derived from committing that crime.[19]

Yet if we say this, we encounter a serious problem. If the benefits of wrongdoing are measured by the inclinations that wrongdoers fail to inhibit, then the amounts of punishment that wrongdoers deserve will also be measured in this way. Thus, since "most have a greater inclination to cheat [on income taxes] than they ever have to murder,"[20] the punishment that tax evaders deserve must be

[19] Ibid., p. 209.
[20] Ibid.

greater than the punishment that is deserved for murder. However, intuitively, the murderer surely deserves the harsher penalty.

We must agree that the strength of one's inclination *to* transgress cannot be what determines the amount of extra benefit one receives *from* transgressing. For related reasons, we must reject the suggestion that the wrongdoer's extra benefit, and so too his deserved punishment, is determined by the amount of profit he receives from acting wrongly.[21] But necessary though these concessions are, they do not support Burgh's final conclusion that there is *no* plausible criterion of degree of benefit; for a further criterion remains untouched. Consider again the murderer and the tax evader. Intuitively, our belief that these persons deserve different amounts of punishment has little to do with any empirically discoverable differences between them. Instead, the crucial difference appears to be moral. If we believe that the murderer deserves a harsher punishment, it is surely because we regard murder as by far the more seriously wrong act. But if so, then the most natural candidate for what determines the murderer's degree of extra benefit is precisely the strength of the moral prohibition he has violated. By this criterion, the reason he has benefited more is not that he has indulged a stronger inclination, nor yet that he has received greater financial or psychic rewards. It is, instead, that he has violated a moral prohibition of far greater seriousness.

By thus equating a wrongdoer's degree of benefit with his act's degree of wrongness, we nicely resolve the problem of proportionality. But in so doing we may appear to stray from the original intent of the benefits-and-burdens account. For how, exactly, is a wrongdoer made better off merely by evading a moral prohibition? How, except by fiat, does such evasion constitute a benefit? To answer this question, we must recall the earlier suggestion that wrongdoers gain extra liberty. As we saw, this suggestion fails when liberty is measured by the strength of the impulse indulged. Nevertheless, we can now see that the suggestion does embody an

---

[21] The proposal that benefit equals ill-gotten gain is incompatible with our intuitions about proportionality because many acts that intuitively call for serious punishment yield little or no profit. For additional criticism, see Richard Wasserstrom, *Philosophy and Social Issues* (Notre Dame, Ind.: University of Notre Dame Press, 1980), pp. 141–46.

important insight. For, in fact, a person who acts wrongly does gain a significant measure of extra liberty: what he gains is freedom from the demands of the prohibition he violates. Because others take that prohibition seriously, they lack a similar liberty. And as the strength of the prohibition increases, so too does the freedom from it which its violation entails. Thus, even if the murderer and the tax evader do succumb to equally strong impulses, their gains in freedom are far from equal. Because the murderer evades a prohibition of far greater force—because he thus "gets away with more"—his net gain in freedom remains greater. And for that reason, the amount of punishment he deserves seems greater as well.

Thus understood, the suggestion that we link degrees of benefit to degrees of wrongness both resolves the proportionality problem and gives content to the claim that wrongdoers gain extra freedom. It also shows exactly why retributive desert is pre-institutional. Since the suggestion makes no essential reference to the law, it clearly allows that persons may deserve punishment even when it is not mandated by legal codes. Even if a high-ranking Nazi has broken no laws, he may still have gained an unfair advantage by violating the moral law as others have not. Of course, none of this will hold unless different acts can be wrong to different degrees; but while that claim is not uncontroversial, there does seem to be a strong case for it.[22]

Thus, all in all, an act's degree of wrongness does seem to offer the most promising measure of the agent's degree of extra gain. I will, accordingly, adopt that measure in what follows.

IV

With this interpretation fixed, we can confront some further difficulties. As we have seen, the benefits-and-burdens account rests on

[22] In particular, we seem forced to presume that one act is more wrong than another in order to make sense of the idea that one obligation can override another in cases of conflict. This presumption, of course, leaves open such questions as whether the relevant notion is cardinal or merely ordinal, whether it explains or is explained by overriding-ness, and so on. However, the account offered in the text seems compatible with a wide range of replies to this question.

two distinct principles of fairness, one synchronic and the other diachronic. It presupposes both that at any given time each person should conform to the moral restraints observed by others and that any unfair advantage enjoyed at an earlier time should be balanced by a corresponding later burden. But on inspection, a principle of diachronic fairness may seem to have counterintuitive implications. For suppose a wrongdoer already has suffered unusually heavy burdens earlier in his life. Then won't a principle of diachronic fairness imply that the extra benefit of wrongdoing already *has* been balanced? And, if so, how can his wrongdoing require additional balancing through punishment? Indeed, if the aim of punishment is to achieve a fair balance of benefits and burdens, then won't punishing him actually be unfair?

To say that the victims of previous hardship are entitled to "free" crimes—to adopt what Gertrude Ezorsky has called the "whole life view" of criminal desert[23]—would be absurd. Thus, to save the benefits-and-burdens account, we must somehow show that diachronic fairness does not require this. We must show, in other words, that only punishment, but not previous hardship, can offset the extra benefits gained through wrongdoing. At first glance, the reason for this difference may seem to be simply that punishment follows the wrongdoer's extra benefits, while earlier hardships have preceded them. But given our "bookkeeping" model of fairness, this response is inadequate. If what is important is only the final balance, then why does it matter in what order the debits and credits are entered?

To meet the objection more adequately, we must recall the special nature of the wrongdoer's extra benefit. As we saw, the most plausible way of understanding that benefit is as an extra measure of freedom from moral restraint. Moreover, as we also saw, the extra benefit's magnitude seems to be determined by the strength of the moral prohibition that is violated. But if the wrongdoer's amount of extra benefit is thus established, then it is *not* determined by the amount of happiness or preference-satisfaction that his act affords

---

[23] Gertrude Ezorsky, "The Ethics of Punishment," in Ezorsky, *Philosophical Perspectives on Punishment*, pp. xxii–xxvii.

him. By contrast, the magnitude of his earlier burden is determined in the latter way. To say that someone has had a hard life is to say exactly that he has had more than his share of unhappiness or preference-frustration. But if the wrongdoer's extra benefit is measured by his act's degree of wrongness, whereas his previous burden is measured on the different scale of preference-(dis)satisfaction, then there is indeed a convincing reason why the later benefit cannot be balanced by the earlier burden. Such balancing is impossible not because the benefit and burden stand in the wrong temporal relation, but rather simply because they are incommensurable.

Besides showing why the benefits of wrongdoing are not balanced by previous hardships, this rejoinder also makes it clearer why such benefits *are* balanced by subsequently imposed punishment. We noted at the outset that punishment is puzzling because it involves the legitimate performance of an ordinarily impermissible act. However, we can now see that it is precisely the ordinary impermissibility of the act performed as punishment that *makes* it a suitable way of balancing the wrongdoer's unfair advantage. Because the wrongdoer has unfairly gained an extra measure of freedom from moral restraint, the natural way to restore a fair balance is to reduce the protection he ordinarily would have gained through moral restraints on the conduct of others. By treating the wrongdoer in what is ordinarily a forbidden way, we strip away part of the protection that moral restraints on our behavior would ordinarily have afforded him. Thus, we remove precisely the sort of advantage he has gained. Because the resulting disadvantage can be assessed in terms of its usual moral wrongness, it can be weighed on the same scale as the wrongdoer's unfair advantage. Thus, it is commensurable with the wrongdoer's extra benefit as his previous hardships are not.[24]

---

[24] Just as we can distinguish between the benefits of wealth and opportunity and the benefit of freedom from moral restraint, so too can we distinguish between the burden of privation and the burden of nonrestraint on the part of others. By pressing the latter distinction, we can answer an objection raised by Jeffrey Murphy in "Marxism and Retribution" (in Murphy, *Retribution, Justice, and Therapy* [Dordrecht, Holland: Reidel, 1979], pp. 91–115). In that article, Murphy concedes that a benefits-and-burdens account *would* justify punishment if society were sufficiently just to provide each citizen with a fair share of its benefits. However, because Mur-

V

With this, we may dismiss the concern that a wrongdoer's extra gains might be offset by any and all sorts of previous hardships. However, a related worry, raised by a subset of the wrongdoer's previous hardships, may seem to remain. If the wrongdoer has previously been wronged or subjected to unjust social arrangements, then he evidently has *not* enjoyed the full protection of moral restraints on others' conduct. Hence, if diachronic fairness requires that his extra freedom from moral restraint be offset by a corresponding loss of protection from such restraint upon others, then its demands do here appear to be met. Thus, we seem to remain committed to the view that wrongdoers who were themselves previously wronged do not now deserve to be punished.

In fact, though, we need not be. Even if X has previously wronged Y, it hardly follows that a fair balance of benefits and burdens is restored when Y in turn wrongs Z. If Y does this, then the original wrongdoer X is still left with the double benefit of moral restraint upon others plus his own freedom from such restraint; and the current victim Z is left with the double burden of moral restraint on his acts plus the absence of restraint on the acts of (some) others. Thus, the original unfairness is not removed but merely displaced. Of course, the unfairness is *not* displaced if the person now affected by Y's (ordinarily) wrong act is not the innocent Z, but rather the very X whose earlier wrong act harmed Y. If it is only X whom Y now harms, then Y's ordinarily wrong act will merely right the balance, and so our account will indeed imply that X deserves no further punishment. But this implication may be acceptable; for if Y's ordinarily wrong act harms the X who has previously wronged Y, then Y's act will in effect be X's deserved punishment.

Since we feel that those who inflict deserved punishment should

---

phy views society as deeply *unjust* to the social classes to which criminals often belong, he denies that criminal acts generally do leave criminals with more than their fair share of benefits. Yet even if wealth and opportunity are distributed unjustly, it does not follow that this is also true of the more pertinent good of other individuals' restraint from wrongdoing. To show that criminals receive less than their fair share of *this* good, one would need a further argument. The prospects for such an argument will be considered in the next section.

not be punished in their turn, the implication that Y deserves no further punishment for his treatment of X is largely consistent with our intuitions. However, it is not *fully* intuitive, for many would balk at the idea that private individuals (as opposed to duly constituted state officials) may inflict the punishment that wrongdoers deserve. There is considerable support for the view that punishment should be inflicted only in the juridical context, and that private punishers are mere vigilantes. Yet our aversion to private punishment can be understood in terms that have nothing to do with desert. It is amply accounted for by Locke's sensible worry that if we do permit private punishment,

> self-love will make men partial to themselves and their friends, and, on the other side, . . . ill-nature, passion, and revenge will carry them too far in punishing others, and hence nothing but confusion and disorder will follow.[25]

Given this explanation of the belief that punishment may only be inflicted by representatives of the state, our account is not damaged by its failure to provide any deeper justification for that belief. But what, now, of the still more widely held view that the state's representatives are at least *among* those who may punish? We saw that Y's extra benefit in wronging the innocent Z does not offset the extra burden that X's earlier wrongdoing inflicted on Y. But, having acknowledged this, mustn't we also acknowledge that Y's extra benefit in wronging the innocent Z will not be offset by the later punitive acts of anyone except Z himself? If Y's wronging Z after he himself was wronged merely left Z with a double burden while X had a double benefit, then doesn't W's punishing Y after Y has wronged Z similarly leave Z with a double burden while W acquires a double benefit? And, therefore, doesn't it follow that no one can administer the punishment a wrongdoer deserves except his original victim? More particularly, doesn't it follow that the state's representatives may not legitimately punish?

The implication that deserved punishment may not be adminis-

---

[25] John Locke, *The Second Treatise of Civil Government* (New York: Hafner, 1969), sec. 13, p. 127. See also sections 124–26 and passim.

tered by just anyone is not entirely unwelcome. Whatever his mistakes, Mabbott was surely right to deny that the wrongdoer is fair game for anyone who wishes to treat him in an ordinarily impermissible way. Still, we would clearly be going too far if we said that deserved punishment may be inflicted only by the wrongdoer's own victim. Thus, we must ask whether our account really does imply this. To see that it does not, we may note, first, that there is a clear difference between performing a normally wrong act that harms a wrongdoer for reasons unrelated to his previous actions and performing a similar act on behalf of his victim. If someone performs a normally impermissible act for the latter reason—if he does so merely to remove the wrongdoer's excess benefit and not for personal pleasure or profit—then he is, in effect, the agent of another. He is, in that case, acting on behalf of the victim or the victim's society. Hence, the moral restraints on *his* behavior are not lifted, and so he receives no double benefit. Second, while punishment does not restore to the victim the protection that effective moral restraints on the wrongdoer would have afforded him, its administration on the victim's behalf does represent at least a symbolic lifting of the corresponding moral restraints on *his* behavior. Thus, it does go some distance toward restoring a benefit that he, but not the wrongdoer, has foregone.[26] Because the resulting balance of benefits and burdens is far from perfect, this account captures the common feeling that punishment never fully sets things right. However, because the resulting balance is the fairest that remains possible after the wrong has been done, disinterested punishment is nevertheless required.

A final difficulty remains. We have argued that fairness may justify a previously wronged person (or his surrogate) in doing what would ordinarily wrong the person who wronged him, but that it cannot justify his acting that way toward others. However, if some-

[26] Because it construes punishment as a (partly symbolic) lifting of a moral restraint on the conduct of the wrongdoer's victim, our account assigns a natural role to the concept of mercy. On the suggested account, the victim of wrongdoing is uniquely situated to display mercy because he is uniquely situated to decline to take advantage of the absence of moral restraints on his conduct. Because the advantage to be restored is his due, he, and he alone, is in a position to refuse it.

one has been wronged not by the actions of any individual, but rather by an unjust social institution, then the distinction between those who have and have not wronged him may seem to break down. Given a universal obligation to resist injustice, hasn't *every-one* who tolerated the unjust institution wronged the victim of injustice, and so gained an unfair advantage at his expense? And, therefore, doesn't our account construe any ordinarily wrong act that the victim performs as punishment for anyone it happens to affect?

Although the issues here are complicated, several factors tell against this conclusion. First, it is far from clear that everyone living in a society containing unjust institutions *has* acted wrongly. Prima facie, this seems unlikely; for the wrongness of one's toleration of injustice depends on such factors as one's awareness (or the degree to which one should have been aware) that the relevant institutions are unjust, and also on one's ability to take meaningful steps to alter the situation. Moreover, and crucially, even if everyone in a society containing unjust institutions has acted wrongly, the wrongdoing is not apt to be serious in all cases. Given the mitigating factors just mentioned, most individuals' toleration of injustice seems at worst marginally wrong. However, if so, then our account will at most allow victims of injustice to treat most others in ways that are ordinarily not seriously wrong. This immediately rules out many ordinary acts of wrongdoing. It may still seem to allow an act such as robbing the federal treasury, which slightly harms many individuals but greatly harms no one. Yet even this is dubious; for if theft may seriously wrong a *single* individual whom it does not greatly harm, then it may also seriously wrong each of *many* individuals whom it does not greatly harm. Of course, none of this implies that there are *no* ordinarily wrong acts which our account licenses the victims of injustice to perform. However, once the limitations on such acts are understood, their possibility ceases to threaten the account.[27]

---

[27] The suggestion that punishment is required to restore a fair balance of benefits and burdens is strongly reminiscent of (and is sometimes assimilated to) a familiar defense of political obligation. According to that defense, we enjoy social stability and opportunities as a result of other peoples' cooperative efforts, so in fairness we

VI

Perhaps the most unusual feature of our account is its interpretation of the wrongdoer's extra benefit. By interpreting that benefit as extra freedom from moral restraint, we avoid most versions of the objection that the magnitude of the benefit does not always match the amount of punishment that the wrongdoer deserves. Yet one form of this objection may remain. In the law, a criminal's sentence is often affected by his act's consequences. For example, an assailant is punished more severely if his victim dies than if he lives.[28] Moreover, many people believe that his extra punishment is deserved.[29] But if the amount of punishment a wrongdoer deserves depends on how much extra freedom from moral restraint he has had, and if his amount of extra freedom depends on how wrongly he has acted, then shouldn't his act's consequences drop out as irrelevant? And doesn't this force us to deny that murderers deserve more punishment than mere assailants?

---

too are required to obey the law and pay taxes rather than "ride free." For versions of this argument, see H.L.A. Hart, "Are There Any Natural Rights?" *Philosophical Review* 64, no. 2 (April 1955), pp. 175–91, and John Rawls, "Legal Obligation and the Duty of Fair Play," in *Law and Philosophy*, ed. Sidney Hook (New York: New York University Press, 1964), pp. 3–18. For criticism, see A. John Simmons, *Moral Principles and Political Obligations* (Princeton: Princeton University Press, 1979), chap. 5. But despite the obvious affinities between the two arguments, they differ in several fundamental respects. First, unlike our benefits-and-burdens defense of punishment, the attempt to ground political obligation in fairness applies only in the context of a cooperative scheme to which most must contribute if any are to benefit. Second, in the political context, the relevant benefits are defined without reference to the moral wrongness of acts, and they span the entire range of advantages that cooperation brings. Third, the current argument, unlike the traditional one, has been found to presuppose a diachronic as well as a synchronic principle of fairness. And, finally, our justification of punishment construes fairness as operating upon preexisting moral obligations, while the traditional argument assigns fairness the more extensive role of creating obligations *de novo*.

[28] In addition, the law imposes harsher penalties for successful criminal attempts than for unsuccessful ones. For discussion, see Lawrence Becker, "Criminal Attempt and the Theory of the Law of Crimes," *Philosophy and Public Affairs* 3, no. 3 (Spring 1974), pp. 262–94.

[29] As evidence of a closely related belief, consider the prevailing attitudes toward drunken driving. Many persons believe that causing a fatal accident while drunk is seriously wrong, yet they feel no remorse about driving when they are drunk themselves, suggesting that they believe that drunken driving is only badly wrong if it issues in serious harm.

Properly understood, it does not, for to say that one's deserved punishment depends on how wrongly one has acted is not yet to specify how wrongness itself is determined. Hence, it is not to deny that an act's wrongness may itself increase with the amount of harm done. If wrongness does increase with harm done, then our account *will* allow that murderers deserve more punishment than mere assailants. Of course, if this is so, then how wrongly one has acted will depend on factors beyond one's control. How wrong an act turns out to be will be a matter of "moral luck."[30] But despite this implication's air of paradox, it does not damage our account. If someone denies that an act's wrongness can depend on factors beyond the agent's control, then he will also deny that amounts of deserved punishment can depend on such factors. Thus, he will simply not have the intuition with which our account is said to be inconsistent.

The more difficult question, of course, is whether that intuition is defensible. Is it *true* that consequences beyond one's control can affect either the wrongness of one's act or the amount of punishment one deserves? Although a full discussion of this question would take us far afield, we may note, in passing, that factors beyond one's control do have other kinds of moral significance. As I shall argue in Chapter 9, various traits and abilities are beyond a person's control, yet still fall within the boundaries of his self. Being constitutive of the person, they do affect both the value of outcomes involving him and the obligations of others toward him. But if factors beyond a person's control can have these sorts of effects, then there is little point in denying that they can also affect the wrongness of his acts. Thus, even if an act's wrongness is not increased by *all* its harmful effects, it may well be increased by some of them.

[30] For penetrating discussion of these issues, see Thomas Nagel, "Moral Luck," in Nagel, *Mortal Questions*, pp. 24–38.

S I X

DESERT AND DIACHRONIC
FAIRNESS

In the last chapter, I argued that the moral basis of desert of punishment is fairness. Because the wrongdoer has had an extra measure
of freedom from moral restraint, his punishment restores a fair
overall balance of benefits and burdens. Since this justification allows an imbalance that exists at one time to be rectified at another,
it presupposes a principle of fairness that is trans-temporal or diachronic. But what is that principle, and how can it be justified in
turn? By getting clear about this, we may not only deepen our understanding of retributive desert, but also connect it to a variety of
more positive desert-claims.

I

There is a whole range of desert-claims that appear to require some
trans-temporal balancing of benefits and burdens. These include
not only claims that persons deserve punishment, but also claims
that persons deserve sums of money, or opportunities, to compensate for wrongly inflicted harm or suffering. In addition, they include many more modest claims that persons deserve relief from
burdens that were *not* wrongfully inflicted. For example, someone
who has had persistent bad luck may be said to deserve a change of
fortune. Finally, and perhaps most important, they include claims
that persons who have worked for others deserve certain wages as
compensation.

Does any plausible diachronic principle underlie all (or most) of
these desert-claims? Since punishment is a burden while compen-

sation, relaxation, and wages are benefits, any such principle would have to apply to both past benefits and past burdens. If it simply required that all past benefits and burdens be offset, the principle would be

DF1: Any burden or benefit that a person sustains at an earlier time should be matched by a commensurate but opposite benefit or burden at a later time.

But DF1 is a nonstarter. Because it requires the offsetting of past benefits as well as burdens, it implies that anyone who has previously prospered now deserves misfortune and ruin. It is merely spiteful to say that just because a person has been fortunate, he now deserves his turn in the gutter. Moreover, quite apart from its spitefulness, DF1 is unmotivated. Barring a mad desire for symmetry, there is simply no reason why every benefit and burden within a given life should be offset.

Clearly only *some* past benefits and burdens can require balancing. But which? One possibility, suggested by our discussion of punishment, is that one's past benefits or burdens only require offsetting when they are out of line with what others have had. According to this suggestion, diachronic fairness requires that benefits and burdens be equalized not *within* lives, but rather *across* temporally extended lives. Adjusted to accommodate the incommensurability of some benefits and burdens, this yields

DF2: With respect to each class of commensurable benefits and burdens, each person's total of those benefits and burdens should, over time, be roughly equal to that of each other person.

Since DF2 is a principle of interpersonal equality, it is initially more plausible than DF1. Yet precisely because DF2 is comparative, it seems inappropriate to some desert-claims within our range. Consider the claim that someone deserves to be compensated for wrongly inflicted suffering. This claim may surely be valid even though the victim's suffering has not raised his lifetime misery total above that of most others. Thus, interpersonal comparisons are irrelevant here.

If this were the only objection, we might rescue DF2 by saying that such non-comparative desert-claims are simply not grounded in diachronic fairness. But there are other problems, too. First, while some principle of interpersonal equality may well be defensible, DF2's egalitarianism is extreme. If all interpersonal inequalities required later rectification, then many widely accepted reasons for inequality would lack moral weight. For example, nobody could deserve anything for his diligent efforts, his superior qualifications, his selflessness or heroism, or his outstanding performance in competition. But my argument has been, and will continue to be, that many such desert-claims do have significant normative force. And even if DF2 were appropriately weakened, it would share with DF1 the unacceptable implication that previous good fortune—in this case, comparative good fortune—can by itself justify present burdens. Of course, DF2 does not *require* that all previously advantaged persons now be disadvantaged; but it does countenance new disadvantages as one way of satisfying its demands. Moreover, where the previously disadvantaged are dead or beyond help, DF2 *does* require that the previously advantaged be burdened, since this is the only (remaining) way of restoring diachronic equality across lives. Thus, DF2 seems almost as spiteful as DF1. Of course, we could eliminate the spitefulness by stipulating that past inequalities may only be offset through additional advantages for the previously disadvantaged. But thus qualified, DF2 would no longer license imposing additional burdens on wrongdoers. Hence, it would not justify deserved punishment.

All in all, DF2 is as hopeless as DF1. Whatever we say about diachronic fairness, its basis cannot be a principle requiring either the balancing of benefits and burdens within lives or the equalization of benefits and burdens across lives. Its basis must be some less symmetrical principle which implies (1) that only some past benefits and burdens be offset, (2) that the occurrences that require offsetting include many more burdens than benefits, and (3) that these burdens and benefits be defined sometimes comparatively and sometimes not. Can we find a principle that has these implications, yet is not unacceptably ad hoc?

93

II

If such a principle exists, its demands cannot be triggered by just any benefit or burden. Rather, the trigger must be some feature that benefits and burdens sometimes possess and sometimes do not. Although there are indefinitely many such features, I believe the most promising for our purposes is the relationship between a benefit or burden and the norm(s) or standard(s) that govern it. More precisely, I suggest that what diachronic fairness demands is not the offsetting of past benefits and burdens *simpliciter*, but rather the offsetting of the violations of independent standards that some of these have entailed.

Let us look at this more closely. I want to say that diachronic fairness demands the rectification of past violations of independent standards. This implies that some norms and standards are temporally specific—that some of them demand that persons enjoy benefits or suffer burdens at particular times, or during particular periods. It also implies that the principle of diachronic fairness is not a ground-level principle, but is a second-level principle that comes into play only when the demands of some other norm or standard have gone unmet. When we make all this explicit, what we get is

DF3: For every good G, every person M, and every period of time P, if M has less (more) of G than he should during P, then M should have correspondingly more (less) of G or some related good than he otherwise should during some later period P'.

Should we accept DF3? If we do, we will be able to explain why diachronic fairness has implications (1)–(3). To explain why only some past benefits and burdens require offsetting, we will be able to say that not all past benefits and burdens have violated independent standards. To explain why many more benefits than burdens require offsetting—why people generally do not deserve penalties merely for doing well—we will be able to say that most distributional standards are themselves minima rather than maxima. In most cases, we do not believe that any amount of a good is inherently too much, but only that certain amounts are too little. When persons do have too much, the reason is generally that their having as much as they do requires that others have too little (either absolutely or in comparative terms). Since our standards are generally floors rather than ceilings, it is not surprising that their violation is generally correctable primarily in the direction of (what would otherwise be) excess. Finally, to explain why only some of the benefits and burdens that require offsetting are comparative, we will be able to say that some but not all of our first-level standards are themselves comparative.

DF3 is thus the sort of principle we are seeking. But before invoking it, we must establish, first, that it is itself defensible, and second, that its demands match those of most desert-claims within our range. Consider, first, the case for DF3. Why, when someone fails to have what he ought at t_1, should he have correspondingly more or less later? If the morally significant units were momentary person-stages, this question could not be answered. In that case, the entity that had too much or too little at t_1 would no longer exist at t_2. But I shall argue in Chapter 9 that it is not the person-stage, but rather the temporally extended person from whom it is an abstraction, who is the truly significant unit. For now, let us simply assume that this (common-sense) view is correct. If so, then DF3's prospects are far brighter; for the temporal specificity of our standards—the fact that they demand that persons benefit or be burdened at specific moments—will not have a metaphysical basis. That specificity will, instead, reflect only the truism that whatever happens must happen sometime. For example, if a moral rule demands that M refrain from harming N at t_1, this will reflect only the fact that t_1 is among the moments at which M might harm N. In general, what is significant about an improper burden or benefit will be not its temporal location, but only its occurrence within a life.

But if so, then its impropriety often will not be irremediable until that life is over. If before a person's death his improper burden or benefit is offset by a later benefit or burden, then his life will at least contain the right overall amount of the relevant benefits and burdens. Of course, the idea that the right amount for someone is the difference between a positive and a negative quantity is more at home in some contexts than others. If the right amount of money for someone is $10, then he does get what he should if he receives $100 but loses $90; but if someone should be caused no pain, he does not get what he should if he is alternately tortured and caused pleasure. Yet even here, he may come closer to getting what he should by being both tortured and caused pleasure than simply by being tortured. In any event, most standards seem far more strongly aggregative than this. Thus, providing an offsetting benefit generally does move someone closer to what the violated standard originally demanded.

We are now in a position to set forth the case for DF3. Fully articulated, the argument appears to be (1) that it is good that the demands of well-grounded standards be met; (2) that it is therefore good that the demands of such standards come as close as possible to being met; (3) that because the standards govern the fortunes of temporally extended persons, they come closest to being met when all deviations from them are appropriately offset; and (4) that it is therefore good that all such deviations *be* offset. In the preceding paragraphs, I offered a conditional justification of (3), but I did not defend (1) or (2). However, to appreciate their strength, we need only consider what it would mean to deny them. To deny (1), we would have to embrace either the contradiction that it is no better that there be good outcomes than that there be bad ones or the immensely implausible claim that it is no better that persons treat others as they should than that they do not. To deny (2), we would have to embrace the scarcely more plausible claim that the value of the satisfaction of well-grounded standards is all-or-nothing, and not a matter of degree. Since I cannot imagine what would motivate these claims, I shall have nothing further to say about them.[1]

---

[1] For related discussion of the connections between compensation and personhood, see Derek Parfit, *Reasons and Persons* (Oxford: Oxford University Press, 1984), pp. 342–43 and passim. Parfit holds that personal identity over time involves no "deep further fact" besides psychological continuity and connectedness, and that this makes it defensible to claim "that a benefit at one time cannot provide compensation for a burden at another time, even when both come within the same life" (p. 343). Thus, Parfit would apparently agree that the primacy of the extended self is necessary (though perhaps not, as I have claimed, sufficient) to establish DF3. For remarks that may bear on the degree to which the demands of our standards are aggregative, see Parfit's note 112, p. 521. Other aspects of Parfit's position will be discussed in Chapter 9.

III

With DF3 thus provisionally secured, let us return to its relation to desert. We introduced the idea of diachronic fairness because various desert-claims appeared to tie what people now deserve to their past benefits and burdens. But is DF3 really the principle that underlies these claims? Does it convincingly link desert of punishment to desert of compensation, relief, and wages? Can we show, in each instance, that what is deserved would rectify a prior deviation from a well-grounded independent standard?

Given our discussion of punishment, retributive desert-claims clearly are grounded in something like DF3. I argued earlier that punishment is a burden aimed at offsetting a wrongdoer's previous extra benefit, and that that benefit should be viewed as an extra measure of freedom from moral restraint. But if so, then what requires offsetting is precisely a deviation from a first-level (moral) standard. Thus, applied to deserved punishment, DF3 seems unproblematical.

What about deserved compensation? Is it also grounded in DF3? If so, then what violations of independent standards does it aim to put right? Since harms are most clearly compensable when caused by wrongdoing, the most obvious candidates may again seem to be violations of moral standards. But I have argued that punishing a wrongdoer both provides him with an extra burden and provides his victim with a (somewhat abstract) extra benefit. Hence, this suggestion would imply that where punishment is administered, compensation for victims is unnecessary. To avoid this implication, as well as to leave room for compensation for non-wrongfully inflicted harms, we must distinguish between the burden of unmatched moral restraint and the burden of pain or loss. Since these burdens differ, so too may the standards they violate. In particular, a single act may violate both a standard that demands that no person treat another in a certain way and one that demands that no person be caused (certain sorts of) harm. Of these standard-violations, the first is offset by punishment, the second by compensation.

Are *all* valid claims to compensation justified in this way? Despite appearances, I think not. As Robert Nozick has noted, we

97

standardly believe that "Something fully compensates . . . person X for person Y's action A if X is no worse off receiving it, Y having done A, than X would have been without receiving it if Y had not done A."[2] But restoring X to the position he would have occupied if Y had not done A may involve either offsetting a burden that X already has suffered as a result of A or forestalling a future burden that X otherwise would suffer as a result of A. Since DF3 requires the offsetting of past deviations from independent standards, it clearly does demand the offsetting of burdens of the first sort. But if an act—even a past act—has not yet imposed a burden, there is, as yet, no standard-violation to be offset. Here DF3 can find no purchase. Thus, DF3 cannot be what dictates prophylactic compensatory action.

What should we make of this? There is little point in denying either that claims to compensation may be aimed at preventing future harms or that some such claims are morally compelling. But what we may say, and what seems sufficient, is that although such claims are not justified by DF3, the reasoning that does justify them is fully compatible with DF3. For when a compensatory benefit will not offset a past harm, but will prevent a future harm that would otherwise be caused by a past act, the justification for providing the benefit lies no further away than the standard that the anticipated harm would violate. For example, the standard that demands the return of a stolen object is the very property right that would (continue to) be violated if the object were not returned. Here, the justification consists not in any displacement of the standard's demand, but simply in its continuation. Whether we call such compensation deserved, or whether we reserve this locution for cases in which DF3 enters, is an unimportant verbal question. What is important is that both sorts of justification are obviously parts of the same overall picture.

Thus, DF3 does justify many claims that persons deserve compensation, as well as all (legitimate) claims that persons deserve punishment. But what, next, of claims that persons deserve relief

---

[2] Nozick, *Anarchy, State, and Utopia*, p. 57. For discussion of some problems raised by Nozick's formulation, see George Sher, "Compensation and Transworld Personal Identity," *The Monist* 62, no. 3 (July 1979), pp. 378–91.

from burdens that did not result from human actions (or were only incidentally the results of such actions)? We do say that someone who has suffered intense or long-standing pain now deserves to be comfortable, and that someone whose endeavors consistently have been frustrated now deserves a change of luck. Moreover, when we say these things, we do base our desert-claims on the subjects' previous burdens. Although we know that each life must contain some hardship, we feel that some lives (or some portions of lives) are excessively harsh. Some amounts of suffering seem so great that persons should not have to bear them. Since these are, in effect, assertions that standards have been violated, the corresponding desert-claims do seem to be traceable to DF3. But the more difficult question is whether standards that do not regulate behavior, but simply affirm that persons should not have to bear certain hardships, are themselves defensible. Though sympathetic to this view, I have no compelling arguments for it. Thus, the most important question about such desert-claims—do they have real normative force?—must be left open.

IV

What, finally, of claims that workers deserve specific wages? Employers and employees often disagree about how much pay workers deserve. Many of their claims are, of course, mere rationalizations. Yet even these reflect a shared conviction that some wages really are deserved. To what degree can this conviction be justified?

We obviously cannot justify all intuitions about what all workers deserve. Such intuitions often conflict and often are tainted by self-interest. In addition, what pass for desert-claims are sometimes appeals to the utility of wage schedules, or to obligations arising from prior agreements or practices. Still, although intuition here is especially untrustworthy, we may make progress in another way. It is uncontroversial that labor is generally considered a burden, and that wages are never deserved until work is actually done. Thus, deserved wages, like other deserved benefits, may be construed as offsetting prior deviations from independent standards. Here again, the justification may involve DF3.

How might such a justification run? Prima facie, there are several possibilities. As David Miller notes, workers have been held to deserve remuneration for either (1) the difficulty, unpleasantness, or danger of their work, (2) the effort they expend while working, or (3) the contribution their work makes to others.[3] If any of these aspects of labor is a burden that violates an independent standard, the claim that workers deserve to be paid may be justified by DF3. Moreover, the amount of pay a worker deserves may depend on the size of the burden to be offset.

Does labor systematically violate an independent standard? Certainly there are limits to the unpleasantness, difficulty and danger that workers should be asked to undergo. Moreover, some necessary jobs may unavoidably exceed these limits. If one does, then DF3 may imply that persons performing it should receive offsetting benefits. Yet even granting this, it remains wildly implausible to suppose that all jobs violate the limits on unpleasantness, difficulty, and danger. To say this of even the safe and rewarding work of a college professor, we would have to invoke a standard that condemns any and all work as unacceptably unpleasant. Such a standard would lack all credibility. Thus, appeals to unpleasantness, difficulty, and danger can at best show that some differences in workers' pay are deserved. For example, garbage collectors, coal miners, and combat soldiers may deserve some extra pay.[4] But the more general question—why, and how much, do *all* workers deserve to be paid?—remains unanswered.

Nor can we answer it by construing deserved wages as benefits required to offset the worker's efforts or contribution to others. Unlike unpleasantness and danger, effort, and perhaps also contribution, is present wherever workers deserve to be paid. Yet, also

---

[3] David Miller, *Social Justice* (Oxford: Oxford University Press, 1976), pp. 102–21.

[4] Miller apparently would disagree. He argues that the unpleasantness, difficulty, and danger incurred by a worker cannot be bases for his desert because this would violate the requirement that "a desert basis consists of personal attributes which are generally held in high regard" (Miller, *Social Justice*, p. 112). But Miller's "requirement" appears to be grounded in nothing deeper than the observation that the bases for positive desert are *usually* traits that we esteem. It is thus merely a piece of verbal legislation that we need not accept.

unlike unpleasantness and danger, neither effort nor contribution appears to violate any independent standard. There is, on the face of it, no reason why people should not exert effort to achieve legitimate goals, or why they should not contribute to the well-being of others. Since these aspects of labor do not violate independent standards, they do not combine with DF3 to call for offsetting benefits.[5]

At this point, the suggestion that DF3 justifies desert of wages may seem decidedly unpromising. But we should not despair. Even if effort and contribution to others do not in themselves violate independent standards, they may still do so *in the context of the typical work situation*. By concentrating on that situation, we may yet see why wages are deserved.

Thus, consider what does happen when one person is employed by another. The worker, by hypothesis, does things that his employer wants done and would otherwise have to do for himself. The worker devotes his time and energy, which he might otherwise employ in pursuits of his own choosing, to advance the employer's project. In so doing, he subordinates his own purposes to those of the employer. Of course, he only does so in expectation of receiving the agreed-upon wage. But since our question is precisely whether the wage has any moral basis beyond the agreement itself (and whether some such agreements are themselves contrary to desert), we must abstract from both the expected wage and the agreement that generates the expectation. When we do, we find activity that is directed at another's purposes at the expense of the agent's own.

But such activity, if it occurred, would clearly run counter to the fundamental tenet that each person's aims, aspirations, and pursuits are valuable in themselves. As we saw in Chapter 4, the premise that each person himself has value leads directly to the conclusion that each person's desires (and, a fortiori, endeavors) confer

---

[5] It might seem that we do not *need* to show why workers deserve to be paid for their efforts, since we established in Chapter 4 that effort confers value on its object. However, the efforts discussed there were focused attempts, made over long periods of time, to achieve single goals. While the efforts of workers who deserve to be paid sometimes fit this description, they just as often do not. Thus, our earlier argument does not apply in all, or even most, of the relevant cases.

value on their objects. From here it is a short step to the conclusion that no one's purposive activity should play a merely subordinate role. Although any degree of mutual purpose-furthering seems legitimate, the one-sided furthering of another's purposes does not. This requirement is not violated when we help others out of friendship or altruism, since in so doing we make the others' purposes our own. But when someone works for another without such a motive, and pursues an outcome that is of interest only to his employer, his labor does create an imbalance. By participating in this one-sided relationship, the worker functions merely as a means.

We are now in a better position to appreciate DF3's role. I have just argued that when a person works for another, his unremunerated labor violates a standard that requires that no one's purposes be subordinated to the purposes of others. This situation is clearly rectified by the restoration of equality between what the worker has done for others and what those others have done for him. Thus, DF3 calls for a response that furthers the worker's purposes in turn. A wage, which the employee can convert to goods or services of his own choosing, is singularly well suited to serve this function. And this, I suggest, is the basic reason the wage is deserved.

This reasoning has much to recommend it. It captures and makes more precise the common-sense idea that desert of wages is somehow grounded in reciprocity.[6] Less obvious, it shows why both the worker's effort and his productivity (and, to a lesser degree, his job's unpleasantness and danger) are relevant to what he deserves. These factors all contribute to his desert because they are all constituents of the situation in which his purposes are maximally subordinated. When the worker exerts effort, he foregoes other activities that would further his own purposes. When his efforts are productive, they further the purposes of others—of his employer and, sometimes, of the employer's customers or clients. When his

---

[6] Although it may seem obvious that an employee's desert rests on an employer's obligation to reciprocate, few have asked why this obligation should exist. Why, if the employer has not agreed to do so, must he match efforts or benefits that were not made or bestowed upon him for his own good? Certainly the most familiar reason for reciprocating—that in receiving benefits from others, we incur debts of gratitude—is inapplicable here. The function of the subordination-of-purposes account is to provide a more adequate reason.

efforts are difficult or dangerous, they thwart the worker's further purpose of avoiding difficulty or danger. Since each element increases the degree of purpose-subordination, none is the sole determinant of desert. Hence, the disputes among the proponents of each are best viewed as debates over the relative importance of these elements.

V

To what degree can these disputes be resolved? What does our account imply about the traditional debate between those who tie deserved wages to workers' efforts and those who tie them to workers' contributions? And what, if anything, does it imply about how much particular workers deserve to be paid?

Given the moral equality of employer and employee, an initially attractive idea is that effort and contribution matter equally. But when we look more closely, we see that despite the parties' moral equality, effort and contribution do not play wholly parallel roles. Rather, even unproductive effort is aimed at furthering the employer's purposes, while effortless contribution is not similarly aimed at preempting the worker's goals. Given this asymmetry, it is clearly the worker's effort that plays the more fundamental role in determining the subordination of his purposes. To capture this, we might say that his contribution determines a smaller fraction of the wage he deserves and his efforts a larger one. But given its structure, our argument provides no non-arbitrary way of specifying the relevant fractions. Thus, it seems preferable to capture the priority of effort by saying that all workers deserve a basic wage to offset their efforts, but that a more productive worker deserves enough in addition to bring his total wage to an amount that offsets his contribution to his employer.

While this suggestion is a step in the right direction, it requires completion by some non-arbitrary specification of *how much* pay offsets a given amount of effort or contribution. Let us consider each factor separately. Where the point of a wage is to offset a worker's efforts, no theoretically precise estimate of how much is deserved seems possible. The only remotely plausible way of achieving precision would be to say that a given amount of effort is offset by a wage that enables the worker to further his own purposes as much as he might have by exerting the same amount of effort. But this is indeterminate until we specify the conditions under which the worker's hypothetical effort would have taken place. For example, if his aim were to put food on his family's table, then the degree to which a given amount of effort would have advanced that aim would depend on his access to land, seed, fertilizer, and tools, and on the quality of these resources. Since we lack a principled specification of these background conditions, our suggestion is hopelessly incomplete. Thus, we must rest content with the vaguer idea that a wage offsets a worker's efforts when it treats his purposes as no less important than those of his employer. To do this, it seems both necessary and sufficient that the wage allow the worker to satisfy his basic needs. Such a wage seems necessary because without food, clothing, and shelter, a worker cannot function as a purposive agent at all. It seems sufficient because it already satisfies purposes that matter to the employee far more than any intended contribution could to his employer.

Does this account imply that persons with special needs, such as costly medical conditions or large families, deserve more for their efforts than others? Although this suggestion is somewhat counterintuitive, I believe it is not easily dismissed. It is, of course, impractical to try to adjust wages to individual needs; but the question is whether this impracticality justifies or merely explains the intuition that deserved wages do not vary with need. I will not attempt to resolve this question here. Nor, for somewhat different reasons, will I try to say how much effort one must exert before deserving a wage sufficient to meet one's needs. In general, the principle seems to be that a workweek cannot be so long as to imply disrespect for a worker's status as a purposive agent. This stricture may be violated either by the absolute amount of labor required or by its comparative magnitude given the prevailing standards. But if the stricture is not violated, there is no more precise way of specifying how much a worker deserves. Within the specified limits, the determination of his hourly wage is properly left to market forces.

What, next, of the wages more productive workers deserve? Here again, it is difficult to find a precise and well-motivated formula for matching wages to contributions. Initially, it might seem that each productive worker deserves a wage that furthers his purposes as much as he has furthered those of his employer. But how much a worker furthers his employer's purposes depends on such extraneous factors as the employer's other resources and the nature of his goals. Hence, this suggestion implies that even some workers who we intuitively feel are productive deserve low wages (since their employers have little need for their products or the income they will bring). It also implies that equally productive workers with different employers may deserve quite different wages. To avoid these implications without detaching desert of wages from the furthering of others' purposes, we must abstract from what is idiosyncratic in specific employers' purposes. In its place, we must appeal to some more objective standard of purpose-furthering. This, of course, raises new problems about the nature of the appropriate standard and its relation to what a worker could earn in an actual or ideal open market. It also raises familiar questions about the relative contributions of workers and owners of means of production, and about the possibility of disentangling different contributions to joint products.[7] But we obviously cannot resolve these questions here. Thus, the exact amounts that workers deserve for their contributions must also be left unspecified.[8]

Concerning the contributions of owners of capital, our account is neutral between Marxist and non-Marxist theories. But on another issue, the account is not neutral. I have argued that a wage is deserved when a worker's receiving it would rectify the subordination of his purposes to those of others. But one person's purposes cannot be subordinated to another's unless both are committed to private rather than common goals. Further, such subordination presupposes that labor itself is not an integral part of the worker's goal.

[7] For opposing views on whether such contributions can be disentangled, see Miller, *Social Justice*, pp. 107–8, and Nozick, *Anarchy, State, and Utopia*, pp. 183–89.

[8] Given these considerations, the idea that women and men deserve equal pay for work of "comparable worth" seems destined to remain controversial. Whether that idea can be formulated in terms that do not involve desert, and a fortiori whether it should be retained as a political ideal, are of course separate questions.

Viewed in this light, our account assumes both the individualism and the alienation of workers from their labor that Marx took to characterize capitalist society. These assumptions, of course, do not commit us to any view about the degree to which individualism and alienation are products of capitalism, or to any position concerning their prevalence under socialism or communism. However, they do commit us to the view that if workers were more communally oriented, or were more inclined to regard their labor as "not only a means of life but life's prime want,"[9] then desert of wages would have far less moral importance.

V I

Yet precisely because our account presupposes that labor is not among workers' primary goals, it may seem to invite a final objection. We all know workers who love what they do and thus do not appear to be subordinating their own purposes when they work. We also know workers who hate their work, and so appear to be subordinating their purposes far more than others with identical jobs. On our account, don't the former deserve far lower wages than their co-workers (if indeed they deserve any pay at all), and don't the latter deserve far more? And, even allowing for the unreliability of our intuitions, aren't such implications unacceptably counterintuitive?

Consider, first, the person who loves his work—the actor whose consuming passion is the theater, the academic whose great pleasures are teaching and writing, the athlete who "would play the game for nothing." Where persons hold such attitudes, their purposes do tend to merge with those of their employers. The convergence is less than total, since even the most dedicated teacher or athlete must want to acquire the necessities of life, while most employers have their own aims in providing work. Still, even allowing for this, willing workers clearly do subordinate their purposes less than others. Thus, our account does seem to imply that they deserve less pay.

[9] Karl Marx, "Critique of the Gotha Program," in *The Marx-Engels Reader*, ed. Robert W. Tucker (New York: W. W. Norton, 1972), p. 388.

But how damaging is this? There is some force to the idea that those who love their work receive part of their pay in "psychic rewards," but the stronger intuition appears to be that willing workers deserve as much pay as others. Thus, to defend our account, we must somehow disarm that intuition. This is, I think, not difficult to do. It is a commonplace that the most committed and willing workers are generally also the best. Thus, although these workers come closer than others to pursuing their own purposes, they also generally do more to advance the purposes of others. In part, the intuition that they deserve to be paid as much as others may reflect a belief that these two factors cancel. But that intuition may also have other sources. For reasons yet to be considered, we believe that merit itself is a source of desert. Anticipating our later discussion, let us say that the meritorious deserve the recognition that a high salary implies. If they do, then the intuition that committed workers deserve to be well paid may also reflect this belief. Another possibility is that we expect even persons who love their work to have a second-level purpose not to be exploited. Or, more simply, we may believe that exploitation is wrong regardless of a worker's attitudes.[10]

In all, we seem well able to account for our intuitions about the desert of willing workers. But what, now, of workers who are unusually *dis*contented with their jobs? An employee who is disaffected and bitter, and would prefer to be almost anywhere rather than at work, may endure as much purpose-frustration as a worker with an especially unpleasant or monotonous job. If the latter deserves additional pay to offset the additional subordination of his purposes, then mustn't this also hold for the former? Yet isn't it highly counterintuitive to say that a worker with negative attitudes deserves a higher wage than his more constructive colleague? Do we really want to say this of the too-familiar professor whose dissatisfaction shows itself in cynicism about his students, despair about his research, and blind antagonism toward all administrators?

In good measure, our reluctance to say that such figures deserve

[10] For related discussion, see Lawrence Becker, *Property Rights* (London: Routledge and Kegan Paul, 1977), pp. 55–56.

more pay than others appears closely related to our reluctance to say that the very committed deserve less. Just as a very willing worker is apt to perform well, a very unwilling one is apt to perform badly. The dissatisfied worker's labor is likely to be relatively unproductive. This means that he is apt to be less deserving than others by one measure even if more deserving by another. In addition, it means that paying him more than others will give him undeserved recognition, and so will blur our recognition of genuine merit.

These facts partially explain why dissatisfied workers do not seem to deserve more pay than others. But I do not think they are the whole story. Rather, I suspect that the intuition also reflects a willingness to take some negative attitudes more seriously than others. If we agree that workers deserve extra pay for jobs that most people find oppressive, monotonous, or unpleasant but do not believe that workers deserve extra pay for jobs that only *they* find unpleasant, the reason may well be that we regard only the former sorts of unpleasantness as objective enough to be morally significant. Some purposes may seem so unreasonable that we believe their subordination does not *call* for rectification. I think, in fact, that this reaction is probably the main source of the intuition that unwilling workers deserve no more pay than others; and I suspect, too, that the reaction is probably defensible. But to defend it, we would again have to range far afield. Thus, having noted the possibility, I will leave the matter here.

SEVEN

DESERT AND MERIT

The discussion so far contains what may seem to be one curious omission. Despite the variety of subjects discussed, we have made little reference to what many consider the primary basis of good desert. This is, of course, the cluster of attributes that fall under the headings of merit, excellence, and virtue. We have not entirely ignored these topics, since diligent effort and planning are themselves meritorious activities. However, in explaining the desert of the diligent and far-sighted, we did not appeal to the meritorious nature of their acts. Moreover, many other forms of merit have not been mentioned at all. In what follows, I will try to rectify these omissions. As before, my main aim will be to discover *why* the deserving parties—in this case, the meritorious—should have what they are said to deserve.

I

Merit spans both the moral and the nonmoral realms. Some persons are said to deserve rewards or acclaim for their morally good or virtuous acts, while others are said to deserve prizes, honors, or opportunities for their accomplishments, abilities, or skills. Moreover, even within each category, there is much variation. The morally meritorious include both people who perform single transcendent acts of heroism or sacrifice and persons whose generosity or compassion is woven through their lives. The nonmorally meritorious include athletes who run faster than others, scientists who discover cures for deadly diseases, and job applicants who score highest on qualifying exams. Given this variety, the relevant desert-claims may seem to have no single justification.

I believe that this is correct. In the next two chapters, I shall argue that the desert of the meritorious and virtuous is grounded not in any single principle or value, but rather in a number of more local sources. By tracing these out, we will complete our discussion of the major justifications of desert-claims. But first, I want to consider two lines of approach which, if successful, would indeed offer unifying justifications of the desert of the meritorious.

The first appeals to the fact that each form of merit is defined in relation to some norm or standard. When we say that someone has displayed outstanding skill, courage, strength, originality, or goodness, we always imply that his performance has surpassed the norm for performances of its type. Because of this, it may be thought that all desert for merit is grounded in some principle analogous to DF3. For if *violations* of independent standards can call for offsetting benefits or burdens, then *surpassings* of such standards may seem able to do the same.

This suggestion, however, dissolves under scrutiny. Its initial appeal lies in the apparent parallel between the violations of standards whose offsetting DF3 demands and the surpassings of standards that merit allegedly entails. Yet on inspection, most displays of merit do not surpass standards at all. To surpass a standard, one must do more than it demands. But standards of excellence do not *impose* demands; rather, they provide criteria for ranking traits or performances. Hence, what most meritorious agents surpass are not the standards that establish their merit, but merely the levels of excellence that others obtain. More important, even when someone really does surpass a standard's demands—when, for example, he performs a supererogatory act—there is no obvious reason for him to receive any offsetting benefit. DF3's justification was that since persons themselves are temporally extended, demands that they receive benefits or burdens at earlier moments may, if unmet, be displaced to later moments. But nothing similar holds if a standard's demands have been surpassed; for in that case, the demands are a fortiori already fully satisfied.

Thus, desert for merit is unlikely to be grounded in any principle analogous to DF3. But a second way of linking merit to standards may seem more promising. When someone displays excellence or virtue, others commonly respond to him with admiration, approval, or gratitude. These attitudes find their natural expression in honor, praise, and reward. But the honors and rewards that our positive attitudes incline us to bestow bear obvious affinities to what the meritorious are thought to deserve. Thus, mightn't the latter's desert be somehow grounded in the tendency of their acts to call forth such responses?

This suggestion is hardly novel. In his discussion of desert of reward in *The Methods of Ethics*, Henry Sidgwick observed that

> [t]his kind of justice . . . seems like Gratitude universalized: and the same principle applied to punishment may similarly be regarded as Resentment universalized.[1]

And in his masterful essay "Justice and Personal Desert," Joel Feinberg follows Sidgwick by contending that

> the services and deprivations which we call "rewards" and "punishments" are conventional means of expressing gratitude and resentment, for these attitudes are prototypically those involved in the "urge to reward" and the "urge to punish."[2]

As Sidgwick and Feinberg both suggest, an "expressive account" of desert applies as naturally to punishment as to reward.[3] Thus, if defensible, it would supplement the justification of punishment provided in Chapter 5. But *is* such an account defensible? Does the desert of the meritorious really reflect our inclination to respond to their acts and traits with gratitude and other positive attitudes?

II

If the question were either "Are we, as a matter of fact, inclined to express admiration and gratitude by providing rewards?" or "Can our actual practices be traced to this inclination?", then the answer

---

[1] Sidgwick, *The Methods of Ethics*, pp. 280–81.

[2] Feinberg, "Justice and Personal Desert," p. 68.

[3] See Joel Feinberg, "The Expressive Function of Punishment," in Feinberg, *Doing and Deserving*, pp. 95–118.

might in general be "yes." But if we left things here, our account would not tell us whether, or why, people really *ought to have* the things they are said to deserve. The account would explain, but would not justify, the practice of rewarding the meritorious. To do the latter, the account must be backed by some principle, value, or argument that shows why individuals or society should exhibit appropriate expressive behavior. It must, in other words, contain a normative as well as a descriptive component.

What form might this normative component take? To appreciate the possibilities, we must distinguish two functions of rewards. As we have already seen, rewards and prizes often serve to express admiration, appreciation, or gratitude. But because such attitudes presuppose beliefs that persons really have displayed excellence or virtue, rewards must also serve a second function. Besides expressing positive attitudes toward merit, they must also mark its existence. Because our natural affective tendencies are well known (and because we know they are well known), bestowing any real or symbolic reward is a way of saying that the recipient really has performed some act or has displayed some trait that is outstanding or excellent. It is, in effect, an assertion or affirmation of the recipient's merit. Though inseparable in practice, the assertive and expressive elements of rewarding are theoretically quite distinct. And because of this, the account's normative component may take either of two forms. If the meritorious ought to be rewarded, the reason may be that, other things being equal, we ought to (1) tell the truth or (2) express admiration or gratitude for merit.

Let us examine each suggestion. In favor of (1), it can be said that obligations of veracity are familiar and unproblematical, and that they hold a prominent place in virtually every moral theory. Still, invoking the principle of veracity here invites two serious objections. First, on most interpretations, that principle is negative rather than positive. It requires that we not say what we know to be false, but it does not require that we say everything we know to be true. Unless others have special rights to our information, usually we may simply remain silent. Thus, our failure to reward merit does not violate the principle as usually conceived. Second, even if we *were* required to volunteer information, no appeal to this requirement would account, at a suitably deep level, for the intuition that what the meritorious deserve is *rewards*. Since information can be conveyed in many ways, there is no essential reason to recognize anyone's merit through desirable or pleasant treatment. Of course, most people find it pleasant just to have their merit recognized, but the vehicle of recognition need not be pleasant in any further way. Instead of providing prizes, rewards, or opportunities, we could record the existence of merit simply by publishing detailed lists. We could even flog or torture in direct proportion to merit. Given our psychological makeup, adopting this convention would be difficult; but it is surely possible. If the convention existed, our suggestion would imply that the meritorious deserved their beatings and abuse.

Because this is so clearly absurd, any adequate version of the expressive account must tie desert more directly to our tendency to respond to merit with good treatment. Instead of appealing to a principle of veracity, it must invoke a principle to the effect that, other things being equal, we ought to express the admiration and gratitude that merit naturally elicits. Yet although this shift would explain why the meritorious ought to receive good treatment, it would also raise new difficulties. For what, exactly, would the operative principle require? Would it demand only that we express admiration and gratitude for merit *if and when we feel them*? If so, then it would require only forthrightness in interpersonal relations. It would impose no obligations on persons who lack the relevant feelings, and so would allow desert to be canceled by ingratitude or indifference. Would it require, instead, that we both feel and express admiration and gratitude toward the meritorious? If so, then our account invites the reply that our feelings are generally not within our control, and so are not subject to obligation at all. To avoid both objections, the principle would have to require that either (1) we cultivate feelings that incline us to honor and reward the meritorious or (2) we act as though we have those feelings, and so provide honors and rewards even when we feel nothing. Yet neither requirement is plausible unless we already believe that the meritorious deserve honors and rewards, and that their desert has real normative force. Since this belief is what we are trying to justify, appeals to such principles do not advance the argument.

No version of the expressive account seems likely to explain why the meritorious should have the prizes, honors, and opportunities they are said to deserve. At one point, Feinberg comes close to acknowledging this. Speaking of the "fit" between human responses and the occurrences that evoke them, he remarks:

> [E]ven when the object of the attitude is logically appropriate, it may still lack a certain kind of propriety. Glee, for example, is an inappropriate response to another's suffering. . . . I am not sure how, if at all, these judgments of moral appropriateness are to be verified; but I suspect that they resemble certain aesthetic judgments—for example, that crimson and orange are clashing colors—more than they resemble judicial pronouncements—for example, that a certain person is to be punished for a crime or that a certain runner is to be awarded the prize for the hundred-yard dash.[4]

In this passage, Feinberg suggests that the reasons for having (and, presumably, for expressing) the "morally appropriate" attitudes are analogous to those that support aesthetic judgments. Taken seriously, this analogy implies that the value that is served by promoting an outstanding employee, or honoring a hero, is of the same general type as the value that is served by wearing a matching shirt and tie. Even when we allow for differences in strength among aesthetic reasons, this implication seems to amount to a concession that the desert of the meritorious lacks serious normative force.[5] In this context, as elsewhere, to aestheticize morality is effectively to deny it.

---

[4] Feinberg, "Justice and Personal Desert," p. 82.

[5] It might be replied that aesthetic judgments *do* have serious normative force insofar as they express aesthetic requirements. For example, a certain chord may be precisely what is required to complete a musical work. In such cases, the appropriate completing element is sometimes held to be "aesthetically necessary." Yet even here, the necessity is only internal to the composition. To show that a chord is necessary to complete a work is not to show that the work is necessary in any further sense.

III

Yet even if the expressive account does not justify all merit-based desert-claims, it may still play a more modest justificatory role. Ironically, the desert-claims to whose justification the expressive account is most pertinent are precisely those from which Feinberg tries to dissociate this account in the passage just quoted. Like the claim "that a certain runner is to be awarded the prize for the hundred-yard dash," they are desert-claims that presuppose conventional structures which establish both tests for excellence and rewards or prizes for passing those tests.[6]

Such conventional structures are of course extremely varied. They range from the rules and bylaws of the National Football League to the arrangements for impromptu footraces to the regulations and criteria that govern the assignment of grades in universities. But despite their differences, these structures all involve conventions that are public knowledge within the relevant communities. These conventions include rules that specify what performers may and may not do; criteria for success and failure in performance; and procedures for awarding prizes, titles, or grades on the basis of that success or failure.[7] Like linguistic rules, the conventions invest brute occurrences with significance they would otherwise lack. In particular, where the conventions exist, the awarding of any prize, title, or grade is a conventional way of signifying that the recipient has satisfied the appropriate criteria of performance. And, knowing this, others naturally believe that the recipient has performed meritoriously. Barring special grounds for doubt, it would be unreasonable *not* to believe that the gold medalist has crossed the finish line first, that the red ribbon winner has grown the fair's second largest tomato, and that the C student has written an adequate but far from outstanding exam.

But if so, then something like the principle of veracity must in-

---

[6] Feinberg, of course, does not deny that conventional structures of rules can affect what persons ought to have, but he often speaks as though what they determine is entitlement rather than desert. See, for example, Feinberg, "Justice and Personal Desert," p. 57. However, for remarks suggesting that those who qualify for a prize *do* deserve it, see ibid., pp. 62–64.

[7] For relevant discussion, see Rawls, "Two Concepts of Rules," sec. 3.

deed apply. If awarding a prize or grade in accordance with fixed rules amounts to making an assertion about how well the recipient has performed, then deviating from those rules must amount to making a *false* assertion about this. Hence, whatever is wrong with making such false assertions must also be wrong with departing from the rules.[8] Moreover, when we examine the situation, we find several things that are wrong. First, if someone who promulgates, referees, or judges a contest knowingly deviates from the rules, and thus makes (or contributes to the making of) a false assertion about a performer's merit, he arguably does violate his obligation of veracity. Second, even where no person is responsible for an improper grade or outcome—even where a good student's D results solely from a computer malfunction or a referee is screened from seeing a crucial foul—there is disvalue simply in the creation of the relevant false beliefs. Because our excellences are matters of pride and importance to us, the mere existence of false beliefs about them is a significantly bad state of affairs. And third, even if neither wrongdoing *nor* false belief is in question—even if, for instance, the foul missed by the referee was seen by fifty million television viewers—there seems to be disvalue in the simple fact that the wrong winner is proclaimed or the wrong grade is assigned. In this limiting case, the disvalue appears to reside solely in the falsity of the assertion itself.

How does this reasoning differ from the appeal to veracity we rejected above? On the current account, the principle of veracity plays a far more restricted role. It is now invoked to establish not that any form of excellence ought to be acknowledged, but only that where there *are* conventions for evaluating performance, their dictates ought to be honored. To justify the conventions themselves, we may invoke quite different considerations. For example, we may appeal to the facts that professional athletic leagues make money,

---

[8] Michael Walzer makes a related point when he writes that "[t]he crucial standard for public honor is desert. Not desert casually or parochially conceived, not the desert of personal friends and enemies: public honor is endorsed and reiterated by private individuals only if it is thought to conform to an objective measure. Hence, it is distributed by juries, whose members deliver not an opinion but a verdict—a 'true speech' about the qualities of the recipients." See Walzer, *Spheres of Justice* (New York: Basic Books, 1983), p. 259 and passim.

that amateur contests provide entertainment and opportunities to compete, and that grading systems give students information about their progress and incentives to study. Having thus divided the labor, we avoid both objections to the argument's earlier version. For, first, since the principle of veracity is invoked only where some affirmation about merit is inevitable, the version of it that applies is not the implausible "Always say what is true," but the weaker and more plausible "Do not say what is false." And second, because we now presuppose a background of existing conventions, we can appeal to facts about these conventions to explain why the meritorious always deserve prizes, awards, and honors, but never forms of unpleasant treatment. Superficially, the explanation is simply that no conventional structure *prescribes* that excellence be recognized through unpleasant treatment. More deeply, it is that if a structure did prescribe unpleasant treatment, then no one would be moved to display the relevant excellence.

By thus appealing to veracity, we can justify the desert-claims that arise when persons display merit in conventionally structured contexts. But what of the desert-claims that arise in such contexts when persons *fail* to display their true merit? As Feinberg observes:

> In a contest of skill in which the winner can be determined by exact measurement, such as a high-jumping contest, there can be no question of who deserves the prize. . . . There might still be controversy, however, over who deserved to win. To be sure, the victor deserved the prize, but who deserved to be victor? Perhaps the man who truly deserved to win did not in fact win because he pulled up lame, or tore his shoe, or suffered some other unforeseeable stroke of bad luck.[9]

Since the athlete who tore his shoe did not satisfy the victory criterion, his failure to receive the prize involves no false assertion about his achievement. Moreover, it seems clear that his luckier rival *should* be proclaimed the winner and *should* receive the prize. Still, there remains a sense in which the unlucky competitor did de-

[9] Feinberg, "Justice and Personal Desert," p. 64.

serve to win. What does this come to, and how does it relate to the victor's desert?

If our account is correct, the connection will be quite close. When prizes or high grades are awarded, the persons who qualify for them are generally the ones with the most skill, ability, or knowledge. Thus, an assertion that someone has qualified for a gold medal or an A is not cleanly separable from an assertion that he was the swiftest runner in the race or had superior knowledge of his subject.[10] In most cases, the two assertions are true or false together. Yet in examples like Feinberg's, the correlation breaks down. When the superior runner comes up lame or tears a shoe, the most able competitor is *not* the one who satisfies the contest's victory criterion. For this reason, awarding the prize to the latter involves one true affirmation (that he satisfied the victory criterion) but also one false one (that he was, at the time of the contest, the best performer). Since prizes are primarily markers of victory, this dissonance cannot require that the prize be diverted to the superior but unlucky competitor. Thus, we continue to believe that the loser had no complaint. Still, we remain uneasy at the (often blatant) false implication that the loser was not the better performer. To vent this unease, we say that the loser "really deserved to win."

All in all, the demands of veracity provide one clear justification for claims that outstanding competitors deserve prizes and outstanding students deserve A's. But veracity is not the only justification for these claims. Rather, given the expectation of rewards that fixed conventions can arouse, the claims may also draw force from the principle that reasonable expectations should be honored. More strongly yet, they may draw force from the related principle that promises (including de facto promises) should be kept. In general, these principles are apt to play a minor role when the deserved prize is a certificate, trophy, or other merely symbolic reward.

[10] The content of the latter sort of assertion can itself vary with the context. In some sports, such as baseball, even dominant teams win only about 60 percent of the time. Where these sports are concerned, the assertion that the winning team was best on a given day will imply little about its more general level of skill. However, if the sport is one in which dominant teams or competitors win with greater regularity, the assertion that a team or competitor was best on a given day may indeed impute superior skill.

Here, the main sources of normative force do seem to be principles and values associated with truth. But where a prize has independent value—where, for example, it is a sum of money or a job—reasonable expectations may supply as much normative force as veracity, or even more. Of course, for this very reason, these cases are no longer clear-cut instances of desert. Where the main grounding of one's claim is a de facto promise, one does not so much deserve the prize as have a right to it.

IV

So far, I have argued that desert for nonmoral merit is often grounded in demands of veracity and fidelity, as these are called into play by the conventions that structure contests and tests.[11] Quite obviously, this justification applies only where such conventions exist. Where persons excel at activities not regulated by conventions—where, for instance, someone excels at balancing a telephone on his nose—the justification does not apply. In these contexts, our argument can find no purchase.

For the most part, this limitation is not troublesome. But there is one important type of case in which desert for merit does seem decisively to outrun the requirements of veracity and fidelity. It is often said that persons deserve to be hired for jobs, or to be admitted to educational institutions, because they are best qualified to do the work or to learn the material. Where such claims are made, their import does *not* seem to be merely that the best-qualified applicant ought to be chosen because existing rules dictate his selection. Rather, what is meant is that the rules *ought to* dictate his selection—that he has a significant prior claim to be chosen. Thus, the desert of the best-qualified appears to have some further (and more strongly pre-conventional) grounding.

---

[11] When persons come to deserve prizes or grades in this way, their desert is in one sense conventional, in one sense not. It is conventional in the sense that the desert-claim would not be justified if the relevant conventions did not exist. However, it is nonconventional in the sense that the principles of veracity and promise-keeping, which supply the normative force, are not mere artifacts of the conventions that govern the parties' performance.

This is not a minor matter. As William A. Galston rightly notes, the idea that the best-qualified or most able deserve to be chosen is "one of the historically and conceptually most important desert-claims."[12] Because it provides a rationale for the widely held ideal of equal opportunity, it is a central (if often unstated) assumption of modern liberal thought. But how is that assumption to be justified? If the best-qualified applicant were always the one who had worked hardest to develop his qualifications, then we might appeal to his past hard work to account for his desert. But as often as not, a person's superior qualifications reflect not his greater past effort, but rather his greater native ability.[13] Since this does not appear to undermine his desert, our justification must appeal to some fact other than effort.

As a first step toward a more adequate justification, we may note that there are close internal connections between jobs and the skills and abilities they require and between education and the ability to learn. No job can be done unless a worker has the requisite skill or ability, so the primary purpose of seeking someone to do a job will only be accomplished if one hires a suitably skilled applicant. Moreover, that purpose will best be accomplished if one hires the most skilled applicant. Similarly, the primary purpose of admitting persons to educational institutions will best be accomplished by admitting those who are most able to learn. In other contexts, internal connections between goods and traits have been taken to provide strong reasons for allocating the goods to those possessing the traits. For example, Bernard Williams has written that "[l]eaving aside preventive medicine, the proper ground of distribution of medical care is ill health: this is a necessary truth."[14] More generally, Michael Walzer has suggested that "for all our personal and collective resources, there are distributive reasons that are somehow *right*, that are naturally part of our ideas about the things

---

[12] William A. Galston, *Justice and the Human Good* (Chicago: University of Chicago Press, 1980), p. 176.

[13] See Rachels, "What People Deserve," p. 156.

[14] Bernard Williams, "The Idea of Equality," in Williams, *Problems of the Self* (Cambridge, England: Cambridge University Press, 1973), p. 240.

themselves."[15] But *why* should an internal connection between a good and a trait—in our case, between an opportunity to perform a task and a person's superior ability to do so—be a significant reason for awarding the good to the trait's possessor?

In one sense, the answer in the current context is clear. As we just saw, the primary purpose of hiring or admitting—to select someone who will work or learn—is apt to be best accomplished if one selects the best-qualified applicant. Moreover, showing that a given action will best accomplish a purpose is a way of justifying the action to anyone who has the purpose. Thus we have already provided a kind of justification of selection by qualification. Yet if we left things here, our justification would at best explain why selecting best-qualified applicants is rational from the hiring officer's perspective. It would not answer the quite different question of why such selection is owed to the best-qualified applicants themselves. Hence, it would fail to capture the desert-claim's real import.

To do that, we must look beyond the act of selecting by merit and consider the attitude toward persons which that act expresses. When we hire by merit, we abstract from all facts about the applicants except their ability to perform well at the relevant tasks. By thus concentrating on their ability to perform, we treat them as agents whose purposeful acts can make a difference in the world. Moreover, by concentrating on abilities that are internally connected to jobs and opportunities that exist to serve independent purposes, we affirm the applicants' involvement in the wider life of the community. For both reasons, selecting by merit is a way of taking seriously the potential agency of both the successful and the unsuccessful applicants. Conversely, when an applicant is selected on some other basis, there is a recognizable if elusive sense in which he and his rivals are *not* taken seriously. And this suggests that we

---

[15] Michael Walzer, "The Idea of Equality," *Dissent* (Fall 1973), p. 403. This idea is developed further in Walzer's *Spheres of Justice.* In that work, Walzer observes that he regards the proper reasons for having goods to be determined by the social meanings that constitute the goods, whereas for Williams, "relevance seems to connect to essential rather than to social meanings" (p. 9). But whoever is right about this, I cannot see that either philosopher has taken the crucial next step and asked exactly what is *wrong* with any particular irrelevant distributive procedure.

may justify selection by merit by arguing that persons *ought* to be taken seriously in the relevant sense.

I believe, in fact, that some argument of this sort does underlie the claim that best-qualified applicants deserve jobs and educational opportunities. It is worth repeating that the argument is not an appeal to consequences. Although the argument emphasizes the internal connections between jobs and qualifications, it does so not to establish the inefficiency, but rather to show the wrongness, of departures from merit criteria. Yet just because of this, the argument raises many further questions. Do the aims of employment and education require selecting the *most* able person, or only a competent one? Whatever these aims require, how is the situation affected by the intimate connections between opportunities and rewards—between desirable jobs and education and the money and prestige that these allow people to acquire? And, most important, what is the force of the claim that departures from merit criteria do not take applicants seriously? To what principle, value, or other consideration does this claim appeal?

V

The first question—whether the aims of employment and education really require the selection of *best*-qualified persons—gets its bite from the facts that jobs done adequately are still done, and material learned adequately is still learned. Given these facts, it may be held that the aims of employment and education are satisfied whenever the chosen applicant's ability exceeds the appropriate threshold. It is granted on all sides that we should not hire persons who cannot do the work or provide education for persons who cannot learn. However, beyond this, appeals to the prerequisites of performance may seem to prove little.

But this objection presupposes a very limited—I think an unacceptably limited—vision of the aims of employment and education. It presupposes that the point of employing someone is merely to insure that the job be adequately done, and that the point of educating is merely to enable someone to master academic subjects in some fashion. In general, however, purposive activity aims not merely at achieving satisfactory results, but at achieving the *best* results that

prevailing conditions allow. A weekend gardener may be resigned
to his small plot, his poor soil, and his lack of time to pull weeds;
and he may therefore be happy to produce tomatoes above a certain
number and quality. Nevertheless, his aim is still to grow as many
tomatoes, and as good tomatoes, as his resources permit. Similarly,
an employer may be quite willing to settle for work whose quality
exceeds a certain threshold, but he nevertheless aims at obtaining
the best work available for the price. Still more obvious, there is no
theoretical limit to the breadth and depth of understanding that education aims to instill. Given these considerations, the aims of employment and education are considerably more comprehensive than
the objection allows. To satisfy them fully, we must indeed choose
best-qualified members of applicant pools.

The second question appears more serious. Thus far, I have spo-
ken as though, when someone is hired or admitted to an educational
institution, he acquires only the chance to work or learn. But this is
clearly oversimplified. Many coveted jobs bring high salaries and
prestige, while many sought-after forms of education lead predictably to similar rewards. Where such connections hold, opportunities to work or learn are also opportunities to acquire wealth and
prestige. Moreover, whatever we say about prestige, being best
qualified to work or learn is clearly *not* internally related to earning
a high wage. Thus, the proper grounds for allocating opportunities
to work or learn need not coincide with the proper grounds for allocating opportunities to acquire the associated rewards. But if not,
then it may indeed seem acceptable to allocate jobs or education on
some basis other than qualifications. As Thomas Nagel puts the
point:

> [W]here the allocation of one benefit on relevant grounds car-
> ries with it the allocation of other, more significant benefits to
> which those grounds are irrelevant, the departure from those
> grounds need not be a serious offense against justice. . . . [I]t
> may be acceptable to depart from the "relevant" grounds for
> undramatic reasons of social utility, that would not justify
> more flagrant and undiluted examples of unfairness.[16]

[16] Nagel, "Equal Treatment and Compensatory Discrimination," p. 359.

To this, we need only add that if Nagel is right, departures from merit criteria may also be defensible on other grounds—for example, that they promote equality (among either individuals or groups), that they meet pressing individual needs, or that they reward past efforts.

This objection to selection by merit is often accompanied by the claim that highly paid workers do not deserve (all) their wages. For this reason, the objection may be taken to assert that deviations from merit criteria are permissible *because* the prevailing reward structure is indefensible. But this interpretation is neither charitable nor necessary. It is not charitable because even if there is no reason for anyone to earn the high wage that attaches to a job, it does not follow that there is no reason for anyone to have the job to which the wage attaches. If merit is a good reason for someone to have a job, it does not cease to be a good reason merely because the job pays an indefensible wage. And the interpretation is unnecessary because the question of how to allocate what in fact are dual opportunities would arise even if the prevailing reward structure were completely acceptable. Given these facts, the strongest version of Nagel's objection is *not* the bad argument just discussed. Rather, it is that when the proper reasons for allocating opportunities to work or learn do not coincide with the proper reasons for allocating the associated opportunities to earn high salaries, it is the latter reasons that ought to dominate.

To insist that this argument can never succeed would be unrealistic. Any kind of moral pluralist must believe—and I do believe—that there are goals so urgent, and needs so pressing, that they simply override the reasons for hiring or admitting by merit. But it is one thing to concede that this may occur and quite another to agree that it generally does. To establish the latter, one would have to show *why* the favored non-meritocratic reasons for allocating opportunities to acquire wealth and prestige are generally dominant over meritocratic reasons for allocating opportunities to work or learn.

Can the non-meritocratic reasons be shown to dominate? To do so, one might argue either that these reasons are themselves weightier than meritocratic reasons or that the opportunities to which they are linked opportunities to acquire wealth and prestige—take priority over opportunities to work or learn. Nagel suggests an appeal of the first sort when he writes that "the presumption [in favor of hiring and admitting by merit] may not be very strong to begin with."[17] But Nagel's only basis for regarding this presumption as weak is his implication that wealth and prestige are "more significant" benefits than opportunities to work or learn. This is inadequate because the strength of a reason for allocating a benefit in a certain way need not be proportional to the significance of that benefit itself. And when we turn from the strength of the competing reasons to the relation between the linked opportunities, we find that this relation if anything favors hiring and admitting by merit. For since one cannot acquire the salary and prestige associated with a good job without actually doing the job—since the salary and prestige attach to the job, rather than vice versa—it is the opportunity to do the job that is naturally prior. Thus, if the priority of one of two linked opportunities can imply that the criterion for allocating that opportunity should also have priority, it is the merit criterion that ought to dominate.

VI

But what, in the end, does the case for this criterion come to? We saw that superior qualifications are internally connected to the aims of employment and education, and that inattention to such connections involves some sort of failure to take applicants seriously. But what, exactly, does this mean? What sort of failure is involved, and why is it normatively significant?

To answer this final question, we must pursue the contrast between the attitudes that underlie merit and non-merit criteria. I suggested earlier that when someone is hired or admitted because he is best qualified, he is treated as a full participant in the relevant productive and creative arrangements. But suppose, now, that someone is selected for reasons other than his qualifications. In that case, his decisive feature may be entirely unrelated to his ability to

[17] Ibid., p. 359.

advance any independent purposes. This occurs when someone is hired because he needs the job so urgently, or because he is the nephew of the company president. Alternatively, his decisive feature may indeed suit him to advance some independent purpose, but only in a way that is unconnected (or merely incidentally connected) to his actions. This occurs when a weak student is admitted to a competitive institution in the hope that his parents will donate a wing to the library, and when members of minority groups are hired to correct the "under-representation" of those groups, or to break down stereotypes. In neither type of case is either the chosen candidate or his better-qualified rival treated as an individual whose actions themselves will matter. Instead, all parties are treated as mere bearers of needs or claims, as passive links in causal chains, or as interchangeable specimens of larger groups or classes.

This contrast makes the core argument for selection by merit easier to grasp. Properly understood, the requirement that we select among applicants on the basis of their qualifications is a consequence of the more general requirement that we treat all persons as rational agents. Because we most readily associate practical reason with deliberation and choice, the general requirement is most often taken to demand that we not coerce others' decisions. But practical reason encompasses not only decisions, but also the acts and intended effects to which these decisions lead. Moreover, it ranges over both acts intended to serve agents' own interests and acts with other aims. Thus, any requirement that we treat persons as rational agents must demand respect not only for their choices, but also for their ability to do things which advance their own and others' ends. Yet, as we just saw, when we select among applicants for reasons other than their ability to perform the tasks that define positions, we treat them as passive recipients of largesse or links in causal chains rather than as active contributors to anyone's ends. By thus disengaging their practical wills from the aims that have generated the positions, we violate the requirement that they be treated as rational agents. For this reason, there must indeed be a strong presumption in favor of awarding opportunities on the basis of the ability to perform the relevant tasks. Even where the tasks are mechanical and repetitive, selecting in this way affirms the applicants' status as choosers and doers, while selecting on other grounds does not.[18]

This, surely, is an important (non-consequentialist) reason for choosing only the best-qualified applicant. But is it also the rationale for the claim that the best-qualified applicant *deserves* to be chosen? On the surface, this may seem doubtful; for while only the best-qualified applicant deserves to be chosen, it is not just he, but all the applicants, who ought to be treated as rational agents. Thus, the proffered reason may seem to be of the wrong form to justify the desert-claim. But this objection is confused. What needs to be shown is not that only the best-qualified applicant is owed *treatment as a rational agent*, but rather that he, and only he, is owed *the contested position*. To establish this, I have argued that only selection by qualification treats all applicants as rational agents, and that under such selection, the best-qualified applicant, and he alone, is owed the position. On this account, what the best-qualified applicant alone is owed just *is* what he alone deserves. Hence, the proffered reason is of the right form to justify the desert-claim.

Indeed, by accepting the account, we bring out an important continuity between the desert of the best-qualified and other forms of desert. On the surface, desert-claims whose bases are abilities to perform future tasks may seem unrelated to desert-claims whose bases are past actions. But given what has been said, these types of desert-claims are indeed connected. They share a vision of the person that is rooted in, and draws its main elements from, the inescapable fact of his agency. Since this vision requires considerable elaboration, I shall defer detailed discussion of it until Chapter 9.

---

[18] Because this argument grounds the desert of the best-qualified in an obligation to respect the applicants' status as agents, it may seem to fail for cases in which qualifications are "passive." For example, for a job as receptionist, the qualifications are apt to include being attractive (or at least presentable). But as long as one's attractiveness is important because it increases one's ability to interact smoothly with others, it does contribute to the efficacy of one's actions. On the other hand, if the receptionist will do nothing, or virtually nothing, but sit and look attractive, we may concede that the resulting desert-claim either lacks serious force or must be justified in some other way. For further discussion of such qualifications, see Alan Wertheimer, "Jobs, Qualifications, and Preferences," *Ethics* 94, no. 1 (October 1983), pp. 99–112.

But even without elaboration, its introduction explains why it seems least objectionable to depart from merit criteria when the rationale for doing so involves some other form of desert. Even ardent meritocrats are not apt to be overly disturbed if a less-qualified applicant is hired because he has worked much harder than his rivals; and we can now see that this intuition is sound. If departing from merit criteria is generally wrong because it fails to respect the applicants' prospective agency, its wrongness is at least mitigated when the countervailing factor is precisely what the applicants have already done.

One other reason for bypassing best-qualified applicants requires brief mention. Sometimes one applicant is best qualified because another was prevented by past discrimination, or by its effects, from developing the relevant skills. Had there been no wrongdoing, the second applicant would have been better qualified. I have argued elsewhere that in such cases we should, if possible, give the less-qualified applicant just enough preference to return him to the competitive position he would have occupied in the absence of wrongdoing.[19] I shall not repeat that argument here. But I do want to stress that if this defense of preferential treatment is otherwise sound, it is far less vulnerable than others to the charge of giving insufficient weight to the desert of the best-qualified. Although compensatory preference is not, strictly speaking, deserved (since its aim is not to rectify past deviations from independent standards, but to prevent future ones), it does share with desert a vision of the parties as agents. It manifests this vision not by basing its selection on either the applicants' actual past actions or their potential future ones, but rather by focusing on the actions that they *would have* been able to perform in a more just world. Although merely possible actions cannot create actual desert, any argument that turns on these actions does acknowledge the parties' status as agents. Thus, here again, the usual wrongness of deviating from merit criteria is at least mitigated.

[19] See George Sher, "Justifying Reverse Discrimination in Employment," and George Sher, "Preferential Hiring," in *Just Business: New Introductory Essays in Business Ethics*, ed. Tom Regan (New York: Random House, 1984), pp. 32–59.

VII

So far, I have argued that desert-claims based on merit are justified in two important contexts. When someone satisfies criteria of performance established by fixed sets of conventions, he ought to receive whatever prizes, recognition, or grades those conventions dictate; and when an applicant is best-qualified for a job or educational opportunity, he ought to receive that opportunity. Yet these desert-bases, however important, do not exhaust the forms of merit that are said to create desert. We also say that persons with interesting ideas deserve to be heard, that superior political candidates deserve to be elected, that authors of outstanding books deserve recognition, and that scientists who discover vaccines or generals who lead victorious armies deserve honors and awards. We cannot plausibly ground these desert-claims in either the principles of veracity or fidelity or the requirement that persons be treated as rational agents. And short of postulating principles or values that merely restate what must be shown, I can envision no other non-consequentialist reason for saying that such persons ought to have what they are said to deserve. Thus, barring further developments, our working assumption—that all major desert-claims have real normative force—must here be abandoned; here, we must settle for a non-justificatory account.

If these desert-claims lack normative force, why do we make them? One possibility, of course, is that we intend them to have normative force, but we simply are mistaken. But why should we *make* such mistakes? To answer this question, we must revert to two of Feinberg's ideas. As we saw, Feinberg connects desert to both (1) the fitness of responding to acts or traits in certain ways and (2) our natural tendencies to express admiration, gratitude, and resentment. I argued above that these ideas are of little help in showing why the meritorious ought to have what they are said to deserve. But I now want to add that they are of far more help in explaining why we *say* that the meritorious deserve things.

Thus, consider the claim that a person with interesting ideas deserves to be heard. At first glance, it may seem unhelpful to interpret this claim as asserting that there is a relation of fitness between the person's ideas and other people's attention. But this interpretation *is* helpful when we factor in relevant background information. It is uncontroversial that people often seek enlightenment and understanding; and, given these aims, it surely *is* fitting that they pay attention to those who can enlighten them, that is, to persons with interesting ideas. Similarly, we all want wise and effective political leadership, so it is fitting that we vote for politicians with viable and just programs. In these and other cases, the deserved response is an appropriate way of achieving a recognizable goal. Hence, we can interpret the desert-claim as asserting precisely that the response fits the goal.

On this interpretation, some of the desert-claims we failed to justify are disguised hypothetical imperatives. When a desert-claim plays this role, it does not assert that anything is owed to the deserving party. It says only that given that party's merits, others will do well to respond to him in certain ways. About some desert-claims, such as claims that wise and skilled politicians deserve to be elected, this seems to tell the whole story. But about others, more must be said. When we claim that an outstanding author deserves recognition, we do not seem to be saying only that a widely held aim is served by having people read his books. We seem to be saying, in addition, something about *him*. A fortiori, when a scientist has discovered a cure for a dreaded disease, the claim that he deserves honors and awards cannot plausibly be equated with any hypothetical imperative. Hence, even if such desert-claims are not justified, our inclination to make them requires further explanation.

To provide it, we must return to Feinberg's other observation, that honors and rewards are natural expressions of admiration and gratitude. Because they are, it is hardly surprising that our willingness to ascribe desert for merit, and to invest such desert with normative force, should occasionally outrun our justificatory resources. When this occurs, the obvious explanation is that we confuse our natural inclination to express admiration or gratitude with a more objective reason to provide the meritorious with honors and rewards. In such cases, we project our inclinations onto the world and call them values or obligations. The tendency to do this—an instance of what Hume called the mind's "great propensity to spread itself on external objects"[20]—can be expected to operate whether or not a given desert-claim is justified. Indeed, the tendency is surely abetted by the belief that a justification is forthcoming. But where desert-claims can be justified, the fact that their prescriptions match our inclinations is unimportant. Like other error theories, this one is most needed, and most illuminating, where justification fails.

[20] David Hume, *A Treatise of Human Nature* (Oxford: Oxford University Press, 1960), bk. 1, pt. 4, p. 167.

EIGHT

DESERT AND VIRTUE

In the last chapter, we distinguished nonmoral from moral merit. Persons exhibit nonmoral merit when they compete or perform with unusual skill or give indication of the ability to do so. Persons exhibit moral merit when they display a virtuous character or perform specific acts of courage, thoughtfulness, or generosity. Where desert-claims are based on nonmoral merit, we found that sometimes they are justified, but at other times they are mere externalizations of our expressive tendencies. What, now, of claims that heroes deserve rewards, or that especially generous or sympathetic persons deserve to fare well? Joel Feinberg's example of "the wife who sacrifices all to nurse her hopelessly invalid husband through endless torturous hours until death"[1] seems the very paradigm of a deserving soul. Reminded that such persons exist, we feel the force of W. D. Ross's claim that there is special value in "the proportionment of happiness to virtue."[2] But Ross, typically, offers no defense of this claim. Can we do better?

I

Quite clearly, the desert of the virtuous cannot have the same grounding as that of the nonmorally meritorious. The rewarding of virtue is not required by the principles of veracity or fidelity, as these are called into play by conventional structures. There are no "virtue contests." Neither, again, are rewards for virtue called for by the requirements that persons be treated as agents, and not as mere links in causal chains or as interchangeable representatives of

---

[1] Feinberg, "Justice and Personal Desert," p. 72.
[2] Ross, *The Right and the Good*, p. 27.

groups. The failure to reward someone denies neither his past nor his present or future agency. We encounter problems of a different sort when we conjecture that attributions of desert for virtue might be mere externalizations of a subjective inclination to express admiration or gratitude. This suggestion has been advanced by F. C. Sharp to explain our judgments of desert "where the object of admiration and approbation is character." According to Sharp:

> [A]dmiration, approbation, and its normal attendant, the impersonal form of gratitude which I have called thankfulness, . . . kindle our interest in the welfare of the admired person and make us judge: The good of those I admire ought to be preferred to the good of those I do not admire; and the good of the more admired ought to be preferred to the good of the less admired.[3]

But whether or not Sharp is right, his suggestion is out of place here. For, as we have seen, psychological explanations of desert-claims are of interest only *after* justification has failed.

And, in the current context, its failure is far from clear. For, first, where persons are said to deserve rewards for specific acts of virtue, their desert may well be grounded in the debts of gratitude that these acts engender. We say that persons deserve rewards for heroically saving drowning swimmers, for returning lost wallets despite their own poverty, for stopping to help stranded motorists or accident victims. In each case, the desert-creating act is one that benefits (or prevents harm to) another person, and it is performed at some cost or risk to the agent. Where persons make sacrifices to benefit others, those others are standardly thought to owe them debts of gratitude. Thus, when we say that the benefactors deserve rewards, the real point may be that their beneficiaries owe them such debts. If so, then these desert-claims will draw normative force from whatever principle generates debts of gratitude.

Before accepting this suggestion, we must consider the objection that debts of gratitude, unlike desert of reward, arise only when benefits actually are conferred. Certainly the claim that gratitude is

[3] F. C. Sharp, *Ethics* (New York: Century, 1928), pp. 125–26.

owed only for actual benefits has often seemed self-evident. It is built into Sidgwick's characterization of "the duty of requiting benefits"[4] and is a background assumption of A. John Simmons's careful recent discussion of gratitude.[5] Yet the intuition that persons may deserve rewards for even failed attempts to provide aid is also compelling. Thus, suppose that someone with other pressing aims has spent hours trying to fix a stranger's car on a lonely road. In this case we may well feel that the Good Samaritan deserves a reward despite his ultimate failure to fix the car. But the rationale of this desert-claim is unlikely to differ from that of a desert-claim based on a successful attempt to help. Thus, it may appear that *neither* type of desert-claim can be grounded in a duty of gratitude.

Yet this objection is not decisive. First, despite what both Sidgwick and Simmons imply, it is far from obvious that only acts that confer benefits can create debts of gratitude. Good Samaritans who unsuccessfully try to help stranded motorists are just as plausibly said to be owed debts of gratitude as to deserve rewards. Hence, if they have not conferred a benefit, then persons may be owed debts of gratitude despite such failures.[6] But second, there is also a sense in which Good Samaritans *have* conferred a benefit. They have benefited stranded motorists by treating them in a way that raises the antecedent probability, relative to the available information, of their receiving other benefits. To see why this is a benefit, consider a different sort of case. Suppose someone is given a ticket to a lottery that has not yet taken place, but whose outcome is already causally determined. Since people willingly (and reasonably) pay for such tickets, they clearly do have value. Hence, to be given one—even one that will eventually lose—is indeed to receive a benefit. Yet if the lottery's future outcome *is* known by all, then being given a ticket that will not win is *not* receiving a benefit. Thus, a given ticket's status as a benefit plainly does depend on the proba-

---

[4] Sidgwick, *The Methods of Ethics*, p. 259.

[5] Simmons, *Moral Principles and Political Obligations*, chap. 7, esp. pp. 163–83.

[6] The claim that persons may be owed debts of gratitude for acts that have failed to confer benefits is defended by Terrance McConnell in his unpublished paper "Debts of Gratitude."

bility, relative to what is known, that it will bring other benefits.[7] And so too, *mutatis mutandis*, does the Good Samaritan's (eventually unsuccessful) attempt to fix the car.

This reply disposes of the worry that unsuccessful attempts to provide aid do not generate debts of gratitude. But there remain many further questions about such debts themselves. Prima facie, debts of gratitude seem too context-sensitive to be governed by any simple moral principle. (We feel that repaying a millionaire with a job is just silly, but that similarly repaying an unemployed person is not; and a heartfelt letter of thanks is appropriate repayment from one who is destitute, but not necessarily from one who is prosperous.) Nor, if any principle of gratitude could be formulated, would its own grounding be clear.

Rather than pursue these matters here, I shall simply assume that, however debts of gratitude are best understood, they must have *some* real normative basis. Granting this, how much of what we believe about desert for virtue is reasonably attributed to them? There is, I think, a spectrum of cases. At one end are heroic or self-sacrificing acts that are aimed at helping others but do not reflect a praiseworthy character. For example, a person who returns to a burning building, and so saves another, may act from hysteria or panic. The companion who looks after a rich widow in her declining years may do so only in the hope of inheriting her fortune. If such persons deserve to be rewarded—as, arguably, they sometimes do—the reason is *only* that their beneficiaries are indebted to them. What they deserve is precisely to be rewarded *by those beneficiaries*. Hence, if the beneficiaries have died or are otherwise unable to discharge their debts, these desert-claims are no longer in place.

Further along the spectrum, things become more complicated. In a second class of cases, the desert-basis is a heroic or self-sacrificing act that does reflect a praiseworthy character. The acts that fit this description include that of a person who resolutely masters his fear in order to rescue someone, and that of a Good Samaritan who

---

[7] A fuller discussion would take up the question of who must be ignorant of the fact that the ticket will lose in order for it to qualify as a benefit, and of why these persons' ignorance is crucial. But there is no need for us to address these matters here. For pertinent discussion, see Sher, "What Makes a Lottery Fair?"

spends hours trying to fix a disabled car without any thought of reward. Here, too, we find foster parents who take in children nobody else wants, physicians and nurses who forego higher incomes to practice medicine in the slums, and the wife who sets aside her own desires to nurse her invalid husband. In part, these desert-claims also draw normative force from whatever debts of gratitude the agents have incurred. Yet unlike the others, these desert-claims do not become inappropriate when the agents' beneficiaries have died or become unable to respond. Indeed, part of the reason the devoted wife seems so deserving is precisely that she knows her invalid husband *cannot* reciprocate. Thus, her desert, and that of others like her, appears to draw most of its normative force from a source other than debts of gratitude.

This impression is confirmed by a final class of cases. In these, our attributions of desert are based on no specific acts. There are people whose entire lives are marked by honesty and fairness, and whose generosity, tact, and sympathy can be counted on no matter what the situation. When we encounter such people, we feel that they deserve to be happy, and to fare well, for reasons independent of their actions. These judgments are directed not at what the deserving parties have done, but simply at what they are. Of course, people who are truly generous or fair must often have acted generously or fairly. But this hardly implies that those actions have placed others significantly in their debt. Often the acts through which persons manifest superior characters are small and unspectacular. Yet the desert of the morally good can hardly be grounded in the many small debts of gratitude they have accumulated.

II

Although an excellent character seems in itself to be a significant desert-basis, it has received perhaps less philosophical attention, and certainly less defense, than any other. It is true that Ross and a few others have held that there is value in "the proportionment of happiness to virtue"; but most who have considered this suggestion have rejected it. And in many discussions to which it might seem relevant, the desert of the morally good is simply ignored. I suspect that this attitude is due partly to a sense that any attempt to match happiness to virtue will be impracticable or self-defeating, and partly to sympathy with Hastings Rashdall's complaint that he

> can see no reason at all why superior moral goodness should be assigned a superior quantity of external goods, that is to say, the means of indulging desires which have no connexion with this superior goodness.[8]

Yet neither reason is decisive. In this section, I try to rebut some common objections to the view that happiness ought to be proportional to moral virtue. In the following two sections, I sketch a positive argument for that view.

Consider first the issue of practicality. There is no doubt that accurate assessments of character are hard to come by. Such assessments require detailed information not only about how a person has acted, but also about how he would act under many alternative conditions. This information is, to say the least, difficult to acquire; moreover, if the information were available, we would not welcome a formal mechanism for evaluating individuals' virtues and character flaws. Quite apart from its intrusiveness,

> [t]he apparatus for detecting such flaws (a "moral police"?) would be enormously cumbersome and impractical, and its methods so uncertain and fallible that none of us could feel safe in entrusting the determination of our material allotments to it.[9]

Thus, any systematic attempt to reward all (and only?) the virtuous seems hopelessly unworkable.

Though we must grant this point, the concession, from our perspective, means little. As we have repeatedly seen, the fact that a desert-claim is justified does not mean that any person is obligated to provide what is deserved. A fortiori, it does not mean that *society* is obligated to provide what is deserved. Hence, even if *nothing*

[8] Hastings Rashdall, *The Theory of Good and Evil*, vol. 1 (Oxford: Oxford University Press, 1907), p. 257.

[9] Joel Feinberg, *Social Philosophy* (Englewood Cliffs, N.J.: Prentice-Hall, 1973), p. 113.

could be done to match happiness to virtue, the question of whether the matching has value—of whether it is a good thing when it does occur—would remain open. But neither is rewarding the virtuous always hopeless. Although judgments of character are too delicate to entrust to bureaucrats, our daily lives and personal relationships often do support such judgments. Hence, even if society cannot recognize or reward virtue, individuals often can. And society might even promote this end indirectly: without introducing an objectionable "moral police," it might, with ingenuity, contrive less intrusive institutions whose tendency was to reward at least the outstandingly good.

A second objection—that attempts to match happiness to virtue are not just impracticable but self-defeating—may seem more telling. This objection turns on the psychological effects of rewards. If virtue were systematically rewarded, then people would try to act virtuously in order to receive rewards. But genuinely virtuous acts are not performed just for the sake of rewards. They are, instead, performed for other, purer motives. Since actions performed for the sake of rewards cannot at the same time be performed (solely) from these purer motives, rewarding people for virtue would actually encourage people *not* to be virtuous. As A. C. Ewing has put the point, "for a man who previously did good actions irrespective of reward to come to do them for the sake of the reward is decidedly a step downward."[10]

There is no formal inconsistency in the idea of a good whose realization extinguishes one of its elements. Other goods, including the quenching of thirst and the satisfying of hunger, display the same peculiarity. Still, even if formally consistent, the thought that the matching of happiness to virtue might discourage virtue is disturbing, and if the matching did have this effect, we might conclude that it is not a good. But *does* it have this effect? As we have seen, the operative forms of virtue consist not of isolated good acts, but rather of fixed character traits. Because such traits are settled dispositions, they seem far too stable to be easily dislodged by other

[10] A. C. Ewing, *The Morality of Punishment* (Kegan Paul, Trench, Trubner, and Co., 1929), p. 132.

motives. A person who is truly generous, fair-minded, and honest is not apt to become less so if he learns that he will fare well as a result of having these traits. Thus, rewarding someone who is genuinely virtuous does not seem likely to worsen his character. At most, the expectation of reward might adversely affect a person who has not yet *formed* a fixed character; a person who, if moved to do what is right for the wrong reason, might never become disposed to act for purer motives. But the facts of moral education make even this worry seem unrealistic. In many cases, behavior that a person first displays in the hope of being rewarded is eventually internalized and thus does become genuinely virtuous.[11]

There remains another version of the concern that rewarding the virtuous is self-defeating. This version locates the difficulty not in the psychological effects of the expectation of reward, but rather in the logical relationship between morality and virtue. As Rawls has put the problem:

> The essential point is that the concept of moral worth does not provide a first principle of distributive justice. This is because it cannot be introduced until after the principles of justice and of natural duty and obligation have been acknowledged. Once these principles are on hand, moral worth can be defined as having a sense of justice; and . . . the virtues can be characterized as desires or tendencies to act upon the corresponding principles. Thus, the concept of moral worth is secondary to those of right and justice, and it plays no role in the substantive definition of distributive shares.[12]

Because virtue cannot be understood without a prior understanding of the principles of morality, Rawls argues that making virtue itself the moral basis of distribution would get things exactly backwards. It would be "like having the institution of punishment in order to punish thieves."[13]

But would it? At worst, a problem might arise if what each agent ought to have were said to depend solely on his disposition to give

[11] See Sher and Bennett, "Moral Education and Indoctrination."
[12] Rawls, *A Theory of Justice*, pp. 312–13.
[13] Ibid., p. 313.

139

others what they ought to have. Because what the others ought to have would in turn depend on their disposition to give the agent what *he* ought to have, it might then be impossible to say what anyone ought to have. Yet even on this reading, no problem would arise if the disposition to give others what they ought to have were merely a readiness to give others *whatever* they ought to have. A fortiori, no problem would arise if the concept of virtue were explicable in different terms altogether. And, in large measure, it clearly is. When we ask what sorts of persons deserve to be happy, we most naturally think of those who are generous, sympathetic, kind, and honest. In all of this, there is no reference to the disposition to reward virtue. Thus, that disposition is at most one among many forms of virtue that create desert. And because it is, we can say, first, that a person deserves to be rewarded if he displays the other relevant forms of virtue; next, that he is additionally deserving of reward if he also displays the second-level virtue of tending to reward others with the first-level virtues; and, finally, that he becomes yet more deserving by ascending still higher up the scale.[14] Thus construed, the claim that the virtuous deserve to fare well embodies no incoherency. At worst, Rawls's argument might show that this claim falls short of being (one kind of) "first principle of distributive justice." However, given the range of other desert-claims already defended, this conclusion seems inevitable anyhow.

If there are better arguments against the view that there is value in the matching of happiness to virtue, I am not aware of them. In the end, the main reason for rejecting this view may be merely that there is no compelling reason to accept it. Yet this may be reason enough. Although Ross was happy enough to accept the value of this matching, we must remind ourselves that appeals to moral primitives often have been misused, and that the multiplication of such primitives is neither elegant nor explanatorily fruitful. Hence, if nothing further can be said, we must presume that there is no special value in the happiness of those with superior characters. But, in fact, there is more to be said.

[14] For a related response to Rawls, see Galston, *Justice and the Human Good*, p. 171.

To appreciate the positive case for holding that there is value in the matching of happiness to virtue, consider first what might seem a misstep by Rawls. Although his subject is clearly desert for vir- tuous character, Rawls three times in the passage quoted above (and often elsewhere) frames the issue in terms of desert for moral *worth*. Taken at face value, this formulation seems both unneces- sary and misleading—unnecessary because Rawls's own argument contains no essential reference to the worth of persons, and mis- leading because one can hold that there is special value in the hap- piness of the virtuous without holding that they are worth more than others.

Strictly speaking, these observations are correct. But at a deeper level, Rawls's introduction of the worth of persons does embody an important insight. For even if this notion is not needed to *formulate* the claim that the virtuous deserve to fare well, it surely *is* needed for that claim's justification. As we saw in Chapter 4, the view that there is value in desire-satisfaction, and far more value in the suc- cess of diligent striving, is most naturally derived from the premise that persons themselves have worth or value. From this starting point we can infer that any objects persons want or seek acquire value in their turn. But if the value of ordinary desire-satisfaction and successful effort is grounded in the worth of ordinary persons, then the further value of any subset of these outcomes seems apt to be grounded in the special worth of some persons. In particular, if the satisfactions or achievements of the virtuous have additional value, this does seem likely to follow from these persons' additional worth.

Thus, we cannot avoid asking whether a superior moral character does increase a person's worth. As posed, the question sounds strange; for the idea that all persons are equal in worth is usually taken for granted. Yet this commonplace may be only a dramatic way of saying that no person has merely instrumental worth. Its point may be simply that no differences in how useful people are can matter unless those to whom persons are useful (that is, them- selves and other people) have some value in themselves. Since this

141

value is logically prior to instrumental value, it cannot (of course) vary *with* instrumental value. But that does not mean that it cannot vary with any *other* differences among persons.

And when we consider the difference between the virtuous and the non-virtuous, we do find factors that point to real differences in worth. To see this, consider briefly the question of why persons have worth at all. At the most general level, the answer seems plainly to lie in the complexity of individuals' mental lives. It is surely the lack of similar mental complexity that explains why trees and stones lack similar worth. But which aspects of persons' mental lives confer worth upon them? Although answers vary, one interesting possibility, advanced by Robert Nozick, is that the crucial aspects include (1) the fact that a person is reflexively conscious of himself as an "I," and (2) the fact that one is "a seeker after value, someone who searches for value and guides her behavior by value considerations."[15] Although (1) and (2) both warrant attention, I shall concentrate on (2).

Does the worth of persons really stem, in part, from the fact that they are capable of regarding some things as more valuable than others, and that they tend to seek the more valuable? There are several reasons to believe that it does. First, unlike other aspects of a person's subjectivity, this one is internally connected to worth itself. When persons "seek value," what they seek is of a kind with what is alleged to arise as a result of their seeking. Thus, Nozick's suggestion satisfies the vague but intelligible requirement that a worth-conferring characteristic be *relevant* to the worth it confers. Second, by saying that part of what confers worth on persons is their own propensity to seek value, we bring together the notions of being a moral subject and being a moral object. We imply that the capacities to give and receive moral treatment are of a piece. Thus, we give expression to the compelling Kantian idea that morality is somehow rooted in reciprocity. And third, by accepting this suggestion, we explain the appeal of several familiar alternative views. As Nozick notes, the "usual suspects" for the role of worth-

[15] Robert Nozick, *Philosophical Explanations* (Cambridge, Mass.: Harvard University Press, 1981), pp. 452–59. The quotation appears on p. 457.

conferring characteristic have included "being rational, being an agent, being sentient, being conscious," and also "ability to plan over time and ability to follow principles, perhaps even free will."[16] On the current account, these are necessary conditions for full human worth; but the deeper explanation of this is that they are necessary for one or both of the truly crucial characteristics of seeking value and considering oneself an "I."[17]

Needless to say, these sketchy observations do not *prove* that seeking value is a worth-conferring characteristic. To establish that fully, we would have to say far more about a number of difficult issues.[18] Yet sketchy as the case for it is, this view seems better motivated than any of its competitors. Indeed, the more usual claims that worth is grounded in freedom or in rationality are standardly given *no* defense. As Peter Singer rightly complains, "contemporary philosophers . . . freely invoke the dignity [and worth] of mankind without needing to justify the idea at all."[19] In any event, I shall assume that the worth of persons *is* due partly to the fact that they have a concept of value and seek to realize it. Those who remain unconvinced may regard my argument as a demonstration of what would hold if this claim were true, or as a study in the etiology of the familiar belief that there is special value in the happiness of the virtuous.

For if seeking value is part of what confers worth on persons, then we *can* conclude that the happiness of the specially virtuous has special value. The first step is to note that the moral virtues that interest us are all heightened and concentrated propensities to seek forms of value. When someone is fair-minded and honest, he automatically seeks to do what is right. When someone is generous, sympathetic, considerate, or kind, he automatically seeks to bring good results. In each case, the person exemplifies, to a higher degree than others, the value-seeking propensity that is crucial to the

---

[16] Ibid., pp. 452, 459.

[17] Nozick suggests this in *Philosophical Explanations*, p. 459.

[18] For suggestive further discussion, see Nozick, *Philosophical Explanations*, pp. 517–22 and passim.

[19] Peter Singer, "All Animals Are Equal," in *Animal Rights and Human Obligations*, ed. Tom Regan and Peter Singer (Englewood Cliffs, N.J.: Prentice-Hall, 1976), p. 159.

worth of persons. And because he does, we may reasonably suppose that he acquires greater worth than do others from his possession of it. As Nozick has put the point:

> In behaving ethically, we transcend our own limits and connect to another's value as value. The life of the ethical person will have greater value or meaning; the moral push consists in the fact that his life will have greater worth.[20]

But if a virtuous person does have greater worth than others, then his desires and sustained efforts will be able to confer correspondingly more value on their objects. Thus, however good it is that an ordinary person's desires are satisfied, or that his diligent efforts succeed, it will be even better if the person who is satisfied or successful is especially virtuous. When this is the case, his happiness *will* have special value.

As just presented, my argument rests on two premises. It assumes that (1) persons derive (some of) their worth from the fact that they seek value, and that (2) the intentional objects of persons' desires and efforts derive value from the fact that they are sought by beings *with* worth. But are these premises really compatible? If something acquires value from the fact that it is sought by a being with worth, then it evidently lacked that value independent of its being sought. But if an object lacks independent value, then how can the fact that a person pursues it enhance that person's worth? When we claim that value flows both from persons to the objects they seek and from those objects to persons, don't we fall into a (human-centered) version of the Euthyphro trap? Aren't we left with no point at which value might really originate?

This objection looks worse than it is. The answer to it is that even if persons do acquire worth from their seeking of value, it does not follow that *all* they seek is value. Even if someone is concerned to promote the good, and to do what is right, he can still diligently strive to further his career, want to watch baseball games, and plan to marry someone he loves. Moreover, he surely need not have these desires and projects merely because he takes their objects to

---

[20] Nozick, *Philosophical Explanations*, p. 612.

have independent value. His value-seeking propensity may, of course, affect the *way* he pursues these goals; it may prevent him from using illegitimate means, or lead him to be especially responsive to the valuable aspects of what he seeks. Still, his having precisely these desires and projects, and not others, is not a response to any special value that he perceives (or takes himself to perceive) their objects to have. Like others, even very virtuous persons simply find themselves preferring (or passionately wanting) some things, being indifferent to others, and being averse to still others. And given this ineradicable residue of brute preference, it remains possible to say both that an agent would have less worth if he were less of a value-seeker and that the worth he thus acquires can devolve on whatever outcomes or objects he seeks for reasons unrelated to their (independent) value.

One other observation can be made. By attributing the desert of the virtuous to the fact that they seek value to a greater degree than others, and thus have greater worth, we can explain the (otherwise puzzling) intuition that only some traditional virtues give rise to desert. I have already suggested that we regard persons as deserving of happiness when they are generous, kind, fair-minded, and honest. To this list, we may add such virtues as being devoted to others and being ready to identify imaginatively with them. Yet we do *not* believe that someone ought to be happy merely because he is courageous, temperate, cheerful, or prudent. Though genuine excellences of character, these traditional virtues intuitively do not affect what people deserve. And the reason, we can now see, is that because courage, temperance, cheerfulness, and prudence are not in themselves tendencies to promote (moral or nonmoral) value, they do not themselves increase a person's worth. Thus, they also do not engender desert. Of course, this does not mean that these virtues never *affect* desert. A person with kind impulses, but not the courage to act on them, surely may be less deserving than another who has similar impulses but is not deterred from acting on them by danger or disapproval. But what does follow is that when a virtue from the second list increases a person's desert, it does so only in combination with, or as an auxiliary to, a virtue from the first list. As Kant famously observed:

Moderation in emotions and passions, self-control, and calm deliberation not only are good in many respects but even seem to constitute a part of the inner worth of the person. But however unconditionally they were esteemed by the ancients, they are far from being good without qualification. For without the principle of a good will they can become extremely bad, and the coolness of a villain makes him not only far more dangerous but also more directly abominable in our eyes than he would have seemed without it.[21]

IV

The idea that persons of outstanding character have greater worth than others is a form of perfectionism. As such, it raises some uncomfortable questions. Having admitted differences in worth, can we stop short of adding that the very talented also have greater worth than others? And what about the wicked? If the virtuous are worth more than others, then mustn't those at the other end of the spectrum be worth less? And, indeed, if the value of one's traits can affect one's worth, then mightn't some persons even have negative worth? If so, what has become of the basic respect that we owe to all persons?

These questions must be taken seriously. If our argument really implies a full-blown moral elitism, then that itself will count as a *reductio*. But are we committed to anything this extreme? We are surely *not* committed to the repulsive claim that the specially gifted are worth more than others; for like the virtues of courage and temperance, one's talents do not correlate with one's propensity to seek value. A person may be smarter, shrewder, and stronger than others, and yet be no more disposed to pursue the good. Things are less clear in the aesthetic realm. When someone has literary or aesthetic talent, or is unusually sensitive to beauty, he may indeed seek aesthetic value to a greater degree than do others. There are persons to whom elegance, grace, and style are all-important. Yet

---

[21] Immanuel Kant, *The Foundations of the Metaphysics of Morals*, trans. Lewis White Beck (Indianapolis: Bobbs-Merrill, 1959), p. 10.

the status of aesthetic value, and its relation to other forms of value, is murky at best. Thus, pending clarification, I think we need not worry that, on our account, the aesthetically gifted or sensitive will turn out to be worth more than others.

The more difficult questions concern persons with *less* than the usual propensity to seek value. If persons do derive worth from this propensity, then mustn't those in whom it is attenuated or lacking be worth less than others? Indeed, if someone is well aware of what has value, but wantonly shuns it, then mightn't he have *negative* worth? And, since the worth of persons is the basis of their rights, won't all this imply that the rights of persons also vary with moral character? Saying this is quite different from saying that wrong-doers (temporarily) forfeit some of their rights. At least on the surface, it seems inconsistent with the widely accepted idea that "[t]he moral community is not a club from which members may be dropped for delinquency. Our morality does not provide for moral outcastes or half-castes."[22] As a corollary, it also seems inconsistent with the idea that all persons should be treated equally by the law.

Yet these implications, too, can be avoided. In large measure, they reflect a failure to distinguish concepts that admit of degrees from those that establish thresholds. When we infer that those who seek value less than others are of lesser worth, and thus that their rights are less significant, we clearly assume that all three notions admit of degrees. But even if value-seeking and having worth admit of degrees, being a right-bearer may not. Since rights are limits on how others may treat us, it makes little sense to say that one person is less of a right-bearer, or has weaker or less meaningful rights, than another. And though it does make sense to say that one person has *fewer* rights than another, it seems arbitrary to single out any particular rights as those that persons lack simply because they are wicked. Thus, the more natural view is that any being capable of seeking value at all has a full complement of moral rights. Having reached the threshold, he has any and all natural rights that any other right-bearer has. And even if someone is so wicked (or so

[22] Gregory Vlastos, "Justice and Equality," in *Social Justice*, ed. Richard B. Brandt (Englewood Cliffs, N.J.: Prentice-Hall, 1962), p. 48.

mentally impaired) that he does *not* reach the threshold, we may still have good reason to extend him honorary but full membership in the moral club. It is often difficult to determine with certainty that someone lacks the crucial capacities. In addition, even very wicked (or very defective) human beings are similar enough to others to make it very difficult to treat them in radically different ways. As Jane English has put it:

> Our psychological constitution makes it the case that for our ethical theory to work, it must prohibit certain treatment of non-persons who are sufficiently person-like. If our moral rules allowed people to treat some person-like non-persons in ways we do not want people to be treated, this would undermine the system of sympathies and attitudes that makes the ethical system work.[23]

Finally, no matter how wicked someone is, it is always seemly to express, through our treatment of him, the continuing hope that his character might improve.

Given these considerations, our argument poses little threat to the universality of human rights. But it surely does imply that the happiness of the wicked is less valuable than that of others. Having argued that persons with a greater-than-usual propensity to seek value are worth more than others, we can hardly deny that those who are specially indifferent or hostile to value—the callous and vicious—are worth less. Nor, therefore, can we deny that less value is transmitted to the objects of their desires and projects. But as long as the issue is not the rights of the wicked, but only the value of their well-being and happiness, this conclusion may simply be

---

[23] Jane English, "Abortion and the Concept of a Person," *Canadian Journal of Philosophy* 5, no. 2 (October 1975), p. 241. The considerations adduced by English appear to apply with far greater force to our treatment of humans than to our treatment of animals. Thus, there may be good reason to treat defective humans, but not animals with similar capacities, as if they have rights. This, I believe, is the way to answer those who hold that because we cannot specify any capacity that all humans but no animals possess, it is inconsistent to say that all humans, but no animals, have rights. For an argument of this sort, see Tom Regan, "Do Animals Have a Right to Life?" in Regan and Singer, eds., *Animal Rights and Human Obligations*, pp. 197–204.

accepted. It is no less plausible that the happiness of the very bad is worth less than that of most others than that the happiness of the very good is worth more.

Can we go further and infer that the happiness of the wicked has *negative* value? And, if so, is there positive value in their unhappiness and suffering? If these things followed, then our argument would provide a theoretical basis for Moore and Ross's approach to deserved punishment. It would thus complement the argument of Chapter 5. Yet as tempting as these conclusions are, I believe they must be resisted. To draw them, we would have to assume that wickedness standardly involves hostility or antagonism to value. In Nozick's terms, we would have to assume that the wicked are anti-responsive to value. But in fact, much of the wickedness that evokes the intuition recorded by Moore and Ross—the intuition that "the wicked ought to suffer"—involves not so much hostility as blank indifference to value. Although evildoers are not always banal self-seekers or drab functionaries, they clearly often are. And of such persons, it seems extreme to say that their very existence has negative (rather than much-reduced positive) worth. Hence, it also seems extreme to say that their happiness and well-being have negative value, or that their unhappiness and suffering have positive value. We may perhaps attribute negative worth to the occasional monster who seeks and relishes the degradation and destruction of others. But such attributions are not reasonable in the less spectacular majority of cases with which any helpful theory of punishment must deal.[24]

---

[24] Even if we accept what our account implies about the wicked, can we also accept what it implies about the mentally impaired? If persons lack the mental capacities that are prerequisites for seeking value (and for having a self-concept), then won't the retarded lack the full measure of human worth? Given our argument, won't this mean that their happiness is worth less than that of normal persons? And isn't this badly counter-intuitive?

To reply, we must distinguish between the mildly and the profoundly retarded. There is no reason why the mildly retarded cannot attain a full measure of human worth. They can have a full sense of self, can seek value, and can display virtues and vices. Hence, our account will not devalue their happiness. It *will* devalue the happiness of the profoundly retarded. However, this need not be counterintuitive as long as their happiness retains as much value, and their suffering as much disvalue, as the happiness and suffering of advanced animals of comparable mental abilities.

NINE

DESERT AND THE BOUNDARIES
OF THE SELF

We have now completed our examination of the major classes of desert-claims. These claims were found to draw normative force from a variety of principles and values. Although this result makes sense of more of what we believe than any appeal to a single principle or value, it seems to leave the concept of desert fragmented and diffuse. Given the diversity of its normative sources, in what sense, if any, is desert a *single* concept at all? In this chapter, I shall argue that the concept does have an important unity, but that this unity exists not at the level of moral principles and values, but at the deeper level of conceptions of the person. As diverse as the relevant principles and values are, they share a common vision of what, in the end, we are.

I

This vision is foreshadowed by a related but more superficial continuity among desert-claims. As Feinberg has noted, "the facts which constitute the basis of a subject's desert must be facts about that subject"[1]—about either his actions or his traits or capacities. Broadly speaking, what persons deserve is always determined either by what they have done or by what, in some important sense, they are. This observation is largely borne out by our previous discussion. Rationales for desert-claims whose bases are personal characteristics were provided in Chapter 7, where we saw why best-qualified applicants deserve contested jobs and opportunities, and in

---

[1] Feinberg, "Justice and Personal Desert," p. 59.

Chapter 8, where we saw why persons of virtuous character deserve to fare well. Rationales for desert-claims whose bases are actions were provided in Chapter 3, where we saw why persons deserve the predictable consequences of their free acts; in Chapter 4, where we saw why persons deserve the objects of their sustained efforts over time; in Chapter 5, where we saw why persons deserve punishment commensurate with the wrongness of their acts; in Chapter 7, where we saw why persons deserve prizes for their competitive performance; and in Chapter 8, where we saw why persons deserve rewards for acts aimed at benefiting others. In addition, the principle of diachronic fairness, elaborated in Chapter 6, requires the offsetting of deviations from standards that govern both the deserving party's actions *and* other facts about him. (The complication that the latter facts may concern the impact of others' actions upon the deserving party will receive attention below.)

Why are (almost) all desert-bases either acts or traits of the deserving person? In part, the answer lies precisely in the plausibility of the principles and values that support particular desert-claims. But there is a further question about why these principles and values *are* plausible—about why persons are the sorts of beings to whom they apply. Why are a persons' acts and traits, but not the tides, the movements of the stars, or the acts and traits of others, among the proper determinants of how he ought to fare? Any answer, it seems, must specify some suitably intimate relation that holds between a person and his acts and traits, but not between him and the tides, the movements of the stars, or the acts and traits of others. It must license a distinction between factors that are external to a person and the acts and traits that are, in some appropriately strong sense, his own. Any adequate answer must also construe the person as enduring over time. If he did not endure, then he could not deserve things at later moments for acts he performed at earlier ones. Thus, desert-claims can only be sustained if a person is an entity who is both stable over time and somehow constituted by his attributes. The tenability of such claims presumes this vision of the self.

To what degree is the vision philosophically controversial? Because it construes the self both as constituted by some of its attributes and as temporally extended, it may seem to raise the traditional problems both of essence and attribute and of personal identity. But we must be careful here. Even if proponents of desert do regard a person as being constituted by some of his attributes, they need not construe those attributes as essential in the sense of belonging to him in every possible world in which he exists at all. Instead, they need only hold that the attributes are somehow internal to him in the actual world. His relation to them, though closer than that between (say) a telephone and its color, need not be as close as that between an object and its essence. For this reason, the familiar problem of identity across possible worlds seems unlikely to arise.

Nor, similarly, does much depend on the resolution of most traditional debates over personal identity. It is true that one major motive for discussing this topic is to show how later person-stages can have enough in common with earlier ones to be responsible for the actions of the earlier stages. But just because of this, no traditional theory of personal identity separates later selves from earlier ones in a way that threatens desert. Similarly, no traditional theory commits us to a damaging separation between selves and their attributes. Neither the mental substance theory nor the view that personal identity depends on some form of physical or psychological continuity implies any special relation between selves and their attributes. For this reason, the contest between these views holds little interest for us. What does interest us is Derek Parfit's provocative thesis that precisely because personhood *is* determined only by psychological continuity, it is not important enough to bear much moral weight. However, Parfit's view, and its bearing on desert, is best considered in a later section.

The conception of the self required by desert seems compatible with many different approaches to essentiality and personal identity. But that does not mean it is unproblematical. On the contrary, anyone who construes the self as both temporally extended and constituted by some of its attributes must resolve a deep tension within his conception. This tension emerges as soon as we spell out *which* attributes must constitute the self. Given the variety of desert-bases, a person's constitutive attributes must include at least his skills, talents, abilities, preferences, and values. But merely to list these attributes is to be struck by their mutability. A person's skills may flourish with attention or atrophy through lack of use. Even the deeper talents and abilities upon which they rest may be destroyed by accident or disease. Moreover, what is true of skills, talents, and abilities holds also for the preferences and values that motivate action. These are notoriously subject to the vicissitudes of experience, exposure to argument and new information, and the processes of maturation and aging. Hence, if the subject *is* partly constituted by these attributes, then the passage of time will bring the loss of (part of) what now makes him what he is. Over time, he will apparently lack the stability that a deserving subject requires. Moreover, if we try to block this implication by assimilating the self to an entity that *does* remain the same while its attributes change, then we will undermine the claim that the person's attributes are related to him in a special, "constitutive" manner. In this way, the two elements of our conception of the deserving subject pull against each other.

There are two further problems as well. First, we have seen that many desert-bases are not attributes, but rather the acts that stem from them. Hence, if every desert-base is a constituent of the self, then persons will be constituted by their acts as well as by their preferences and abilities. But is this really a coherent supposition? Doesn't the notion of an act already presuppose at least the independence of the agent, if not his metaphysical priority? Moreover, questions of coherence aside, wouldn't the constitution of the self by its acts mean a decisive breakdown in its trans-temporal stability? Yet if we deny that the self is constituted by its acts, and insist that it is constituted only by the preferences and abilities that generate acts, then won't it be mysterious that persons can deserve things not only for what they are but for what they have done? These questions suggest the need for more discussion of the crucial "constituting" relation. They also suggest that any adequate theory of the deserving self must include a component theory of the relation between the self's traits and its acts.

There is yet another troublesome aspect of the "constituting" relation. Proponents of desert clearly must regard this relation as holding at least between the self and its basic abilities and character traits. They may also have to say that the relation holds between the self and its acts. But how far beyond this must they go? Must the relation also hold between a person and his whims and incidental beliefs? Between a person and his hair color? Between a person and his genealogical history? If not, what is it about these attributes that warrants their exclusion? We obviously must deny that *some* sentences of the form "Jones is _____" record constitutive facts about Jones; but where, and on what principled basis, is the line to be drawn?

II

Ultimately, these questions must be confronted directly. But before addressing them, I want to consider briefly a very different conception of the self. According to this view, the true self is *not* a being constituted by a set of (merely contingent) attributes, but instead is precisely what is left over when we abstract away from all such attributes.

The view to be considered is not entirely new to us. As Michael J. Sandel has argued, it can be extracted without undue strain from a Rawlsian argument we considered earlier.[2] As we saw, Rawls seems to maintain that because the talents and abilities with which a person is born are unchosen, they are undeserved and "morally arbitrary." Thus, persons do not deserve the benefits that flow from the actions their talents and abilities make possible. Taken at face value, this argument was found to be unconvincing. But Rawls's remarks about "moral arbitrariness" can also be taken in a different way. They can be construed as an elliptical way of saying that a person's talents and abilities are external to his "core self." On this reading, the fact that our talents and abilities are unchosen and undeserved does not directly undercut our capacity to deserve things. Rather, it supports a vision of the self that is incompatible with desert. As Sandel has put the point:

[2] Michael J. Sandel, *Liberalism and the Limits of Justice* (Cambridge, England: Cambridge University Press, 1982).

Rawls is not committed to the view that a person can only deserve a thing he produces if he deserves everything he used in producing it, but rather to the view that no one possesses anything in the strong, constitutive sense necessary to a desert base. No one can be said to deserve anything (in the strong, pre-institutional sense), because no one can be said to possess anything (in the strong, constitutive sense). This is the philosophical force of the argument from arbitrariness.[3]

Should we accept Sandel's interpretation of Rawls? As a rendering of Rawls's (current) intentions, it is clearly inadequate. In a recent essay, Rawls has stated that his theory is meant only to organize and make clear "the shared fund of implicitly recognized basic ideas and principles" of our present political culture.[4] His aim is to elucidate "the conception [of justice] we regard—*here and now*—as fair and supported by the best reasons" (emphasis his).[5] Since Rawls believes that our current political culture construes society as an association of free and equal persons who disagree deeply about many moral and philosophical matters, he holds that no satisfactory account of our basic principles can favor one metaphysical theory over another. And so Rawls explicitly denies that his

> [d]escription of the parties [in the original position] . . . presuppose[s] some metaphysical conception of the person, for example, that the essential nature of persons is independent of and prior to their contingent attributes, including their final ends and attachments, and indeed, their character as a whole.[6]

This disavowal is questionable. Let us simply grant that the aim of political theory should be to systematize a society's shared convictions, including its metaphysical convictions, and that in our society there is no overt consensus about any metaphysical view of

[3] Ibid., pp. 92–93.
[4] John Rawls, "Justice as Fairness: Political not Metaphysical," *Philosophy and Public Affairs* 14, no. 3 (Summer 1985), p. 228.
[5] Ibid., p. 238.
[6] Ibid., p. 238.

the person. Let us grant, too, that Rawls is right to say that his theory captures certain attitudes of persons in our society toward themselves—that

> [w]hen we describe a way in which citizens regard themselves as free, we are describing how citizens actually think of themselves in a democratic society should questions of justice arise.[7]

Even granting all this, we cannot conclude that Rawls's theory is truly agnostic about the metaphysical view that persons are not constituted by their contingent attributes; for his account of "how citizens actually think of themselves" may itself imply precisely this view. Even if Rawls's device of the original position does accurately capture shared beliefs, both it and those beliefs may commit us to viewing ourselves as independent of our contingent attributes. Of course, this commitment would exist in tension with our overt lack of an official metaphysic; but such tensions (and even far more blatant inconsistencies within our belief system) are hardly unfamiliar. Moreover, and crucially, the case for deriving principles of justice from the choices people would make in ignorance of their contingent attributes surely *does* become stronger as the metaphysical connection between persons and their attributes is thought to weaken. This is why Sandel's interpretation of Rawls carries weight.

All in all, it is far from clear that Rawls is entitled to disavow the view that persons are independent of their contingent attributes. But what Rawls means is less important than what his arguments establish. We have seen that Rawls wants to assign some prominent role to the fact that our "natural assets" are unchosen and therefore "morally arbitrary." Thus, we must consider the possibility of an argument that moves from "*X* did not choose his 'natural assets' " to "*X* is not constituted by those 'natural assets' " and thence to the conclusion "*X* does not deserve anything for the acts that stem from those assets." Yet upon examination, this argument is no less problematical than the version of the anti-desert argument we rejected

[7] Ibid., pp. 242–43.

earlier. It is true that we acknowledge, as a "fixed point" of our moral scheme, the principle that persons are not responsible for what they have not chosen and could not have avoided. But while this principle may establish that persons are not *responsible for having* their basic preferences and abilities, it does not thereby show that they are not *constituted by* those preferences and abilities. For it is perfectly consistent to say that persons are not responsible for having certain characteristics, yet that precisely these characteristics make them the people they are.

We can, indeed, go further. Assertions of the form "*X* is not responsible for having *C*, but is nevertheless made what he is by *C*" are not merely consistent, but are unavoidable on any account of the person, including the one that Sandel attributes to Rawls. For suppose that we *are* essentially distinct from our empirically determined preferences and abilities, and that our crucial feature is just our ability to make choices. Suppose we are autonomous selves who best express our basic nature by choosing and pursuing our own vision of the good within the constraints of a just society. Even so, we could no more have chosen to *be* such autonomous selves than we could have chosen our more specific preferences and abilities. The supposition that we might so have chosen would only attribute to us some yet prior nature, and so would contradict the claim that our Rawlsian autonomy expresses our nature. Yet if we have *not* chosen our autonomy, then we are no more responsible for having it than we are for having our empirically determined preferences and abilities. Hence, the question of what is constitutive of the self must be settled on other grounds.

So far, I have argued only that the view that selves are not constituted by their contingent attributes draws little support from the fact that persons have not chosen the attributes with which they were born. But the problems with that view go far deeper. The nonempirical self, if it existed, would be a metaphysically extension-less point—a pure subject, distinct from all its characteristics. However, as Nozick has noted in his critique of Rawls:

> Whether any coherent conception of a person remains when the distinction [between a person and his talents, assets, abili-

157

ties, and special traits] is so pressed is an open question. Why we, thick with particular traits, should be cheered that (only) the thus purified men within us are not regarded as means is also unclear.[8]

Here Nozick questions not just the defensibility, but the very coherency, of the idea that we can understand what persons really are by abstracting from all that is merely contingent about them. This criticism is apt to strike a responsive chord. But what, exactly, does it come to? It will not do to complain that featureless selves exist nowhere in the empirical world, for this is merely a consequence of the fact that they are abstractions from selves that *do* exist. Instead, the worry must be that the abstraction has somehow gone too far, that in stripping away *all* the self's empirical characteristics, we do not leave enough of it to fill the role of the moral subject. But what is this role, and why should such a self not be able to fill it?

Although Nozick himself does not press the point, his concern may well center on the subject's capacity for agency. As we have seen, the self that Sandel and Nozick attribute to Rawls is construed as distinct from both the empirical preferences and values that standardly motivate choice and the empirical skills and abilities through which choice is implemented. Yet, on the other hand, that self must be characterized precisely by its autonomy—this much follows from Rawls's claim that the selves that are "modeled" by the original position are "free and equal persons." But if the self *is* shorn of all its actual preferences and values, then on what basis could it freely chose? If we deny the influence of anything that might serve as a reason, then aren't we left with choices that are capricious and arbitrary? And again, if the self is stripped of all its actual abilities, then how could it possibly act on its choices? If it cannot *do* anything, then mustn't any exercise of its "freedom" be hopelessly ineffectual? Indeed, if it really lacks *all* abilities, then won't it lack even the ability to *choose*? And, thus, won't even ineffectual choices lie forever beyond its reach?

With these questions, we reach an important juncture. Although much remains to be settled, it is now clear that the attributes that

---

[8] Nozick, *Anarchy, State, and Utopia*, p. 228.

are pertinent to desert are importantly bound up with our agency. No being that did not stand in some suitably intimate relation to its preferences, values, skills, talents, and abilities could choose and act in the full sense. Thus, if our agency is an inescapable feature of our makeup, then so too may be our status as deserving subjects. Further, by getting clearer about what our agency requires, we may shed light on the crucial constituting relation.

III

If we *can* identify the deserving self with the self that agency requires, we will finally capture what has proved to be an elusive link. It has been apparent from the outset that there is some important connection between desert and action. However, as we saw, the link is captured neither by the thesis that all desert-bases *are* actions nor by the thesis that all desert-claims draw normative force from the value of autonomous acts. Can it now be captured by the more complicated thesis that all desert-claims presuppose precisely the conception of the self that is forced upon us by the inescapability of our agency?

Neither the content of this thesis nor the argument for it is straightforward. For one thing, if our capacity to deserve things requires defense, then so too does our capacity to act. As obvious as our agency seems, its inescapability cannot here be taken for granted. More serious, even if our agency is inescapable, what this implies about our relation to our preferences and abilities—how and in what sense we must be *constituted by* them—remains to be spelled out. In addition, the view that the self is constituted by its preferences and abilities must be reconciled with its capacity to endure while those preferences and abilities change. And the other problems raised earlier—about desert-bases that are *not* constituting traits, about the distinction between constituting and non-constituting traits (and, we may add, about "inauthentic" preferences)—must also be resolved.

Let us begin by asking whether, and in what sense, attributions of agency really are inescapable. To appreciate the case for their inescapability, we must recall certain very familiar features of practical reasoning. In particular, we need to remind ourselves of both its pervasiveness and its point. To approach the world from a practical standpoint is precisely to ask oneself *what to do* within, upon, or to some portion of it. Deliberation, planning, and the formation and execution of intentions are all aspects of this approach. Even cognition, insofar as it involves the gathering and active processing of information, is inseparably bound up with it. But if so, then our commitment to a view of ourselves as agents must run at least as deep as our propensity to deliberate and plan. Since even hopeless situations evoke reflexive deliberative activity (and since even a passive acceptance of one's lot requires an active intention to abstain from further deliberation aimed at improving it), the propensity to deliberate and plan is clearly a fixed feature of our mental makeup. Thus, the view that we are beings who can implement our plans and intentions—that we are agents—must be a fixed feature as well.

Though sketchy, these remarks suggest a clear rationale for the view that our agency is inescapable. But how and in what sense does this imply that we are *constituted by* our preferences, abilities, or other traits? At first glance, this may seem not to follow at all; for despite our unavoidable agency, we certainly can dissociate ourselves from particular preferences or abilities. We do so whenever we refuse in principle to act upon or exercise them. Yet on closer inspection, the mere possibility of disavowal does not seem sufficient to defeat the implication that one is constituted by a preference or ability. The more pertinent question is whether, in any given case, one actually has dissociated oneself; and to that question, the answer is often "no." Moreover, even when we do disavow a preference or ability, our disavowal must itself be grounded in some higher-order preference or value, and must draw upon some further ability. Hence, we cannot possibly disavow *all* our preferences, values, or abilities. And any preference or ability that is *not* explicitly disavowed will automatically enter into any deliberation to which it pertains. Thus, despite the possibility of disavowal, the relation between persons who deliberate and their (non-disavowed) preferences and abilities remains especially and peculiarly close.

Can we be more precise? To give exact content to the claim that persons are constituted by their preferences and abilities, we must look more closely at the deliberative standpoint, and in particular at the requirements it imposes. Because deliberation aims at decisions about which act(s) to perform, the prospective agent's preferences, values, skills, and abilities are never themselves its primary subjects. To deliberate is precisely to look *through* one's preferences, abilities, and related traits to the available actions themselves. Of course, we can always step back to ask ourselves what we really do prefer or value, and what we really can accomplish; but when we do, we deliberate only at one remove. All first-level deliberation remains oriented to action; and so from its perspective, one's preferences and abilities are not within view. They are not a part of what is to be chosen, but rather are background conditions that make choice possible. Hence, a person engaged in practical reasoning is not in a position to distinguish between the acts that his preferences and values incline him to perform, the acts that his skills and abilities enable him to perform, and the acts that *he* might perform. To him, the primal fact is that any of the contemplated acts *would* be his; and so from his standpoint, preferences, abilities, and self are merged. Given this fact, we can indeed make sense of the claim that persons are constituted by their preferences, abilities, and related traits. To do so, we need only equate the constituting relation with the relation that deliberating agents must take to hold between those traits and themselves.

Should we accept this equation? To do so would be to invoke the deliberative perspective both to give content to our notion of constitution and to establish the notion's general applicability; but there is no a priori objection to this. We may wonder, though, whether any appeal to the deliberative perspective can be general enough to show that *all* persons are constituted by their preferences and abilities. It is true that if the deliberative perspective is unavoidable for anyone, then it is unavoidable for everyone. However, it is also true that each person can deliberate only about his own possible actions. Thus, at best, our argument may appear to show that each person must regard *himself* as constituted by his preferences and abilities. From this, it does not follow that anyone must

161

regard *all* persons as constituted by their preferences and abilities. Hence, we may seem not to have shown that anyone is compelled to believe that all persons are the sorts of beings to whom desert-claims can apply.

This objection obviously has some force. Because the deliberative perspective is a perspective of particular individuals, the most our appeal to it can directly show is that we each must adopt a certain view of ourselves. Even so, our awareness of the many physical, psychological, and behavioral likenesses between ourselves and others cannot help but influence us to extend this view to others. Given these likenesses, the simplest theory of the person clearly does not make any radical distinction between self and others. Hence, considerations of overall coherency must tell strongly for an extension of our view of ourselves. They must support the position that all selves are constituted by their preferences and abilities if any are.

Even by itself, this rejoinder seems strong enough to disarm the objection that our argument is not general enough. But there is also a deeper, if more speculative, reply. Besides appealing to coherence to show that we should generalize our view of ourselves despite the inaccessibility of others' deliberations, we may invoke our capacity for imaginative identification to show that the deliberations of others are *not* entirely inaccessible to us. We must concede, of course, that an ability to identify imaginatively with those deliberations is not a requirement of our own agency. However, such an ability does seem to be required if we are to be moved by the interests of others. Hence, it may also be required if we are to respond to the demands of morality. But if so, then a belief that others as well as ourselves are constituted by their preferences and abilities is apt to be a prerequisite for *moral* agency. At the very least, there is a strong analogy between the question of why our vision of ourselves should be extended to others and the question of why something's being a reason for someone else should make it a reason for us. If this analogy can be sustained, then a generalization of the vision of ourselves required by our agency will draw support from any successful defense of the moral point of view. The case for it will be, at worst, no weaker than the case for morality itself.

Is even a fully generalized version of that vision really adequate to the demands of desert? Even if all persons are constituted in the specified sense by their preferences and abilities, don't many puzzles remain? In particular, don't we still owe explanations of (1) how deserving selves can remain the same while their constituting preferences and abilities change; (2) why desert-bases are most often actions and not constituting traits such as preferences and abilities; (3) why some preferences appear "inauthentic," and so do not seem constitutive of agents; and (4) which traits *besides* preferences and abilities are constituting elements of the self? Without answers to these questions, the metaphysical basis of desert will remain problematical.

Consider first the question of how a deserving self can remain the same if its constituting preferences and abilities change. On some interpretations of "constitution," this question is simply unanswerable. But because our account extracts its notion of constitution from the standpoint of deliberation, its situation looks more promising. Because it is very often directed at future actions, deliberation itself may impose requirements on the way we view the future selves who will perform those actions. Hence, these requirements themselves may provide reasons to believe that persons can persist longer than their constituting preferences and abilities.

What, then, does deliberation require us to think about our future selves? As we just noted, persons often deliberate about acts that they cannot immediately perform. When someone decides to perform such an act, the immediate outcome of his decision is not the act itself, but rather an intention to perform it. To entertain such an intention is not necessarily to expect to survive until one implements it. A person can certainly intend to do something that he believes he is unlikely to live long enough to do. All the same, to intend to do something is at least to believe that any person who *does* perform the intended act will be a continuation of one's current self. No act performed by any other person would count as a discharging of one's intention. Because of this, there is indeed a sense in which the intending agent must identify with the person who will carry out his intention. And, by the same token, anyone who merely deliberates about what to do in the future, but has not yet decided on a course of action, must also regard *him*self as continuous with any person who will perform whichever act he finally does choose. He must identify not only with his current preferences and abilities, but also, in the specified sense, with the later person who will perform the chosen act.

Does the latter sort of identification commit the deliberating agent to believing that the relevant future self will retain all his current preferences and abilities? Upon examination, we see that it clearly does not. Even intending an action is quite compatible with acknowledging that many of one's current skills and abilities may have deteriorated by the time one performs it. It is also compatible with acknowledging that by that time, many of one's current preferences and values may have changed. As we will see later, intending an act is *not* compatible with acknowledging that before one acts, one will relinquish the very preferences or values that now motivate one's intention. However, because we deliberate *before* we form any definite intentions, the person who merely deliberates is not committed even to this. He is not committed even to believing that he will retain the preferences or values that would now motivate the future acts he is contemplating.

With these points in mind, we can answer the objection that if persons are constituted by their preferences and abilities, they cannot have the duration of deserving subjects because they cannot remain the same while their constituting preferences and abilities change. The notion of constitution that is required by the deliberative perspective implies not that persons must fail to outlast their constituting traits, but rather just the opposite. Although our prospective agency does require that we identify with the preferences and abilities that make our actions possible, it also forces us to project ourselves further into the future than any of our present preferences and values need extend. Consequently, the notion of constitution that it defines has precisely the right degree of strength for us. It is strong enough to explain how persons can deserve things because of their constituting traits, yet not so strong as to imply that the very same deserving subjects cannot exist after their currently constituting traits have changed.

V

Earlier in this chapter, I suggested that the vision of the self that is associated with desert seems compatible with most traditional views of trans-temporal personal identity. But I also suggested that we would eventually have to come to grips with Derek Parfit's claim that if such identity depends entirely on the psychological relations between person-stages, it is less morally important than we have thought. Keeping in mind what has been said, I now want briefly to examine Parfit's position. Although this part of the discussion is, strictly speaking, a digression, it is justified both by the intrinsic importance of Parfit's views and by the reflected light that those views shed on our own position.

Parfit's views are most fully developed in his recent book *Reasons and Persons*.[9] There Parfit argues brilliantly for what he calls the "reductionist" approach to personal identity. On this approach, personal identity is said to be determined entirely by the relations that hold between the states of persons which exist at different times. In particular, on Parfit's view, the crucial relation, designated *R*, is said to combine direct memory-, desire-, and intention-connectedness with indirect memory-, desire-, and intention-continuity. According to Parfit, someone is identical with a given future person if and only if (1) he stands in *R* to that future person, and (2) he does not stand in *R* to any *other* future person. And because this is *all* that personal identity involves, Parfit argues that several important conclusions follow. Because personal identity requires that *R* hold uniquely, while being *R*-related to two future selves would not be nearly as bad as being *R*-related to none, Parfit concludes that personal survival matters less than most of us think. Because we have fewer desires and intentions directed at distant than at near

---

[9] Derek Parfit, *Reasons and Persons* (Oxford: Clarendon Press, 1984), pt. 3.

165

future times, and because memory fades over time, Parfit concludes that personal identity is not all-or-nothing, but is a matter of degree. And because personal identity involves *only* a relation among psychological states and not any "further fact," Parfit concludes that personal identity is a less *deep* phenomenon than many have thought.

To what degree does any of this threaten desert? At least in Parfit's view, the answer is unclear. When he considers desert of punishment, he draws only the hedged conclusion that

> [n]on-reductionists believe that personal identity involves a deep further fact, distinct from physical and psychological continuity. It is a defensible claim that only this fact carries with it desert for past crimes, and that, if there is no such fact, there is no desert. . . . But a different view is also defensible. We can defensibly claim that psychological continuity carries with it desert for past crimes.[10]

And when he considers a principle of diachronic fairness analogous to DF3 (which was advanced in Chapter 7 as the underlying rationale for desert of punishment and some other sorts of desert-claims), Parfit similarly concludes that

> [w]e can defensibly claim that a benefit at one time cannot provide compensation for a burden at another time, even when both come within the same life. . . . But, as with earlier arguments appealing to the further fact, though this new conclusion is defensible, it can also be defensibly denied.[11]

Nevertheless, despite Parfit's own caution, the general tendency of his position is clearly to fragment the deserving self, and so to devalue desert. For this reason, it will be helpful to show how the deliberative perspective provides a counterweight to his arguments.

The way it does so is *not* by undermining Parfit's arguments for a reductionist view of personal identity. There is nothing in delib-

---

[10] Ibid., p. 325.
[11] Ibid., p. 343.

eration that implies that such identity must be determined by some "further fact" distinct from the relations among psychological states. Rather, the deliberative perspective commits us to a kind of identification with our future selves that is based on no facts at all. To deliberate about our future acts is not to rely on any factual evidence that it will be we rather than others who will perform those acts. It is, instead, simply to presuppose something of this sort. If we did not accept this presupposition, then we could not begin to try to decide what (*we* are) to do. A fortiori, we could not consider implementing extended action plans whose unity resides precisely in the fact that they will advance purposes that we will continue to entertain while the action plans play themselves out. These forms of identification with future selves, though based on no facts, are nevertheless clearly rational. They are as rational (and are so for some of the same reasons) as counter-factual judgments in which identity across possible worlds is stipulated rather than grounded in facts of resemblance or common origin. In both cases, the identification is rational because it is a prerequisite for a specially important way of speaking or thinking. And because of this, our relations to our future selves seem both more intimate and more morally significant than a cursory examination of the R-relation would suggest.

To what degree are these observations compatible with Parfit's position? The situation here is somewhat complicated. In one respect, the claim that deliberation presupposes identification with future selves is a natural complement to Parfit's account. Because such identification is not grounded in any knowledge of the R-relation, it can easily (though wrongly) be thought to be grounded in knowledge of some other fact. Thus, our proposal may well explain the appeal of the "further fact" view that Parfit rejects. Yet even if it does, its main thrust runs partially counter to Parfit's position. Because the proposal strongly suggests that the connections between stages of persons' lives *are* morally important, its tendency is to block Parfit's (implicit) devaluation of desert. Thus we cannot simply assume that the proposal is correct. We must, instead, bring it into confrontation with Parfit's arguments.

167

Although Parfit deploys many more arguments than we can consider, the most important for us concern the division of consciousness. As Parfit notes, severing the brain's hemispheres actually does seem to divide consciousness into two separate "streams." When this occurs, neither "stream" contains any direct awareness of the other's contents. We can go on to imagine more fanciful cases in which brains are entirely split apart and are then transplanted into two different bodies. Since even half a brain can perpetuate consciousness, each post-division person could then be R-related to the original. And if such division were expected, but had not yet occurred, then the person who was to undergo it might deliberate about what each post-division self would do. He might, for example, consider the possibility "that one resulting person roams the world, and that the other stays at home."[12] On our account, this deliberation requires that he identify with both post-division selves. However, as we have noted, Parfit believes, and argues persuasively, that personal identity is best understood as a one-to-one relation. If it is, then the agent *cannot* be identical to both post-division selves. Since he nevertheless can deliberate about the actions of both, our proposal that all deliberation presupposes identification with the person who will act may seem clearly false.

But this is not clear at all. Let us simply grant that someone might coherently deliberate about the doings of two post-division selves, but that if he thinks clearly, he will realize that he cannot *be* both. Even so, his deliberation may still require identification with both future selves, for *identifying with* them is not the same as believing he is *identical to* them. We saw above that persons who deliberate must identify with their current preferences and abilities, yet need not (and indeed cannot) consider themselves simply to be those traits. In a partially similar fashion, someone who deliberates may identify with one or more future persons—may believe that he is choosing for that person or those persons, and so that any resulting actions will be partly his own—without believing that he simply *is* that person or those persons. One may imaginatively collapse the temporal distance between himself and a future agent, and thus

12 Ibid., p. 261.

try to reach a decision that in a sense belongs to both, without also collapsing the logical distance between them. Of course, since any actual division of consciousness is extremely unlikely, almost all actual identification with a future self probably *is* accompanied by the belief that one is identical to that self. Still, at least in theory, the two attitudes remain clearly distinct.

Moreover, by taking seriously the difference between these two attitudes, we can begin to explain *why* the identification that deliberation presupposes is morally significant. We just saw that when a deliberating agent identifies with a future self, he presumes himself to be choosing *for* that future self. He knows that he (or a successor self) may change his mind; but he also knows that a combination of inertia and trust in previous decisions will probably prevent this. Hence, he knows that his choice is indeed likely to contribute importantly to the future self's actions. But if so, then any evaluation of the future self's actions must at the same time be an evaluation of the deliberator and his present choices. Conversely, any evaluation of the deliberator and his present choices is simultaneously an evaluation of the later actions to which his present choices will probably contribute. And given this evaluative reciprocity, the moral importance of persons, considered as extended stretches of *R*-related consciousness, is both confirmed and explained. For if the moral status of earlier choices is intertwined with that of later actions, then the morally significant unit must indeed be the whole succession of earlier and later selves.

Even so, a problem may seem to remain. At the beginning of the chapter, I suggested that desert-claims, though grounded in diverse moral principles, are nevertheless unified by the fact that they all presuppose a single conception of the self. On that conception, persons are both constituted by their preferences and abilities and extended over time. To flesh out the conception, and also to show why we were forced to accept it, I appealed to the demands of deliberation and practical reason. But under pressure from Parfit's arguments, I have conceded that deliberating agents need *not* be identical to the future selves at whom their deliberations are directed. In light of this, haven't I abandoned my original thesis? For doesn't the concession in effect imply that deliberation does *not* force us to accept any conception of the temporally extended self?

In one sense, this is true. Assuming personal identity is one-to-one, if someone were going to divide, the future selves with whom deliberation forced him to identify would not be later stages of him. There would be no extended persons spanning such division. Yet even so, the fundamental point remains. Even if branching selves are *not* temporally extended persons, they are still *like* such persons in the crucial respect. When they deliberate before branching, their earlier elements must still identify with both later elements in morally significant ways. Hence, there is no reason to deny that they themselves could be bearers of desert. And, in fact, our intuitions strongly suggest that they could. If a person worked very hard for twenty years and then divided, each successor self would intuitively deserve success as much as a single successor. If someone did something foolish and predictably harmed both successors, both would intuitively deserve the consequences as much as one. If someone acted wrongly and then divided, both successors would intuitively deserve punishment. It may seem less clear that division would preserve desert of compensation; if it did, then a wrongdoer who harmed one might owe compensation to two. Yet on inspection, even this seems acceptable; for compensating two seems no worse than paying the same amount for expensive rehabilitation of one.

A further point may be made. We are considering the objection that one's deliberations need not be aimed at one's own future acts. But we must remember that the possibility of branching is only theoretical. In actuality, we cannot form intentions about what to do after our brains have been separated. Hence, the later selves with whom we identify always *are* later stages of us. Since this is only a contingent fact, it does not save the conclusion that there must exist temporally extended persons of the sort required by desert. But do we really need to prove anything this strong? What we really want to know is only how to think about the temporally extended persons whom we already know a posteriori to exist. And nothing yet said invalidates the conclusion that we must regard *these* persons as just the sorts of beings that desert requires.

VI

Yet neither is that conclusion decisively established. Before accepting it, we must complete some unfinished business. I have argued that the inescapability of the deliberative perspective compels us to view ourselves as both constituted by our preferences and abilities and extended over time, and that coherence requires us to extend this view to others. By taking this line, we have seen why persons remain the same when their constituting traits change, and why desert is unaffected by Parfit's reductionist view of personal identity. But other questions remain. I suggested earlier that we must also show why desert-bases are more often actions than traits, why some preferences seem "inauthentic" and thus not constitutive of agents, and how, in principle, to distinguish constituting from non-constituting traits.

Why, if persons are constituted by their preferences and abilities but not by their actions, do they more often deserve things for their actions? Indeed, if actions are too short-lived to be constituents of selves, then why assign them *any* independent standing as desert-bases? To answer these questions, we must somehow show that actions, though shorter-lived than constituting traits, are no less intimately related to persons. But this is easy to do if our view of persons as constituted by their preferences and abilities is itself dictated by the deliberative perspective. The aim of deliberation is precisely to decide upon courses of action. Hence, if its demands shape our conception of the person, then agency already lies at the heart of that conception. Though shorter-lived than constituting traits, one's actions must in another sense be even deeper expressions of one's nature. Actions must belong more deeply to the person because traits would not even *be* constituents of him if it were not for their contributions to his actions. And so it is hardly surprising that persons so often deserve things for what they do rather than for what they are. Given the logical priority of action, anything else would be anomalous.

Consider, next, the fact that some preferences do not seem to be constituting elements of an agent. In general, the preferences that evoke this reaction are just the ones that pose problems for the com-

171

patibilist position on free will. They include the preferences of addicts and compulsives, the preferences caused by brain lesions and other organic disorders, and at least some preferences resulting from indoctrination or "brainwashing." Such preferences provide counterexamples to the compatibilist claim that a person acts freely when he acts as he wants or prefers; for although the compulsive is doing what he prefers to do, he surely is not acting freely. As many have noted, the most promising compatibilist response to such cases is to amend the definition of freedom to require that the preferences that motivate free acts cohere with the agent's broader motivational structure. In addition to acting on his preferences, the free agent must in some sense endorse them. Since persons do not endorse their compulsions, this explains why compulsives are unfree.[13] Thus amended, compatibilism invites reformulation as the view that free acts are motivated by constitutive rather than external preferences. Yet appealing as this view is, it invites a further question: why *should* a preference that lacks congruence with the agent's other desires and character traits be considered external to him?

Once again, our general account of why (most) preferences are internal to an agent provides a natural answer. That account grounds the claim that an agent is constituted by his preferences in the demands of the deliberative perspective. If this is correct, then we need not say that an agent is constituted by all of his preferences. Instead, we may say only that an agent is constituted by whichever preferences can contribute to his deliberations. But, not coincidentally, the preferences that are at odds with the other parts of an agent's motivational structure are badly suited to make such contributions. A preference that someone prefers not to have will resist integration with his other preferences and values. It will therefore be difficult to fit into a larger, more comprehensive action

[13] See, for example, Gerald Dworkin, "Acting Freely," *Nous* 4, no. 4 (November 1970), pp. 367–83; Harry Frankfurt, "Freedom of the Will and the Concept of the Person," *The Journal of Philosophy* 68, no. 1 (January 14, 1971), pp. 5–20; and Gary Watson, "Free Agency," *The Journal of Philosophy* 72, no. 8 (April 24, 1975), pp. 205–20. For enlightening distinctions and criticism, see David Shatz, "Free Will and the Structure of Motivation," *Midwest Studies in Philosophy* 10 (1986), pp. 451–82.

plan. And a preference that is insensitive to countervailing reasons
will not allow compromise in the name of rational decision-making.
It will simply dominate or be dominated. In these and other ways,
preferences that conflict with one's wider motivational structure are
not accessible to practical reasoning. Hence, it is not surprising that
they seem external to agents.

Consider, finally, the broader distinction between constituting
and non-constituting traits. How, in principle, should we draw the
boundaries of the self? Given what has been said, the answer here
should be obvious. Just as the deliberative standpoint determines
which *preferences* are internal to agents, so too does it determine
which *other* facts are internal to them. Once again, the criterion is
whether we are forced to consider a given trait a part of ourselves
when we are trying to decide what to do. We have already seen why
skills and abilities, as well as most preferences and values, fall
squarely within the boundaries of the self. But in addition, we can
see why other facts, such as facts about what others think about us,
or about our own genealogical histories, require different treatment. These facts, though in some sense about us, are not taken for
granted when we contemplate alternative courses of action. When
they enter our deliberations, they do so only in the manner of
purely external facts. Hence, we need not regard them as constituting elements of us. And so they do not strike us as proper bases of
desert.

Are there counterexamples to this way of drawing the distinction? Two sorts of cases come to mind. There are, first, our physical
attributes—our size, musculature, facial structure, and the like.
Though not presupposed by deliberation, these attributes intuitively seem at least more nearly constitutive of us than do many
other facts. Moreover, as in beauty contests, they sometimes do
give rise to desert. Yet bodily attributes, though prima facie troublesome, pose little real difficulty. Their intermediate status is explained partly by their causal relations to the abilities that deliberation does presuppose, and partly by the simpler fact that we
generally act by moving our bodies. Given such facts, our agency
and our embodiment are just too intimately connected to be cleanly

173

separable. And so the impression that our physical attributes are not entirely external is hardly surprising.

The other class of counter-examples may seem more significant. According to DF3, persons sometimes deserve things because their past burdens or benefits have failed to satisfy relevant distributional standards. Hence, the bases of desert must include past deviations from such standards. But deviations from distributional standards are often due either to the acts of others or to no acts at all. For example, when a person deserves to be compensated, the reason is standardly that another has wrongly imposed some burden upon him. When this is so, the basis of the wronged person's desert is not, by our criterion, a constituting element of him. Hence, we seem unable to retain both our criterion of constitution and the claim that all desert-bases are constituting traits of deserving parties.

I think, in fact, that this is correct, that we cannot keep both the criterion and the claim that all desert-bases are constituting traits. But then, why *should* we make the latter claim? Our argument has been that all desert-claims are unified by a distinctive vision of the self—a vision of persons as both constituted by (most of) their current preferences and abilities and extended over time. But this does not imply that all desert-claims must draw equally on both elements of that vision. Some desert-claims, such as those that attribute desert for past actions, plainly do draw on both elements. But others, just as unproblematical, do not. When we say that persons deserve things because of their current abilities, character traits, or actions, we clearly draw only on the assumption that persons are constituted by their present traits. And, just so, when we say that persons deserve things because they have had less or more than their proper shares in the past, we draw only on the assumption that the morally significant entities endure over time. In both cases, there is more to our full conception of the deserving self than the relevant desert-claim presupposes. But in neither case is the full conception thereby undermined.

TEN

WHY THE PAST MATTERS

In the last chapter, I discussed the vision of the person that desert presupposes. In this chapter, I shall take up a closely related presupposition about morality and time. When we say that someone deserves something, we often imply that what he has done or suffered at an earlier moment determines what should befall him, or the way he should be treated, now or in the future. It was precisely to square our vision of the self with this implication that we had to show that a person must be regarded as temporally extended as well as constituted by (some of) his attributes. But even if the view that the past matters is consistent with an unavoidable vision of the self, we have yet to see whether it is independently defensible. Here, appealing again to the demands of the deliberative perspective, I shall argue that it is.

I

It is fitting that the deliberative perspective should provide an answer to the question of why the past matters, for that question only arises because we are temporally situated in a way that makes deliberation possible. If we were not temporally situated, but viewed the world *sub specie aeternitatis*, we could still ask why an event's normative status should be affected by its relations to earlier occurrences—why, for instance, a person should deserve punishment at t_2 for an act performed at t_1, or why one's diligent efforts at t_1 . . . t_n should confer value on one's succeeding at t_{n+1}. However, lacking the notions of past, present, and future, we would not be able to raise the more difficult question of how what is behind us can affect the normative status of what is ahead. We could not ask how (po-

175

tential) future occurrences of no intrinsic importance can acquire value from, or be made obligatory by, their relations to events that have already faded from the scene.

But, of course, we *are* temporally situated. We do occupy a particular temporal location, prior to some events and subsequent to others. And so the moral significance of the past *is* problematical. In part, our sense of difficulty may reflect a belief that the past no longer exists. If past events are nonexistent, then it may seem that any value-conferring features they once had must be nonexistent as well. But both this inference and its premise are controversial, so it is worth stressing that the problem is independent of them. Even if the past does (in some sense) exist, we must explain how it can extend its normative reach into the future. That it cannot do so is, of course, a central assumption of consequentialists, who share the belief that what has value lies entirely in the future or (specious) present.[1] Thus, in asking why the past matters, we confront the consequentialist challenge at its deepest level.

Before taking up the challenge, I want to make two terminological stipulations. First, it will be useful to have a name for the view that an act or occurrence is called for because it would stand in a certain relation to some antecedent act(s) or event(s). In one respect, this is the polar opposite of the view that an act is made right by its causal relation to good consequences. But in another respect, the two views are alike: they both construe (at least) rightness in relational terms; and in this, they both differ from (one important version of) deontology, which holds that an act is made right simply by its intrinsic characteristics. To emphasize both its structural af-

---

[1] This is overstated in two ways. First, some philosophers who hold that we should maximize desire-satisfaction are willing to allow that certain desires may have objects that can be realized only when the desires (or, indeed, the persons having them) no longer exist. This view, though recognizably consequentialist, implies that the valued relation of satisfaction may hold between a current event and a desire that is now past. Second, although G. E. Moore is generally considered a consequentialist, we have seen that he held that certain "organic unities," such as evil followed by pain, have values that are greater than the values of their parts considered individually. Given this view, Moore in effect held that we should punish a wrongdoer because of the trans-temporal relation that would hold between the painful effect of the punishment and his earlier act of wrongdoing. For discussion, see Moore, *Principia Ethica*, pp. 311–16 and, more generally, pp. 27–36 and 183–225.

finity to and its divergence from consequentialism, I shall call the view under discussion *antecedentialism*.[2]

The second terminological stipulation concerns the scope of antecedentialism. Because consequentialism and deontology are both views about what makes acts right, we might view antecedentialism too as a thesis about rightness. But this would be unduly restrictive. Many antecedential claims are less about an act's rightness than about an outcome's value. When we say that a hard worker deserves to succeed, or that a risk taker deserves the predictable consequences of his folly, we do not imply that anyone acts wrongly by not providing what is deserved. In previous chapters, I expressed what is common to duties and values by using the neutral expression "normative force." Let me now add that any feature of an act or event that gives rise to a claim's normative force is a *reason*. Antecedentialism, then, will be the thesis that any feature of an act or event that is a reason for its occurrence beforehand may remain a reason afterward.[3]

This thesis should not be misunderstood. It does not assert merely that features of acts or events that are reasons in prospect remain reasons *for those acts or events* once they are past. Instead, it asserts that features of acts or events that are reasons in prospect may be reasons for *other* acts or events once the originals are past. Because these other acts and events have not yet occurred, antecedentialism is not vulnerable to the objection that there cannot be reasons for what is already fixed or unalterable. Of course, in avoiding this objection, antecedentialism assumes that the features of

[2] For further discussion of the issues just raised, see George Sher, "Antecedentialism," *Ethics* 94, no. 1 (October 1983), pp. 6–17.

[3] Because an agent may consider performing a future act and yet not perform it, the claim that features of future acts are reasons raises obvious questions about the ontological status of possible them. I shall not discuss these questions except to remark that despite them, the claim that features of acts (or facts about acts) are reasons for acting is an extremely natural one. For other formulations that seem to embody this claim, see Nagel, *The Possibility of Altruism*, p. 47, and Kurt Baier, "Moral Reasons," *Midwest Studies in Philosophy* 3 (1978), p. 67. For an account that attempts to establish a theoretical link between rational deliberation and a possible-worlds ontology, and so may explain the appeal of such formulations, see Robert Stalnaker, "Propositions," in *Issues in the Philosophy of Language*, ed. Alfred F. MacKay and Daniel Merrill (New Haven: Yale University Press, 1976), pp. 79–91.

one occurrence may be reasons for another; but that assumption is widely accepted in other contexts. It is uncontroversial that if X's doing A in the future is desirable, this can be a reason not only for X to do A, but also for Y to permit X to do A, and for Z to advance X's performance of A. And if an intrinsically valueless event would bring about another that does have value, then the features that make the second event valuable provide a derivative reason for the first to occur.

Thus, antecedentialism cannot be rejected on the grounds that the features of one occurrence are never reasons for another. But it might still be objected that this phenomenon is only intelligible when both occurrences lie in the future. As we just saw, when a feature of one future act is a reason for another, the explanation is generally that the performance of the second act will promote the performance of the first. Similarly, when a feature of a future event is a reason for another's occurrence, the explanation is generally that the second event will cause the first. But when a given act or event is past, no other act or event can promote, forestall, or otherwise affect it. Thus, we may seem unable to flesh out the claim that a feature of a past act or event can be a reason for a future one.

This worry is legitimate, but it is far from conclusive against antecedentialism. The short answer is that its central assumption—that a future act or event cannot affect one that is past—is badly overstated. It is true that future acts or events cannot *causally* influence the past, but causality is not the only sort of influence that might be relevant. A future act or event might also affect one that is past by entering into a new trans-temporal relation to it. In so doing, the future act or event would change the past occurrence by altering its significant relational properties. Moreover, according to antecedentialists, this is just what does happen when we reward the deserving or punish the guilty. By doing these things, we change unrewarded past efforts or acts of virtue into rewarded ones and unpunished crimes into punished ones. Thus, by saying that we can no longer affect past occurrences, the consequentialist simply begs the question.

Still, it is not yet established that such alterations in trans-temporal relations—such mere "Cambridge changes"—really are morally significant. To show this, we need an argument that reasons retain their force in retrospect. As I have said, I shall seek this view's rationale in the demands of deliberation and practical reasoning. More specifically, I shall argue that if we denied that reasons retain their force in retrospect, we could not coherently form certain very familiar sorts of intentions. Since an ability to form these intentions is central to deliberation itself, this would mean that we could not coherently deliberate. But we have seen that deliberation is unavoidable, so the view that reasons are retrospectively efficacious must be unavoidable too.

Quite obviously, the viability of this argument depends on its details. But before turning to these, I want briefly to anticipate an objection. Because deliberation always aims at action, appealing to its demands may at best seem capable of showing that reasons *for acting* are retrospectively efficacious. But antecedentialism is not just a thesis about reasons for acting. It also attributes retrospective efficacy to reasons *for events to occur*. And indeed, since most desert-claims are grounded in values rather than in obligations, it is this type of reason that seems most pertinent to desert. Thus, isn't our argument doomed from the start?

The full answer to this objection will emerge as we proceed. But even now, it should be clear that deliberation is less exclusively action-oriented than the objection suggests. It is true that deliberation always culminates in action or in intention to act, but the *goal* of action is often to produce some non-actional result. And even where an action has no further goal, its effects are always relevant to the decision about whether to perform it. Because deliberators must look beyond potential actions to their effects, the value or disvalue of those effects—the reasons for and against their occurrence—are also relevant to their deliberations. And because of this, it would not be surprising if any demands that deliberation imposed upon reasons for acting applied also to reasons for events to occur. At the very least, this cannot be ruled out a priori.

II

Paradoxically, the aspect of deliberation that is most pertinent to the retrospective efficacy of reasons is precisely its orientation toward the non-immediate future. When we deliberate, we weigh alternatives that we find individually attractive but jointly incompatible. In the simplest cases, we resolve our deliberations by immediately performing one or another of the possible acts. But because some acts can be performed only at future times, we cannot always resolve our deliberations in this way. Instead, we must sometimes enter a state that does not issue in action immediately, but which *will* lead to it at the appropriate later time. This is, of course, the state of intending to act. Because an intention fixes one's readiness to perform the chosen act, it is a kind of bridge between one's present and future self. In forming it, the agent necessarily envisions his current readiness to act as carrying forward until the appropriate future moment.

An agent who forms an intention to perform a given act need not be certain that the intention will survive until it discharges in action. We can form intentions while acknowledging that we are likely to form new preferences, or that our will is likely to fail before we act. Yet even in cases of these sorts, there are limits to the concessions an intending agent can make. At least where his future preference for an alternative act is clearly envisioned, the agent cannot genuinely intend to pursue his chosen course of action unless he is resolved to resist and struggle against that preference. If he is not resolved to resist the disruptive influence, but rather passively accepts it in advance, then he does not wholeheartedly intend to carry his project through. At best, he intends to carry it through until the moment at which he expects to give in.[4]

Our account of deliberation is complicated by the fact that some acts cannot be performed immediately. But a further complication

[4] The claim that someone who intends to do X must be resolved to resist any anticipated preference not to do X seems related to certain familiar theses about decisions and predictions. One such thesis is advanced by Stuart Hampshire and H.L.A. Hart in "Decision, Intention, and Certainty," *Mind* 67, no. 265 (January 1958), pp. 1–12. In that paper, Hampshire and Hart argue that there is "a necessary connection between certainty [in the knowledge of one's present and future voluntary acts] and intending to do something" (p. 1). This is puzzling because they also admit that a person may have evidence that he will *not* do what he intends. However, the puzzlement vanishes if their real point is not that the agent knows with certainty that he *will do* what he intends, but rather only that he knows he is resolved to resist any contrary impulse or preference. On this reading, Hampshire and Hart's claim implies my own.

is also relevant. When we deliberate, we often must choose between acts that will have to be performed at *different* future times. The incompatible but valued alternatives may include one act, A_1, which can only be performed at t_1, and another act, A_2, which cannot be performed until t_2. When any such choice is in question, we may decide to sacrifice either the earlier act for the later one or the later for the earlier. We decide to sacrifice the earlier for the later when we resolve to get our work out of the way so that we can watch an appealing television program, or to postpone an important announcement to achieve maximum dramatic effect. We decide to sacrifice the later for the earlier when we resolve to watch an appealing early program and do our work afterward, or to help a friend with a task at the cost of neglecting a later obligation or foregoing a later pleasure. When we decide to sacrifice the earlier for the later, we may do so either because foregoing the earlier is a means of achieving the later or, more simply, because the alternative acts are physically or logically incompatible. However, when we decide to sacrifice the later for the earlier, it can only be because the alternative acts are incompatible, for a later act cannot be a means to an earlier one.[5]

Obviously, much more could be said about the structure of the choices that confront us when we deliberate. But rather than pursue this, I want to apply what has already been said to our problem about the retrospective force of reasons. To focus discussion, let us consider one particular instance in which someone is deliberating about his future conduct. Suppose that at t_0, an agent M acknowledges an obligation to help a friend paint his living room at t_1. But suppose that M also believes at t_0 that he should confer with a student at t_2, and that painting at t_1 will prevent this by causing M to

---

[5] Although deliberation often clearly requires the weighing of competing act-sequences, there has been some debate about the sorts of act-sequences we should end by choosing. Holly Goldman, in "Date Rightness and Moral Imperfection," *The Philosophical Review* 85, no. 4 (October 1976), pp. 449–87, argues that one should undertake the best act-sequence he is apt to succeed in carrying out. An opposing view, that one should undertake the best *available* act-sequence, is defended by Patricia S. Greenspan in "Oughts and Determinism: A Reply to Goldman," *The Philosophical Review* 87, no. 1 (January 1978), pp. 77–83. Nothing in my argument rests on the outcome of this debate.

miss the only bus to campus. If M paints at t_1, then the best thing he can do at t_2 is to go home and read. Assume, finally, that M believes that his reason for helping his friend at t_1 is substantially stronger than his reason for meeting with his student at t_2, that neither act can be performed at any other time, and that M has no independent reason to ride the bus and only a very weak reason to read. Under these conditions, M will plainly have grounds for choosing the sequence [paint, read] over the sequence [ride, confer]. In making this decision, M will be deciding to sacrifice the later for the earlier.[6]

We may disagree, of course, with M's assessment of the relative strength of his obligations. But if we set this aside, we will regard M's decision to miss the conference to help with the painting as completely straightforward. But now let us attribute a new belief to M. Suppose that M denies what the antecedentialist affirms, and that he accepts the non-antecedentialist principle

(NA) A feature of an act or event is never a reason for anything once the act or event is past.

This new belief of M's complicates things. On the new supposition, M may still believe that his strong obligation to paint at t_1 is now, at t_0, a good reason to forego the conference at t_2. However, he must also believe that his strong obligation to paint at t_1 will no longer be a good reason to miss the conference when it actually comes time to make the sacrifice. At t_2, when the painting is finished, its features will no longer be a reason for anything, and so a fortiori will no longer be a reason for him to miss the conference. At that time, M will be left to do something that was settled upon in response to a consideration that no longer *warrants* any response. And because

---

[6] Although M's strong reasons for painting and conferring are moral while his weak reasons for riding and reading are not, this configuration is not significant. My argument would also apply if all the relevant reasons were moral, or if they were all nonmoral. Also, although I assume that moral and nonmoral reasons can be combined and assessed on a single scale, this assumption is made only for convenience. A somewhat different version of the argument could be constructed if the assumption were rejected.

M knows this at t_0, his decision to sacrifice the later act for the earlier one seems somehow irrational, somehow self-defeating. But what, exactly, does this mean, and how is it to be defended?

III

To see why M's decision is irrational, we must understand the full implications of his acceptance of (NA). I shall discuss these implications in the next two sections. In this section, I will argue that (1) because M accepts (NA), he is warranted in expecting his preferences to shift at t_1. More particularly, M is warranted in expecting that until t_1 he will prefer reading at t_2 to conferring at t_2, while after t_1 he will prefer conferring at t_2 to reading at t_2. In the following section, I will argue that (2) because M is thus warranted in expecting his preferences to shift, he cannot rationally intend to read rather than confer. Taken together, (1) and (2) should explain why M's decision is undermined by his acceptance of (NA).

Consider first (1), the claim that M's acceptance of (NA) warrants his expectation that his preferences will shift at t_1. Because (NA) is a thesis about reasons, (1)'s truth will obviously depend on the relation between an agent's reasons and his preferences. Thus, to assess (1), we must first clarify that relation. Unfortunately, this will require some digression at the outset.

A common-sense way of representing the relation between reasons and preferences is to say that of any two alternative acts, an agent will tend to prefer the one he believes to be supported by the stronger reasons. On any but the widest reading of "stronger reasons," this connection will occasionally break down because of the agent's weakness or irrationality; but since this does not affect what M is entitled to expect, we can ignore it. However, there is a further problem here that we cannot ignore. As I have just used it, the phrase "stronger reasons" is importantly ambiguous. On one interpretation of that phrase, each act is considered in isolation from all others, and the relevant reasons are only those that support each alternative by itself. On a second interpretation, each act is considered in relation to others, and the relevant reasons are those that support the various act-sequences to which each alternative belongs. On the first interpretation, our generalization asserts that an agent prefers A to B at t if he believes at t that the reasons for A, considered by itself, are stronger than the reasons for B, similarly considered. On the second interpretation, it asserts that an agent prefers A to B at t if he believes at t that the reasons for some available act-sequence to which A belongs are stronger than the reasons for any available act-sequence to which B belongs. Because each version of the generalization is plausible in some contexts, the two versions of it appear to reflect two quite different conceptions of preference. To mark the distinction between them, I shall call the first conception of preference *atomistic* and the second *holistic*.[7]

The distinction between atomistic and holistic preferences is plainly important. However, before we can apply it to our problem, we must refine it. I have said that an agent holistically prefers A to B when he believes that some available act-sequence to which A belongs is supported by stronger reasons than any available act-sequence to which B belongs. However, if an agent knows that A is impossible, then he cannot regard it as belonging to *any* available act-sequence, and so a fortiori cannot hold any such belief about it. Yet despite this, someone may still prefer an impossible act to a possible one, and moreover may do so precisely on the basis of its relations to other acts. He may, in short, still have a holistic preference for the impossible act. To allow for this, we must extend what we have said about holistic preferences. Instead of saying that an agent's holistic preference depends on the reasons he takes to support the *available* act-sequences to which each alternative belongs, we must say that it depends on the reasons he takes to support the act-sequences to which each alternative belongs *in the closest possible world in which each alternative act can be performed*. If both alternatives can actually be performed, then that world will simply be the actual world. If they cannot, then it will be the closest nonactual world.

Although this extension is clearly called for, it raises a further

---

[7] Here and in the remainder of this section, my thinking has been clarified by discussion with Hilary Kornblith.

problem of interpretation. For how, exactly, is the phrase "closest non-actual world" to be understood here? For our purposes, there are again two possibilities. If the acts to be preference-ranked are A and B, and if A was rendered impossible by some previous act C, then one close non-actual world in which A and B are both available is a world that is like the actual world except that in it, C is causally compatible with A. A second close non-actual world in which A and B are both available is one that resembles the actual world in every respect *including* C's causal incompatibility with A, but in which C has not yet been performed. Of these alternative worlds, the first differs from the actual world by lacking a certain causal connection, while the second differs rather with respect to the agent's temporal location. To capture the difference between them, let us call a holistic preference with the first sort of associated world *contracausal*, and one with the second sort of associated world *contratemporal*. A holistic preference whose alternatives are all available in the actual world we may call *simple*.

With all of this in mind, we can now return to (1), the claim that M's acceptance of (NA) warrants his expectation that his preferences will shift at t_1. Although (1) initially seemed clear, we can now see that it is not. Because there are several ways of viewing the relation between reasons and preferences, there are also several ways of interpreting (1). On which interpretation, if any, is (1) true?

(i) Suppose, first, that we understand preference atomistically. In that case, we can concentrate entirely on the reasons that M regards as telling for reading and conferring when these acts are considered by themselves. At t_0, M believes that his reason for conferring is stronger than his reason for reading, and (NA) does not imply that this will change before t_2. Hence, on this interpretation, M is not warranted in expecting any change in preference at t_1, and so (1) is false.

(ii) Suppose, next, that we understand preference holistically. In that case, we must explain how M can expect to prefer either reading *or* conferring after t_1, when one or the other of these acts will no longer be available. Suppose we resolve this problem by letting M anticipate postulating a contracausal world in which whatever he has done at t_1 does not rule out either reading or conferring at t_2. In that case, M is clearly justified in believing that after t_1 he will prefer conferring to reading. However, on the same contracausal assumption, M is also justified in believing that *before* t_1 the best act-sequence is [paint, confer]. Hence, his holistic preference before t_1 must also be to confer rather than to read. But (1) asserts that M is warranted in expecting to prefer conferring to reading only *after* t_1. Hence, this interpretation again renders (1) false.

(iii) Suppose, finally, that we understand preference holistically but resolve the problem of how M can expect to prefer either reading or conferring after t_1 in the other possible way. Instead of letting M anticipate postulating a contracausal world, let us have him anticipate postulating a contratemporal world in which reading and conferring are both still available as they are at t_0. In that case, M's preferences before and after t_1 will reflect the reasons that he believes at those moments to tell for the various act-sequences available at t_0. But although the act-sequences to be considered before and after t_1 are the same, M's acceptance of (NA) guarantees that his attitude toward them will differ at the two moments. Before t_1, M will believe that his strongest single reason is his reason to paint; and so he will regard the sequence [paint, read] as supported by the strongest reasons. Before t_1, M will prefer reading to conferring. However, after t_1, M's acceptance of (NA) will commit him to the view that the features of painting are not reasons at all; and so he will then regard the sequence [ride, confer] as supported by the strongest reasons. After t_1, M will prefer conferring to reading. But this is just the shift that (1) describes. Because M seems warranted in expecting it at t_0, our third interpretation appears to make (1) true.

There is, however, a possible objection here. The crux of the argument has been that after t_1, M's acceptance of (NA) will force him to discount his previous reason for painting at t_1, and so will force him to reverse his judgment that the [paint, read] sequence is supported by stronger reasons than the [ride, confer] sequence. But this reasoning may seem to ignore the fact that it is not yet t_1 in the contratemporal world in which both sequences are available. Because it is not yet t_1 in that world, the features of painting are still reasons there no matter *what* time it is in the actual world. But if so, then M seems warranted in expecting that even after it is t_1 in the actual world, he will view the [paint, read] sequence as supported by stronger reasons than the [ride, confer] sequence. Because he therefore seems warranted in expecting his preference for reading to survive until t_2, our argument may appear to fail.

If this objection is sound, there is no obvious sense in which M's acceptance of (NA) warrants his expectation that his preferences will shift at t_1. But is the objection sound? We must concede that in a world in which it is earlier than t_1, M's acceptance of (NA) does not commit him to believing that the features of painting at t_1 are not reasons. However, upon closer inspection, this seems beside the point. The real question is not whether M must believe *in the contratemporal world* that the features of painting are not reasons, but rather whether he must believe this after t_1 *in the actual world* when he compares the various act-sequences that are available in the contratemporal world. To compare these sequences, M does not have to take up the temporal perspective of the contratemporal world. He can weigh the reasons for performing the acts in each sequence without pretending that it is any earlier than it actually is. In view of this, the most natural temporal standpoint for M—and indeed the only one that seems pertinent to his actual preferences—is that which M occupies in the actual world. Because an assessment of the competing sequences from this standpoint after t_1 can be expected to yield a preference for conferring, our argument for (1) will stand after all.

IV

It is not surprising that there is a sense in which M's acceptance of (NA) warrants his expectation that his preference will shift at t_1. Because M accepts (NA), he is bound to regret his commitment to reading after t_1; and so it is natural that in some sense he will then prefer conferring. But while the truth of (a version of) our first thesis is not unexpected, its bearing on M's rationality is far from clear. It is not always irrational to decide upon an act on the basis of a preference that one expects to shift before the act is performed. A person who decides to stop smoking while expecting to backslide makes a similar decision, yet that decision seems eminently rational. Even when we add that M's acceptance of (NA) implies that his holistic preferences will shift regularly and systematically, his position is not obviously untenable. Thus, our thesis (2), that M's decision is irrational, plainly requires further argument.

To see the case for (2), we must consider not only M's expectations about his future preferences, but also the stance toward those preferences to which his decision commits him. It was suggested earlier that when an agent forms an intention to perform a future act, he must be resolved to resist any anticipated preference for an act that is incompatible with the act he intends. However, the preference for conferring that M expects to acquire at t_1 appears to be of just this sort. Thus, M's position will be untenable if (2a) the preference he expects to acquire at t_1 is among those that his decision commits him to resolving to resist, while (2b) this resolution is blocked by the very commitments that shape his expectations. To complete my argument, I shall now defend each claim in turn.

Let us begin with (2a). At first glance, (2a) appears to be a straightforward consequence of the more general principle that

(P) An intending agent must be resolved to resist any expected preference for an act that is an alternative to the acts he intends.

But a closer look reveals a complication. What, exactly, is the temporal scope of (P)'s notion of an alternative act? More particularly, does (P) require only that an intending agent be resolved to resist any expected preference for an alternative act that will still be available *when the preference arises*? Or does it require, more broadly, that he be resolved to resist any expected preference for an alternative act that is available at the earlier moment *when the intention arises*? Assuming that the relevant preferences are holistic—an assumption that must itself be defended in due course—the first formulation requires only that the agent be resolved to resist any expected holistic-simple preference for an alternative act, while the second requires also that he be resolved to resist any expected holistic-contratemporal preference for an alternative act. Because the preference for conferring which M expects to acquire at t_1 is holistic-contratemporal—because M will no longer be able to confer when his preference for conferring arises at t_1—only the second interpretation of (P) renders (2a) true.

Prima facie, this seems to tell heavily against (2a), for the second interpretation of (P) appears much less plausible than the first. The most obvious reason why an intending agent should be resolved to resist an expected preference for an alternative act is that, by taking this stance, he maximizes his chances of realizing his current intention. But a preference that will only arise when the newly preferred alternative is no longer available is no threat to the realization of an agent's intention. Thus, there appears to be no reason to be resolved to resist an expected holistic-contratemporal preference for an alternative act. Yet this is less damaging than it looks, for the proposed rationale for (P) is deficient on independent grounds. If the point of resolving to resist an expected preference for an alternative act is only to maximize the chances of realizing one's intentions, then there is *no* point in forming such a resolution when it is known that the resolution will hinder rather than advance the performance of the intended act—when, for example, the agent knows that he is more likely to do what he intends if he simply ignores his expected preference for doing otherwise. Moreover, the resolution is also pointless when it is known to be causally superfluous—when, for example, the agent knows that someone else will reinforce his intention if he falters. But, in fact, the resolution plainly *is* required in these and related instances. Thus, a purely instrumental rationale for (P) is not credible. Whatever else is true, the intending agent's resolution to resist his anticipated refractory preference is not required merely as a means to an end.

Although these considerations reduce the appeal of the narrower interpretation of (P), they also pose a puzzle. If the point of being resolved to resist an anticipated preference for an alternative act is not to further the realization of one's intention, then why *must* an intending agent take this stance? The answer lies, I think, in an extension of what we said earlier about the subjective nature of intention. We saw above that an intention is a natural outcome of a decision to do something that cannot (best) be done immediately. It is a state envisioned by the agent as fixing his current readiness to act,

189

and as preserving that readiness until he *can* act. But in the cases we are considering, the intending agent's readiness to act is a direct result of his acceptance of certain reasons. These reasons are what render his readiness to act comprehensible to him, and so he cannot intelligibly envision that readiness as persisting intact without envisioning the reasons as persisting intact as well. He can indeed expect to acquire a future readiness to perform the same act on the basis of new reasons; but insofar as this is what he expects, he cannot regard his current decision as what settles the matter. Because of this, he cannot regard himself as entering a state that will automatically link decision with action, and so he cannot properly regard himself as intending the action at all.

Once all of this is understood, we can sketch a clear alternative rationale for (P). The key to this rationale is that practical reasoning, which generates the reasons that an intending agent must envision as persisting intact, is itself holistic. In view of this, the intending agent must evidently envision not just his current reasons, but also a corresponding holistic preference, as persisting intact until he acts. But if so, then he obviously cannot envision himself as acquiring a new and incompatible holistic preference before then. If he does envision this, his imaginative identification with his future acting self will again break down. Hence, it is hardly surprising that someone who intends a given act must be resolved to resist an expected holistic preference for an alternative act. This resolution is required because it is his only way of dissociating himself from an expectation that conflicts with the vision of his future self demanded by his intention.

Because it is not vulnerable to counterexamples as our earlier suggestion was, this way of understanding (P)'s rationale seems preferable to the earlier account. In what follows, I shall assume that it is correct. But even so, there is still a question. If it is to tell for (2a), the proposed rationale for (P) must support (P)'s wider interpretation. It must show that an intending agent must be resolved to resist an expected holistic preference for an alternative act even when the alternative will no longer be available when the preference arises. It must show, in other words, that he must be resolved to resist an expected holistic-contratemporal as well as a

holistic-simple preference for an alternative act. But because a deliberating agent weighs only available act-sequences, the preferences whose continued existence he must envision are exclusively
holistic-simple. Hence, it may seem that the conflicting future preferences that he must be resolved to resist are exclusively holistic-
simple as well.

This conclusion, however, does not follow. It is true that the preferences whose continuation must be envisioned by an intending
agent are indeed holistic-simple *when they are formed*. Still, the
passage of time will soon render unavailable some of the acts in the
sequence whose comparison determines them. Hence, after an in-
terval, these preferences will no longer reflect the agent's view of
the reasons supporting actually available act-sequences. Instead,
they will reflect his view of the reasons supporting act-sequences
that are available in a contratemporal world whose time is that of
the original decision. But if so, then their continuation will be incompatible with his acquisition of preferences for alternative acts
available in that world. Thus, it is the latter expected preferences
that he must be resolved to resist. Since these expected preferences
are holistic-contratemporal, the wider interpretation of (P), and so
also (2a), is borne out.

I have just argued that M must be resolved to resist his expected
preference for conferring even though he knows that he will no
longer be able to confer when the preference arises. Yet this, by itself, does not invalidate M's decision to paint and then read. Many
agents, such as the smoker mentioned above, make rational decisions embodying similar resolutions.[8] Thus, to complete our argument, we must show that M's decision is somehow different from
these others. This is the point of claim (2b)—the claim that M's

---

[8] The comparison of M and the smoker may appear misleading, for what the
smoker expects to undergo may seem to be less a reassessment of reasons yielding a
realignment of holistic preferences than a simple lapse of willpower. However, the
force of this objection is obscure, for it is difficult to say where one's reasons and
holistic preferences end and his will begins. Moreover, and more important, the objection is irrelevant; for the smoker's decision and accompanying resolution would
be no less rational if what he expected *were* a clearcut revision of his holistic preferences.

ability to resolve to resist his expected preference is blocked by the very commitments that shape his expectation itself.

The argument for (2b) is straightforward enough. When we consider the smoker who expects to backslide, we find that his expected preference for a return to smoking is not internally related to any belief or attitude that he currently holds. His expectation of it is based solely on evidence provided by his and others' past behavior; and it is because of this that he can rationally be resolved to resist his expected preference. But in M's case, the expected preference has a very different source. It is true that M could not expect his preference to shift at t_1 if he did not have evidence that he will continue to believe (NA), and that he will continue to draw certain conclusions from it. However, it is also true that M's evidence for this is just that, in the past, he has generally continued to hold beliefs that he initially regarded as well grounded and has generally drawn the proper inferences from them. But this evidence obviously presupposes that M now believes that (NA) *is* well grounded, and that he *should* draw the relevant conclusions from it. Thus, unlike the smoker's, M's expected contrary preference is internally connected to his current belief structure. It is expected not as an adventitious arrival, but rather as the proper consequence of a continued true belief. Any resolution to resist it will therefore set M against a future conclusion that he believes will be warranted. But taking such a stance is just as irrational as forming an intention while accepting the fact that one's current preferences will not persist. Hence, we seem amply justified in accepting (2b) as well as (2a).

We can now see why M's decision at t_0 seemed irrational and self-defeating. The crux of the problem is that because M accepts (NA), his decision to sacrifice the later act for the earlier one commits him to an expectation that he can neither rationally accept nor rationally reject. To avoid incoherency, M must abandon one of the elements that generate the situation; and given the reasonableness of the decision itself, it is plainly his acceptance of (NA) that will have to go. Neither, it seems, can M reject (NA) here but retain it in other contexts—where the intended sacrifice is past, where none is in question, or where the reasons of other people are concerned. This maneuver might resolve M's immediate difficulty, but if M executed it consistently, he would constantly be repudiating his previously held beliefs that particular reasons have retrospective force. In that case, his belief system would be unstable. In addition, M would be unable to explain why some reasons have retrospective force while others do not, and so his position would lack theoretical simplicity. Similarly, M cannot hold that only the features of actions, but not the features of non-actional events, remain reasons in retrospect; for a variant of our argument shows that he would then be unable coherently to intend to bring about a valuable event at t_1 at the cost of not performing a desirable act at t_2. In general, no selective rejection of (NA) is tenable. Having ascribed retrospective force to some reasons, M cannot avoid extending it to all of them.[9]

[9] My argument that reasons must be viewed as exercising retrospective force is related to a number of other discussions in the recent literature. Thomas Nagel, in *The Possibility of Altruism* (sec. 2), defends a similar (though more general) claim in a rather different way. Alan Gewirth, in *Reason and Morality*, attempts to draw other moral conclusions from the requirements of agency and practical reasoning. And Charles Fried, in *An Anatomy of Values* (chaps. 2 and 3), discusses the internal coherence of action plans in an illuminating way.

E L E V E N

DESERT, RIGHTS, AND
JUSTICE

In the preceding two chapters, I discussed several metaphysical issues associated with desert. This discussion, though difficult, was
necessary if we were to understand the vision of persons and their
relations to the past that is characteristic of desert. But now we
must return to more explicitly normative concerns. Having delin-
eated desert's metaphysical underpinnings, I want to end by locating it in relation to such other moral notions as rights and justice.

That desert and rights are distinct is suggested by the fact that
persons often deserve such things as success, competitive victory,
and wages, to which they have no rights, and equally often acquire
rights to property and opportunities that they do not deserve.
Moreover, when the demands of desert conflict with those of rights
(and perhaps also with those of justice), the latter usually appear to
take precedence. For example, when a dissipated and vicious person
inherits a fortune while far better people must struggle to survive
on almost nothing, we do not say that the heir should be made to
yield the fortune to those who are more deserving. Instead, we say
that the heir has a right to the fortune, he should be allowed to keep
it. If some deny this, it is only because they believe that there *is* no
serious right to inherit. Thus, any thorough study of desert must
relate its demands to those of rights and justice; and any defense of
it must confront the objection that its demands are too weak to be
morally significant.

In this last chapter, I will try to meet this objection. I will do so
not by defending the implausible view that the demands of desert
do take precedence over those of rights and justice, but rather by

arguing that claims involving the three notions usually answer quite different questions, and thus generally do not impose conflicting demands. In saying this, I shall propose a way of elaborating Feinberg's suggestive remark that

> "[d]eserve," "fitting," and "appropriate," on the one hand, and "right," "entitlement," and "rule," on the other, are terms from altogether different parts of our ethical vocabularies; they are related in such a way that there is no paradox in saying of a person that he deserves (it would be fitting for him to have) certain modes of treatment which, nevertheless, he cannot claim as his due.[1]

As I understand them, the "different parts of our ethical vocabulary" which desert and rights represent are precisely the fundamental notions of value and obligation. For, as I shall now argue, most (though not all) significant desert-claims are grounded not in anyone's obligations, but rather in the value of persons' coming to have what they deserve.

I

Some desert-claims plainly cannot be justified except through appeals to value. When a person deserves the predictable consequences of his earlier free acts, there is generally no one who morally ought to promote or provide what is deserved. Similarly, when hard workers deserve to succeed, others are seldom obligated to help them succeed. Where such desert-claims are concerned, the justification can be *only* that there is value in the deserving party's having what he deserves; and not surprisingly, the arguments of Chapters 3 and 4 did take this form. Moreover, although Ross does acknowledge a prima facie duty to promote the matching of happiness to virtue, the argument of Chapter 8 did not rest on this. Instead, I defended the claim that virtuous persons deserve to be happy by arguing that such persons are themselves worth more

[1] Feinberg, "Justice and Personal Desert," p. 86.

than others, and hence that their happiness must be worth more as well.

Thus, some of our arguments clearly have been appeals to value. But the status of other arguments is less obvious. In Chapter 7, I tried to show that the best competitor's desert of victory and the prize, and the student's desert of his grade, reflects the demands of veracity. In Chapters 5 and 6, I argued that desert of punishment, compensation, and wages reflects the demands of diachronic fairness. In Chapter 8, I argued that desert of reward for heroic or helpful acts sometimes draws force from the requirements of gratitude. And, again in Chapter 7, I argued that the desert of the best-qualified reflects the requirement that persons be treated as agents whose activities can make a difference. On one natural interpretation, these demands and requirements are precisely *obligations* to tell the truth, act fairly, display gratitude, and respect the status of persons as agents. And this interpretation is reinforced by the fact that I have repeatedly invoked the *principles* of veracity, diachronic fairness, and gratitude (and might also have invoked a principle of respect for persons as agents); for we naturally view principles as prescribing types of personal behavior, and thus as codifying individual obligations.

But although we *can* regard many of the foregoing arguments as appeals to obligations, that interpretation is not forced on us. As we have seen, the desert of the virtuous is most plausibly grounded not in the obligation to make virtuous persons happy, but in the value of a state—the happiness of the virtuous—which that obligation promotes. Just so, a competitor's desert of his prize, and a student's desert of his grade, might draw its normative force not from obligations to make true assertions or inculcate true beliefs, but rather from the value of true assertions or beliefs themselves. And the same might hold, *mutatis mutandis*, of the other arguments cited.

Should we interpret these arguments as appeals to value rather than to obligation? This question has no all-or-nothing answer. Rather, we must ask, of each argument (1) whether the obligation to which it might appeal is an obligation to promote some independently specifiable and valuable outcome, and (2) if so, whether the desert-claims that the argument justifies would retain their force if the valuable outcome did not ensue despite the best efforts of all those obligated to promote it. If an argument satisfies both (1) and (2), it is likely to be an appeal to value; if it does not, it is likely to be an appeal to obligation.

With this in mind, consider first the argument that desert of victory, prizes, and grades is grounded in veracity. This argument does seem to satisfy (1); for the truth of the assertions and beliefs that emerge when persons are judged to satisfy conventional criteria of victory or performance is clearly distinct from the actions of rules committees, referees, and graders. The truth of those assertions and beliefs is also a plausible locus of value. In addition, the argument seems to satisfy (2), since a person's desert may persist, and may continue to impose demands, when he fails to win a contest or receive an appropriate grade for reasons unrelated to human dereliction. When a referee trips and fails to see a crucial play, he need not fail to fulfill any moral obligation. Even so, the losing competitor still deserves to win, and his desert still retains its normative force. Hence, the desert-claim's demands must stem not from anyone's obligation to promote the accurate recording of the competitors' merits, but, more simply, from the fact that such accuracy is a significant good in itself. Nor is this interpretation undermined by our ability to appeal to a *principle* of veracity; for this principle may specify what is desirable as easily as what is obligatory. In this context, the principle appears to assert only that the world is significantly better when the relevant assertions and beliefs are true.

Similar reasoning applies to the argument that desert of punishment, compensation, and wages is grounded in the demands of diachronic fairness. Here again, requirement (1) appears to be satisfied, since the fact that a past deviation from a standard is now offset is both analytically distinguishable from the act that produced the offsetting and a plausible candidate for the possession of value. Moreover, requirement (2) is also satisfied, since desert of punishment, compensation, and wages may outstrip the ability (and a fortiori the obligations) of individuals to provide what is deserved. For example, a wrongdoer may escape punishment not because any po-

197

liceman or judge has failed to do his job, but simply because he is clever or lucky. Even so, the wrongdoer continues to deserve punishment; and his desert retains its normative force. Similarly, persons may deserve compensation when the resources to provide it are unavailable, and they may deserve wages that market conditions prevent employers from paying. Because these desert-claims, too, impose demands that go beyond the demands of any obligations, the arguments of Chapters 5 and 6 must also appeal not to any obligation to rectify deviations from independent standards, but instead to the superior value of the rectification of such deviations. Of course, if the violated standard was itself an obligation, then the act of rectifying the deviation may itself be obligatory. Nevertheless, the *case* for the rectification must rest not on this obligation, but on the value of a broader pattern that encompasses both the possibility and the actuality of the act that fulfills the obligation.

Having come this far, we may be tempted to suppose that our remaining arguments are also appeals to value. But this conjecture, though appealing, does not really fit the facts. For when we examine these arguments—the appeals to gratitude and to the requirement that persons be treated as agents—we are hard pressed to find independent outcomes which the relevant obligations might promote, and from whose value the arguments might draw their force. Because displays of gratitude and respect for agency promote no valuable outcomes except, trivially, that benefactors are shown gratitude and persons are treated as agents, the appeals to these requirements seem best interpreted as straightforward appeals to obligation. Against this, one might argue that the relevant desert-claims sometimes do extend beyond all obligations—that a hero deserves the reward that his intended beneficiary was unable to provide, or that a best-qualified applicant deserves the job that, due to an unavoidable computer error or a postal delay, went to another. But these desert-claims either have no normative force or have only such force as is attributable to other, related considerations (for example, that heroic acts often betoken a superior character). Thus, our inclination to make them does not seem to save the value-interpretation here.

This does not matter, however, for our aim is not classification but comprehension. Because the notion of desert has probably evolved through a series of analogical extensions, there are unlikely to be any strict necessary and sufficient conditions for its application. But there may still be significant generalizations that hold of most desert-claims, and that support illuminating comparisons between desert and other moral concepts. By taking the value-interpretation as one such generalization, we can answer the objection that desert is systematically dominated by rights, and thus is too weak to be significant.

For although rights-claims and desert-claims both appear to provide answers to the single question "Should person X have Y?" we have just seen that a more discerning rendering of the question that desert-claims generally answer is "Is there something about person X's constituting attributes or actions that would make it a good thing for him to have Y?" By contrast, I now want to argue that when rights-claims appear to compete with desert-claims, the question to which *they* typically provide answers is "Are there at least some persons who have serious obligations to provide X with Y, to protect X's possession of Y, or to refrain from preventing X from having Y?" If this is correct—if rights-claims and desert-claims do answer different questions—then the conflict between them will be only apparent. Hence, the dominance of desert by rights will be only apparent too.

It is not plausible to say that *all* rights-claims are answers to questions about others' obligations toward the right-holder. As David Lyons notes, the "correlativity thesis"—the doctrine that "when I have a right, some other person or persons are under an obligation to me (to provide some service or benefit, for example, or to refrain from interfering with my behavior)"—applies only to the species of right that Hohfeld called a "claim-right."[2] It does not apply to Hohfeldian "liberty-rights," which assert only that the

[2] David Lyons, ed., *Rights* (Belmont, Calif.: Wadsworth, 1979), p. 5. See Wesley Newcomb Hohfeld, *Fundamental Legal Conceptions* (New Haven: Yale University Press, 1919; reprinted 1964).

right-holder himself is not obligated to refrain from a specified activity, and neither does it apply to what Hohfeld called "powers" and "immunities." But because liberties, powers, and immunities carry no implication that persons should have the things to which they have rights, the rights-claims they generate do not even seem to compete with desert-claims. Thus, they are irrelevant to our concerns.

What about claim-rights, which do seem to compete with desert? As we just saw, these rights are widely (and plausibly) said to be correlated with obligations. Prima facie, this may itself seem to establish that they are grounded in obligation. But we must be careful here. In the preceding section, I argued that some desert-claims are also (roughly) correlated with obligations, yet draw their normative force not from the obligations, but rather from the values that they in turn promote. Thus, to be fair, we must now ask whether the same might hold of claim-rights. Where claim-rights are negative—where they require only that others not interfere with the right-holder—this means asking whether they are grounded in the value of each person's freedom to run his life as he sees fit.[3] Where claim-rights are positive—where they require that the right-holder be provided with needed goods or services—it means asking whether they are grounded either in the value of his freedom, which cannot be fully realized unless his needs are met, or in the value of his well-being or flourishing itself.[4]

But upon examination, none of these suggestions are plausible. There may indeed be a sense in which all rights are linked to such values as liberty or well-being;[5] but if a claim-right drew its force directly from any such value, then each person would have a right

[3] For discussion that connects rights with freedom of choice, see Hart, "Are There Any Natural Rights?" and T. M. Scanlon, "Rights, Goals, and Fairness," in *Public and Private Morality*, ed. Stuart Hampshire (Cambridge, England: Cambridge University Press, 1978), pp. 93–111. However, neither philosopher accepts the view that rights-claims are direct appeals to the value of freedom.

[4] The distinction between negative rights and rights to be provided with things is itself problematical; for critical discussion, see Henry Shue, *Basic Rights: Subsistence, Affluence, and U.S. Foreign Policy* (Princeton: Princeton University Press, 1980).

[5] For sophisticated discussion of how the linkage might work, see Scanlon, "Rights, Goals, and Fairness."

to whatever would sufficiently enhance his liberty or well-being. In addition, the strength of one's right to something would be directly proportional to that thing's tendency to promote one's freedom and well-being. Needless to say, this is not how rights behave. Instead, an object or mode of treatment may greatly increase the options open to X, but X may nevertheless have no right to it. In addition, our freedom and well-being can be undermined by unavoidable factors, such as scarcity and disease, to whose absence *nobody* has a right. At best, the value of what is unattainable can generate rights in what Feinberg calls the "manifesto sense"—potential rights that have normative force only to the extent of being "determinants of *present* aspirations and guides to *present* policies" (emphasis his).[6] In all of this, the behavior of claim-rights stands in sharp contrast to that of desert; for when persons deserve happiness, success, good grades, victory, punishment, or compensation, their desert *is* equally breached by any and all occurrences that prevent the valuable outcome.

Thus, desert-claims and rights-claims do seem to answer different questions. When we say that persons deserve things, we generally answer questions about what it would be good for them to have; when we attribute rights, we generally answer questions about what others ought to do or refrain from doing.[7] And because the questions are different, their answers do not compete. Properly understood, desert-claims are neither weaker nor stronger than rights-claims.

Why, then, do desert-claims so often *appear* weaker? To answer this question, we need only recall that most contexts of inquiry are practical, and that even when inquiry is theoretical, any attempt to apply it must eventually lead back to some conclusion about what we or others ought to do. Given these facts, the explanation of the apparent weakness of desert-claims is simply that the overwhelm-

---

[6] Joel Feinberg, "The Nature and Value of Rights," in Lyons, *Rights*, p. 90.

[7] This is not to say that rights-claims provide answers to any and all questions about how persons ought to act. For example, it is sometimes said that rights-claims are only in place where the right-holder is entitled to demand that others treat him as they should, and to complain if they do not. But any such suggestion either will have no effect on my argument or will reinforce the view that rights-claims answer different questions from desert-claims.

ing majority of questions about what persons ought to receive just *are* questions about what we (or others) ought to do.

To illustrate this, let us briefly consider one example. Suppose a farm has been in a family for generations, and that the current farmer has two sons who want it. One son is careless and mean-spirited but was promised the farm long ago, while the other has no claim to the farm but is hard-working and decent. When we consider this case, we reluctantly conclude that the first son should have the farm; but our reason is *not* that his right takes precedence over the second son's desert. Instead, the reason is that the question we are really asking—"To which son should the farmer give the farm?"—is one to which only the rights-claim provides an answer. Here the rights-claim prevails by default. If, instead, our question had been "Which son's having the farm would make the world a better place?" then we would not have hesitated to answer "the second." In that case, it would have been not the rights-claim, but rather the desert-claim, that appeared to dominate.[8]

III

By thus separating questions of value and obligation, we defuse the objection that desert is too weak to be morally significant. However, in so doing, we may seem to invite the related objection that desert is hopelessly impractical. For if desert-claims tell us only what has value, then desert may seem to have no bearing on how we should act.

This objection, however, is a non sequitur; for even if desert-claims do not themselves dictate actions, the values from which they draw their force may surely have an important influence on the obligations that do. There is no reason to expect that influence to be straightforward or direct, but if there is significant value to persons' getting what they deserve, then this must (of course) affect

[8] Significantly, the desert of the best-qualified, which we saw to be grounded in obligation rather than in value, does not seem automatically to give way to rights. Indeed, the claims of the best-qualified are sometimes themselves expressed *as* rights. This confirms the suggestion that when other desert-claims do seem to give way, it is because they provide answers to different questions than do rights-claims.

others' obligations toward them. Moreover, because rights are grounded in obligations, it must affect the nature of rights as well.[9]

Can we be more specific? Can we explain (or predict) the ways in which desert impinges on obligations? Clearly we cannot do so in any detail; for the degree to which a potential outcome's value affects any person's obligations depends on too many factors. It depends (at least) on the value's overall urgency; the ease or difficulty with which the person could promote the value; the comparative ease or difficulty with which others could promote it; the person's prior commitments to promote values such as this one; and the other obligations (including obligations to promote other values) with which the obligation would conflict. Besides being unquantifiable, these factors can be expected to interact in complex ways. In addition, there is an unresolved general question about the degree to which personal discretion supersedes the demands of even the most urgent values.[10] Given all this, it is clearly unrealistic to seek many specific conclusions about obligations to promote deserved outcomes.

Yet even so, some things can be said; for in some cases, the nature of the value that grounds a desert-claim may itself determine whether, and how, the desert-claim obligates. Consider, in this regard, two cases in which persons were said to deserve things that *no* others were obligated to provide. One case concerned a man who carelessly left his umbrella at home despite predictions of rain. Of this man, we said that he does deserve the soaking he gets, but that nobody is obligated to see to it that he gets wet. There is no one with a duty to prevent him from buying a new umbrella en route, or to pour water on his head if the skies clear. Similarly, of the

---

[9] However, for defense of the view that we cannot infer from "*X* ought to be punished" to "We ought to punish *X*," see Elizabeth Wolgast, "Intolerable Wrong and Punishment," *Philosophy* 60, no. 232 (April 1985), pp. 161–74.

[10] For discussion, see Charles Fried, *Right and Wrong* (Cambridge, Mass.: Harvard University Press, 1978), chap. 6 and passim; Bernard Williams, "Persons, Character, and Morality," in *The Identities of Persons*, ed. Amelie Rorty (Berkeley: University of California Press, 1976), pp. 197–216; Susan Wolf, "Moral Saints," *The Journal of Philosophy* 79, no. 8 (August 1982), pp. 419–39; Marcia Baron, "On the Alleged Moral Repugnance of Acting from Duty," *The Journal of Philosophy* 81, no. 4 (April 1984), pp. 197–220; and Lawrence Blum, *Friendship, Altruism, and Morality* (Boston: Routledge and Kegan Paul, 1980).

writer who had worked for years on his novel, we said that he does deserve to succeed, but that nobody is obligated to *help* him succeed.

To see why these desert-claims imply no obligations, recall the arguments upon which they were found to rest. I argued in Chapter 3 that the first man's soaking is valuable because it is part of what he has chosen—because it is a predictable consequence of his free decision, and so inherits value *from* his exercise of freedom. But if so, then what has value—what he deserves—is only that he be soaked *in the way that he predicted or could have predicted*. As the case was described, it was no part of his prediction that anyone else would take steps to bring about the soaking. Hence, such intervention, far from producing the valuable outcome, would actually block it. And something similar holds of the persistent author. Because his success has acquired value from his own past years of effort, it is only the object of *those efforts* that now has value. The efforts were directed at *his* writing a successful book. Hence, any intervention by a second, more gifted writer would again interfere with, rather than promote, the valuable outcome. There are, of course, many less pure cases in which diligent agents do not care how their long-pursued ends are produced. A hard-working shopkeeper might be just as happy becoming rich through the intervention of another as he would be doing it on his own. Yet even so, his efforts are, in a sense, directed only at the latter outcome. Thus, it is hardly surprising that others are not (strongly) obligated to promote his deserved success.

In these cases, the nature of the relevant values explains why no one is obligated to provide what is deserved. But in other cases, the nature of those values explains instead why some persons and not others *are* obligated to provide what is deserved. Thus, consider desert of wages, which obligates primarily employers, and desert of compensation, which obligates primarily those who have inflicted compensable harm. Since these forms of desert are grounded in the value of diachronic fairness, which demands the offsetting of earlier lapses from independent standards, any obligations they generate are apt to apply primarily to those who were implicated in the original violations. The standard that pertains to wages construes each person's aims as having a worth that is independent of any other person's aims. Hence, any lapse from it will naturally call for rectification by the very person or group to whose purposes the deserving party's aims were subordinated. It is not surprising, therefore, that a worker's employer—the person or group to whose purposes his aims *were* subordinated—must pay the deserved wage. Again, since the standards that pertain to compensation forbid the infliction of certain sorts of harms, any deviations from them are best rectified by precisely the persons who inflicted the harm. Thus, it is also unsurprising that those persons bear the primary obligation to compensate.

This, of course, is not the end of the story. Even where only specific persons are obligated to provide what is deserved, many or all others may have related obligations. For example, even if only an employer is obligated to pay a deserved wage, others may be obligated to see that he does what he should do. Although no one is likely to be obligated personally to convince or coerce him, we may all be obligated to press for legislation that would have the same effect. In promoting such legislation, we indirectly increase the likelihood that employees will be paid what they deserve. Since the vehicle of our efforts is part of a larger system of institutions that may be either just or unjust, our obligations to promote deserved outcomes here merge with our obligations to further social justice. Thus, by considering these obligations, we are led to reconsider the vexed relation between desert and justice.

IV

With this, we return to our starting point. From the outset, I have tried to develop an account of desert that preserves its normative independence from institutional arrangements. It was with this in mind that I attempted to rebut Rawls's frontal attack on pre-institutional desert and argued that desert-claims can be justified through appeals to a variety of non-institutional considerations. If my arguments have been even roughly correct, and if we follow Rawls in construing justice as the equitable structuring of large-scale social arrangements, we may indeed conclude that justice is not prior to desert. But neither can we understand justice solely in *terms* of desert. Despite desert's importance, it is surely not plausible to say, with John Hospers, that "justice is [simply] getting what one deserves."[11] Instead, the truth is more complicated than either reductive position allows.

For, on the one hand, a social institution, brought into existence because it is just, may importantly influence what persons deserve. It may do so, first, by shaping the skills, preferences, and values that contribute to the performance of desert-creating actions (or that are themselves desert-bases); second, by establishing the framework of alternatives within which agents decide which actions to perform; third, by establishing the conventions that give many actions their meaning; and, finally, by providing the backdrop of justice (or injustice) that some sources of desert require. Moreover, these factors may act singly or in combination. Some desert-claims, such as those whose basis is virtuous action or character, are affected by just institutions only to the extent that these institutions influence the formation of character traits. Other desert-claims, such as those whose basis is diligent effort, are affected in this way, but also because institutions structure the rewards that attach to actions, and so determine which projects persons find it reasonable to pursue. Still others, such as claims whose basis is superior competitive performance, are affected in both ways, but also in that institutionally established conventions may define the very acts that create the desert. And yet others, besides being affected in all the foregoing ways, cannot arise at all unless society's basic institutions are just (or unjust). As we saw in Chapter 3, the expected consequences of free choices do not inherit value unless the choices are made from among justly structured alternatives. In addition, one obviously cannot deserve compensation for the effects of unjust practices if the practices are not, in fact, unjust.

Thus, a society's justice clearly can have a variety of influences on an individual's desert. But what, now, of the converse relation? Is a society's justice at all affected by the degree to which its citizens

---

[11] John Hospers, *Human Conduct: Problems of Ethics*, shorter ed. (New York: Harcourt Brace Jovanovich, 1972), p. 361.

tend to *get* what they deserve? In Rawls's view, it cannot be; for justice as fairness is designed to be neutral toward all conceptions of the good. It is precisely to guarantee this neutrality that Rawls deprives his contracting parties of all information about the values they hold in the actual world. Given their ignorance, the parties cannot accept any principles that presuppose substantive judgments of worth. Thus:

> The criterion to each according to his virtue would not . . . be chosen in the original position. Since the parties desire to advance their conceptions of the good, they have no reason for arranging their institutions so that distributive shares are determined by moral desert.[12]

Similarly, the parties have reason to reject all other principles that prescribe the promotion of values upon which desert-claims rest.

If we accept Rawls's design of the original position, these conclusions are exactly what we should expect.[13] But once we step outside of Rawls's theory, it becomes far less clear why we should welcome them. For if a given person's having something really would have value—if the world really would be a significantly better place if he had it—then, other things being equal, why *shouldn't* a just society promote his having it? If desert-claims do have a rational basis, then why shouldn't their satisfaction be among the elements of an ideally just scheme? In short, why isn't the question not whether a social ordering promotes *any* values, but instead whether it promotes the *right* values?

To these questions there may seem to be an obvious answer. A society cannot promote the right values unless its representatives

---

[12] Rawls, *A Theory of Justice*, p. 313.

[13] In independent discussions, Michael Lesnoff and James Sterba have suggested that those in Rawls's original position might acknowledge desert at least to the extent of deciding that hard workers should receive rewards beyond those needed to satisfy the difference principle. See Lesnoff, "Capitalism, Socialism, and Justice," in *Justice and Economic Distribution*, ed. Arthur and Shaw, pp. 139–49, and Sterba, *The Demands of Justice* (Notre Dame: University of Notre Dame Press, 1980), chap. 2. Yet even if Lesnoff and Sterba are right (and even if the resulting principle closely resembles our own principle of diachronic fairness), the Rawlsian contractors will remain unable to acknowledge the other values that we have found to underlie various desert-claims.

know which values these are. But people disagree deeply over what has value, and no person or group is in a privileged position to resolve the disagreement. Moreover, as Rawls himself notes, appeals to value in political argument are often disguised assertions of prejudice.

> When it is said, for example, that certain kinds of sexual relationships are degrading and shameful, and should be prohibited on this basis, if only for the sake of the individuals in question irrespective of their wishes, it is often because a reasonable case cannot be made in terms of the principles of justice. Instead, we fall back on notions of excellence.[14]

Thus, don't respect for the opinions of others and a fitting awareness of our own fallibility and partiality require us to settle for a "value-neutral" social framework?

Upon inspection, they do not; for if our fallibility and potential bias did rule out all principles presupposing substantive views about value, then they would also rule out all other moral principles. There is deep disagreement not only about what has value, but also about what is right and just; and if condemnations of deviant sexual conduct can reflect mere personal distaste, then claims about the just distribution of wealth can no less easily reflect mere envy or greed. Because controversy, fallibility, and bias are general conditions of normative inquiry, they do not distinguish between principles that do and do not dictate the promotion of forms of value. Instead, the relevant distinction is between defensible and indefensible normative claims. But the argument of the preceding chapters was precisely that it *is* defensible to attach value to such deserved outcomes as the happiness of the virtuous, the success of hard workers, and the punishment of wrongdoers.

Thus, to establish that social justice does not require the promotion of deserved outcomes, we cannot appeal merely to the controversiality and fallibility of our judgments about value. Instead, we must find some deeper reason why deserved outcomes, though valuable, are no concern of society. But, at least on the surface, the

[14] Rawls, *A Theory of Justice*, p. 331.

208

prospects for finding such a reason appear dim. When a liberal society abjures the promotion of an official set of values, it does so to
allow each citizen to determine and pursue his own "vision of the
good." Thus, precisely in declining to take a position, the society
attempts to promote the higher value of autonomous choice.[15] This,
of course, is just the value that underlies several important types of
desert-claim. Moreover, in promoting autonomy, a society may
also be forced to promote other values associated with desert. For
example, as Robert Simon has observed, Rawls's

> liberty and fair opportunity principles allow and may even re-
> quire the assignment of great weight to just such contingencies
> [as the results of the genetic lottery]. After all, how one is
> praised or blamed, whether others resent or approve of one's
> actions, whether one is hired or fired, are all likely to have
> great effect on one's life.[16]

Although pursuing these issues in detail would require nothing less
than a full theory of liberalism, the values that underlie desert-
claims do not seem at all easy to avoid. Thus, pending persuasive
counter-argument, the presumption appears to be that considerations of desert *can* affect a society's justice as well as be affected by
it. This means, at a minimum, that a society is not just if its institutions systematically prevent persons from having what they deserve, and, more strongly, that a fully just society will actually promote deserved outcomes to the greatest feasible extent.

To what degree *can* a society promote deserved outcomes? Here
again, there is no reason to expect an all-or-nothing answer.
Rather, this will depend on both the ease with which different desert-bases can be discovered to exist and how readily specific deserved outcomes can be fostered by societal incentives or constraints. Some desert-claims, such as claims that wrongdoers
deserve punishment and that best-qualified applicants deserve op-

---

[15] As Vinit Haksar has put it in *Equality, Liberty, and Perfectionism* (Oxford: Oxford University Press, 1979), "Rawls' well-ordered society cannot be set up without
appealing to perfectionist ideals; for instance, we have seen that the view that autonomous life is essential to human well being is a kind of perfectionism" (p. 221).

[16] Simon, "An Indirect Defense of the Merit Principle," p. 229 and passim.

portunities, seem often to satisfy these requirements.[17] Others, such as claims that victims deserve compensation and hard workers deserve to succeed, either pose greater problems of discovery or are more likely to conflict with other demands of justice. And still others, such as claims that persons of good character deserve to prosper, seem altogether to escape society's effective control. We do not retract the view that desert affects justice, but only bow to the requirements of common sense, when we say that just institutions must pay more attention to the former desert-claims than to the latter.

If these remarks are correct, then justice itself is, in two senses, a pluralistic notion. It is pluralistic, first, because the desert-claims that just institutions must acknowledge have no single justification, and, second, because how well a society promotes what is deserved is not the *only* thing that determines its justice. Also required, at a minimum, is that it treat its citizens equitably, safeguard their basic rights (whatever those ultimately are), and provide an adequate range of opportunity for all. It is possible that these requirements are traceable to some common source; but on the whole, our (re)introduction of pre-institutional desert clearly diminishes the prospects for a unified account of justice.

In the recent literature, moral and social philosophers have taken to criticizing their opponents for not sufficiently attending to the differences between individuals. Thus, Rawls, in a now-famous passage, has argued that utilitarianism, in "extending to society the principle of choice for one man . . . does not take seriously the distinction between persons."[18] And Nozick, in criticizing Rawls's treatment of natural talents as a common asset, has argued that "[s]ome will complain, echoing Rawls against utilitarianism, that this 'does not take seriously the distinction between persons.' "[19] It is, I think, an implication of what I have said that both complaints

[17] Of course, if the desert of the best-qualified is not grounded in a value, then the reason that society ought to promote it cannot be that society ought to promote what has value. However, it will still be plausible to say that we should design our social institutions to treat persons as we ourselves ought to treat them.

[18] Rawls, *A Theory of Justice*, p. 27.

[19] Nozick, *Anarchy, State, and Utopia*, p. 228.

are sound, but that an exclusive emphasis on rights-generating activities would be yet a third instance of the same regrettable tendency. Just as persons are more than utilitarian centers of preference-satisfaction or -frustration, and more also than featureless Rawlsian centers of volition, so too are they more than the bargain-strikers and improvers of resources who dominate Nozick's political philosophy. Because each of these theories focuses too exclusively on one aspect of persons, each abstracts from their full particularity, and so ignores many morally significant differences between individuals. In emphasizing the various action-related attributes by which deserving selves are constituted, and the different ways in which personal attributes and actions may alter the world's structure of values, I have tried to suggest a different and richer picture. For how better to capture the moral importance of the differences between persons than to say that each person uniquely deserves things for precisely what he does, and for precisely what he is?

INDEX

LIBRARY OF CONGRESS CATALOGING-IN-PUBLICATION DATA

Sher, George.
Desert.

(Studies in moral, political, and legal philosophy)
Includes bibliographical references and index.
1. Justice (Philosophy) I. Title. II. Series.

B105.J87S54 1987   170   87–2823
ISBN 0–691–07745–2 (alk. paper)